Music in Theory
and Practice

Bruce Benward

University of Wisconsin · Madison

Music
in Theory
and Practice

VOLUME II

WM. C. BROWN COMPANY PUBLISHERS
Dubuque, Iowa

Book Team

Ed Bowers, Jr., Publisher
Robert Nash, Editor
Gordon Stromberg, Designer
Ruth Richard, Manager, Production-Editorial Department
Mary Jones, Production Editor
Laura Kraft, Design Layout Assistant

Wm. C. Brown Company Publishers

Wm. C. Brown, President
Larry W. Brown, Executive Vice-President
Ann Bradley, Director of Marketing Strategy
Jim Buell, Director of Information Management
John Carlisle, Assistant Vice-President, Production Division
Robert Chesterman, Comptroller
David Corona, Design Director
Lawrence E. Cremer, Vice-President, Product Development
Richard C. Crews, Publisher
Ray Deveaux, National College Sales Manager
John Graham, National Marketing Manager
Linda Judge, Director of Personnel/Public Relations
Roger Meyer, Assistant Plant Superintendent
Paul Miller, Vice-President/Director, University Services
Roy Mills, Assistant Vice-President/Plant Superintendent
Ed O'Neill, Vice-President, Manufacturing
Dennis Powers, Director of Information Services

Consulting Editor

Frederick W. Westphal
California State University, Sacramento

Copyright 1977 by Wm. C. Brown Company Publishers

ISBN 0–697–03596–4

Fourth Printing, 1979

Printed in the United States of America

223993

Contents

v

Preface

The chapters in Volume II follow logically from MUSIC IN THEORY AND PRACTICE, VOLUME I. This text continues the study of the Romantic period, introduces some of the larger forms (sonata allegro and rondo), supplies students with a basic knowledge of both 16th and 18th century polyphony, and finally furnishes in some detail the path of music from the Romantic period through the present day.

In some ways this is a considerable undertaking, but when one considers that students nowadays are performing and hearing music representing a wider range of style periods than ever before, it behooves educators to provide them some understanding of the great panorama the art provides.

As mentioned in the preface to Volume I the most interesting class discussions always result from conversations about specific compositions studied. Since this volume also focuses attention on music (not abstract discussions of theoretical formulae) it takes full advantage of the natural fascination students have for music literature, and the author often finds himself simply a third party in an involved and sometimes student dominated seminar.

For this volume especially the author adheres to the principle that no two compositions are the same and should therefore not be analyzed the same. Each composition demands its own special analysis, and thus students should never be restricted to one type of analysis and should be encouraged to invent and fashion new and novel ways to get at the basic understructure of each new composition studied.

The author wishes to acknowledge the generous assistance provided by Professor Les Thimmig in the preparation of the later chapters of this Volume. His scholarship is unquestioned, and his advice and counsel was most appreciated.

The texts, *Music in Theory and Practice/Volumes I and II*, are accompanied by the following learning aids:

Student Workbooks
Instructor's Resource Manual

1
Variation Technique

VARIATION PRINCIPLE

The transformation of a melody, harmony, or rhythm, with changes or elaborations. A varied form of a melody, harmony, or rhythm especially one of a series of such forms developing the potential of the subject or theme.

Music at almost any level contains the element of variation. The following excerpt illustrates a short melody that utilizes the principle of variation:

Illustration showing the variation principle at work in a short eight-measure melody

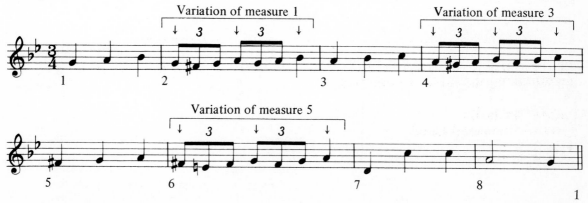

The continuing struggle in musical composition to obtain variety and yet preserve unity finds a welcome friend in the variation technique. Diversification that affords variety is balanced by the common link of unity with its built-in preservation of the prototype (the original theme or subject).

These tones supply the unity (commonality) which links the two phrase members

These tones supply the variety (diversification) which increases interest

The key to variation technique is the adoption of some kind of basic pattern that remains recognizable no matter how much variety is introduced. This basic pattern then becomes the guiding force throughout the entire composition or section within a larger work.

Two forms in which the technique of variation is an integral factor are: *Continuous Variations* and *Theme and Variations* (also known as *Independent Variations*).

TWO VARIATION FORMS

Continuous Variations

A type of variation form in which the variations are fused together in the continuous flow of the composition. One of the most common types of continuous variations is that which employs a *Ground (basso ostinato)*. The ground usually consists of a short melody of four to eight measures that is maintained in the lowest voice and is repeated throughout the composition. The *Chaconne* and *Passacaglia* are examples of continuous variation.

The following excerpt from a composition by André Raison predates the better-known Passacaglia by Bach.

Typical composition in continuous variation form
Upper melody is <u>different</u> for each statement of the ground:

Raison (1654–1719): Passacaille

1st statement of GROUND (basso ostinato)

2nd statement of GROUND (basso ostinato)

3rd statement of GROUND (basso ostinato)

4th statement of GROUND (basso ostinato)

OBSERVATIONS CONCERNING "THE PASSACAGLIA" BY RAISON

A   The ground is four measures long.

B   Some years later Bach added another four measures to the same ground and used it as a basis for his *Passacaglia in C Minor* (organ).

C   Above the ground is a two-voice contrapuntal texture, which for the most part could stand alone (without the ground).

D   The harmony for each tone of the ground alters but slightly from statement to statement.

E   Beginning with the third statement the ground is decorated somewhat and on occasion contains rhythmic changes. Nevertheless, the original tones of the ground are present in each statement no matter how ornamented the line.

F   The name *Continuous Variations* derives from the fact that there is little if any pause between the statements of the ground (as demonstrated here), and the pauses in the upper melody do not always coincide with the end of the ground statement.

COMPOSITION IN CONTINUOUS VARIATION FORM

About the Composer

Henry Purcell, an English composer (1659–1695), was the most original and creative composer of his time. He was active in almost every field and medium of musical composition—theater music, church music, court odes, secular and sacred songs, odes for various occasions, and instrumental music. In his own day he was perhaps as well known as a performer as he was a composer, and he was at one time organist at Westminster Abbey.

About the Composition

Dido and Aeneas, an opera, was written in 1689 and was composed for the students of a boarding school in Chelsey. Although Purcell may have been aware of the limitations imposed when writing for a group of amateurs, this work turned out to be one of the finest operas of the Baroque period. The libretto (text) was adapted by Nahum Tate from the poem *The Aeneid* by Vergil, a Roman poet (70–19 B.C.). The plot is somewhat complex and involves malicious plans to part Dido and her lover, Aeneas.

The aria (song from an opera or oratorio), "When I Am Laid in Earth," is the climax of the opera and is sung immediately after Aeneas's departure to the underworld. It is to be sung with great pathos and feeling representing the tragic situation resulting from the separation of the two lovers.

Purcell: Aria "When I Am Laid in Earth" from the opera *Dido & Aeneas*

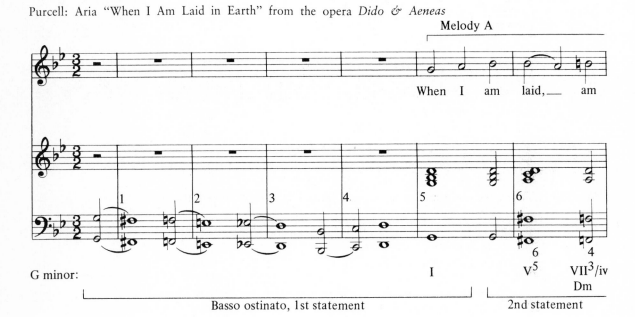

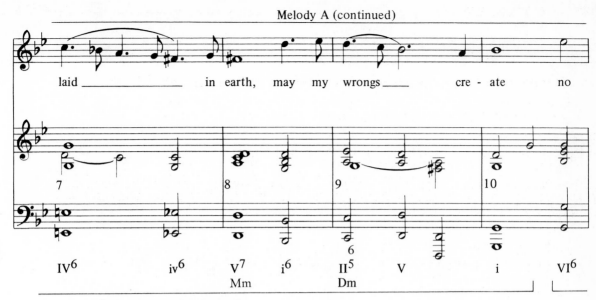

2nd statement (continued)

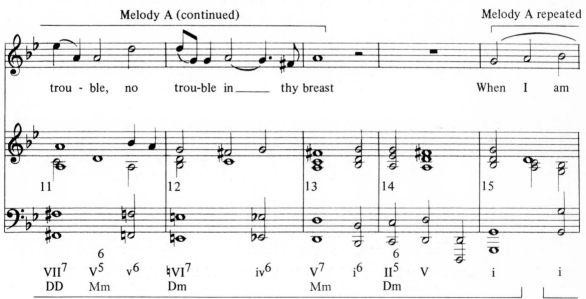

Basso ostinato, 3rd statement

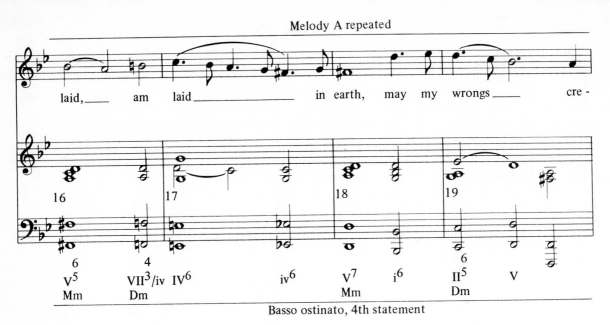

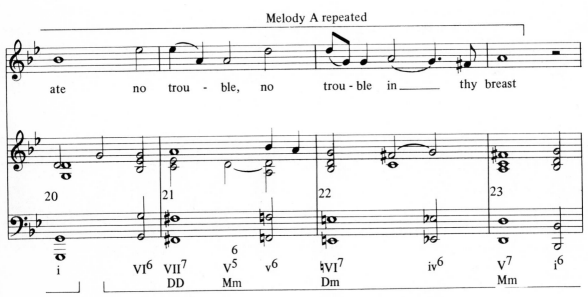

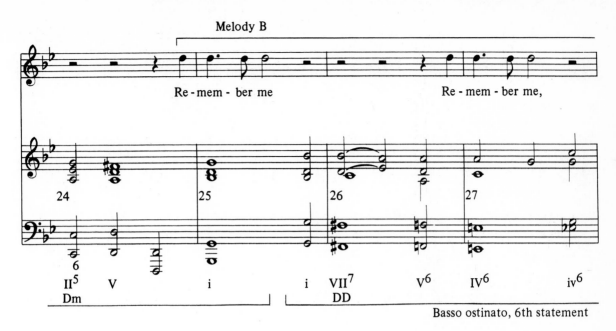

Basso ostinato, 6th statement

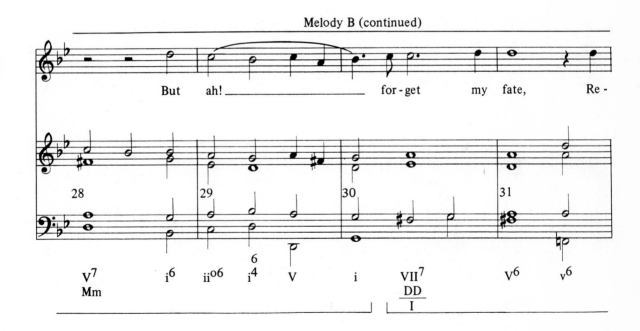

Melody B (continued)

Melody B repeated

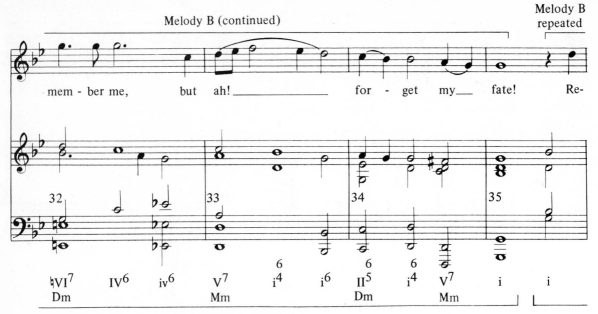

mem - ber me,   but ah! _____   for - get my___ fate!   Re-

32   33   34   35

$\natural VI^7$ IV^6 iv^6 V^7 i^4_4 i^6 $II^5_{...}$ $i^4_{...}$ V^7 i   i

Dm   Mm   Dm   Mm

Basso ostinato, 7th statement

Melody B repeated (continued)

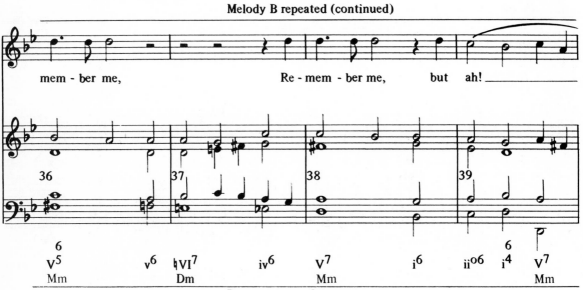

mem - ber me,   Re - mem - ber me,   but ah! _____

36   37   38   39

V^6_5 v^6 $\natural VI^7$ iv^6 V^7 i^6 ii^{o6} i^4_4 V^7

Mm   Dm   Mm   Mm

Basso ostinato, 8th statement

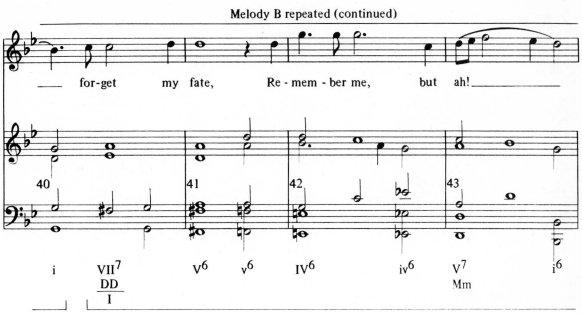

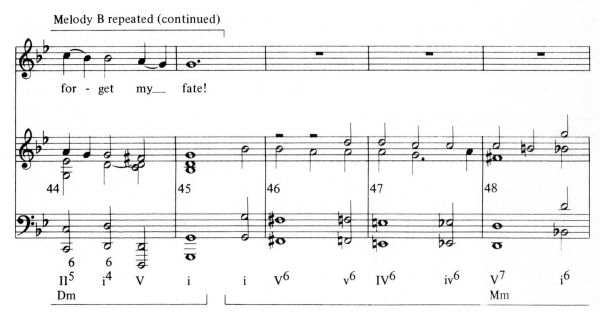

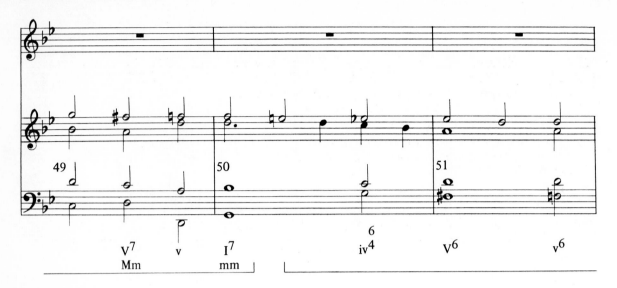

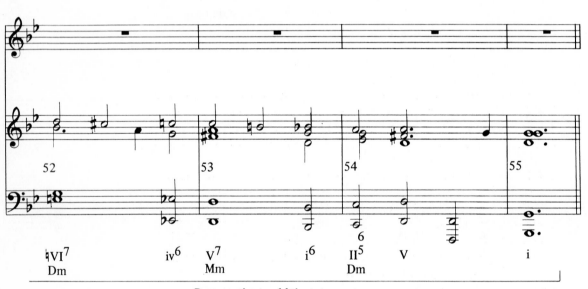

Basso ostinato, 11th statement

Analysis of "When I Am Laid in Earth"

GROUND MEASURES	*GROUND STATEMENT NUMBER	WORDS	VOICE MELODY MEASURES	MUSIC RELATIONSHIPS	TWO-PART FORM
1–5	1	When I am laid in earth, may my wrongs create no trouble in thy breast.	5–13	A	
5–10	2				A
10–15	3	When I am laid in earth, may my wrongs create no trouble in thy breast.	15–23	A	
15–20	4				
20–25	5	Remember me, but ah! forget my fate.	24–35	B	
25–30	6				
30–35	7	Remember me, but ah! forget my fate.	35–45	B	B
35–40	8				
40–45	9				
45–50	10				
50–55	11				

* Ground statements do not coincide with the words.

SOME OBSERVATIONS REGARDING THE ANALYSIS OF
"WHEN I AM LAID IN EARTH

A   The ground is five measures in length.
B   The ground remains in the bass in every statement.
C   The ground is not decorated (as in the Raison illustration on pages 2–3).
D   The 1st, 10th, and 11th statements are without vocal melody.
E   The four sections of the vocal melody (A A B B) do not always coincide
     with the ground statements (the first A of the melody ends in the 4th
     measure of the ground).
F   The harmonic realization of the ground varies from statement to state-
     ment, but the differences are generally slight, and there is more
     similarity in harmonizations than alteration.
G   Some unifying factors:
     1   Eleven successive statements of the ground.
     2   Each of the differing phrases of the voice melody is repeated once,
          thus the highly organized form: A A B B
H   Some factors providing variety:
     1   The varying texture of the orchestral part (here transcribed for
          piano or organ).
     2   The lack of conformity between the endings of the vocal phrases
          and the statements of the ground.
     3   The subtle and mild differences in harmonic realizations from state-
          ment to statement of the ground.

THEME AND VARIATION FORM

A theme (often in sectional form) stated simply and generally ending with an authentic cadence is followed by a series of variations. The variations ordinarily follow the form of the theme. Theme and Variations differ from Continuous Variations in at least two respects:

A   Each individual variation is a complete composition in itself while in the continuous variation no specific statement of the ground is so constructed.

B   The Theme and Variation form offers the composer a broader approach since the possible ways of providing variety are not restricted by the narrow confines of a recurring bass ground. The basic pattern in the Theme and Variation is not restricted exclusively to statements in the lowest voice (as in the Continuous Variation).

The ways in which variety may be introduced into the variations in the Theme and Variation form are boundless. It is possible to change the harmony but retain the melody and rhythm intact, change the melody but retain the harmony and rhythm, or change the rhythm and preserve the harmony and melody. In other words some vital aspect of the theme must be kept to maintain unity while diversification can be obtained through changes in other parameters.

The following excerpts illustrate some of the more orthodox techniques of variation. The theme chosen is the first phrase of "God Save the King," better known in the United States as "America," and is excerpted from Beethoven's set of variations (composed in 1803). Of course Beethoven employed the entire melody, but for purposes of space conservation only the first phrase is selected.

Beethoven: Sieben Variationen uber das Volkslied "God Save the King"
        (Seven Variations on the Folksong "God Save the King")

EMBELLISHED MELODIC LINE

One of the most common techniques employed in the variation form is that of the embellished melodic line. Taken from the Beethoven set of variations, this particular variation employs the melody in the upper line, but it is highly decorated with sixteenth notes. Note also that the harmony, although maintained basically, is laced with a few extra chords (in addition to those found in the theme).

Arpeggiated decoration of the theme

Beethoven: Variation VII

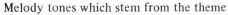

Melody tones which stem from the theme

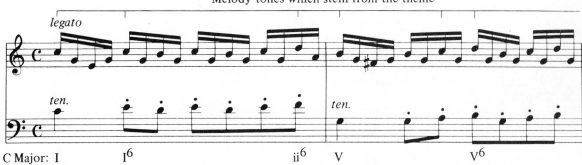

C Major: I   I⁶   ii⁶   V   V⁶

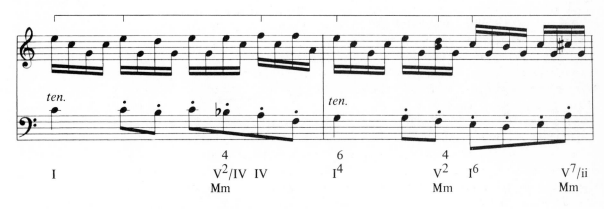

Introduction of a Different Rhythm

Change of Meter

Embellished Melodic Line

This particular example illustrates three common techniques all in the same variation.

A   The dotted eighth plus sixteenth note figure is introduced as a new rhythm (not found in the theme itself), and it is repeated thirteen times in the space of six measures.

B   Instead of the 3/4 meter found in the theme, 4/4 meter is employed in
    this variation.
C   The melody is embellished as previously described.

Beethoven: Variation VI

CHANGE OF MODE

INTRODUCTION OF AN ALBERTI BASS FIGURE INSTEAD
OF BLOCK CHORDS

EMBELLISHED MELODIC LINE

In the Theme and Variation form when the mode is changed from
major to minor or vice versa, the parallel rather than relative minor (or
major) is usually observed. Ordinarily variations retain the same tonic as
the theme. Note also the rather obvious use of Alberti Bass instead of the
block chords found in the theme. Again, the theme is decorated in the upper
voice, this time with a gently undulating motion that weaves in and around
the basic tones of the original melody.

Beethoven: Variation V

CHANGE OF HARMONY

CHANGE OF TEMPO

CHANGE OF MOOD

In the following variation the entire mood of the theme changes, the melody begins in a different key, but modulates back to the original near the end of the variation. To contribute to the mood the tempo changes to adagio, and the complexion of the variation becomes more plodding and prophetic. The melody itself is couched in the key of *F* major, but it is harmonized in *D* minor, which is another item adding to the variety.

Beethoven: Variation VII

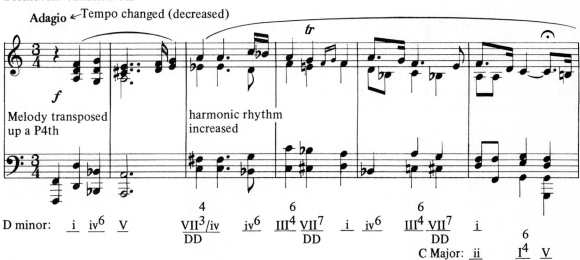

HARMONIC ELABORATION

HARMONIC MOTIF

MELODY TONES CHANGE REGISTER FROM TONE TO TONE

This variation assumes a broader consistency, the harmony spreads the texture over a three-octave span, and the melody tones dip about from octave to octave. At one point a melody tone is deleted entirely (measure 2). A motif consisting of a dominant 7th chord proceeding to its tonic occurs in measures one, two, and three. The motif is primarily harmonic since the emphasis and interest at the moment centers on the 7th chord and its resolution in each of the three measures. Harmonic elaboration occurs when triad tones are arpeggiated and sounded in different octaves.

Beethoven: Variation IV

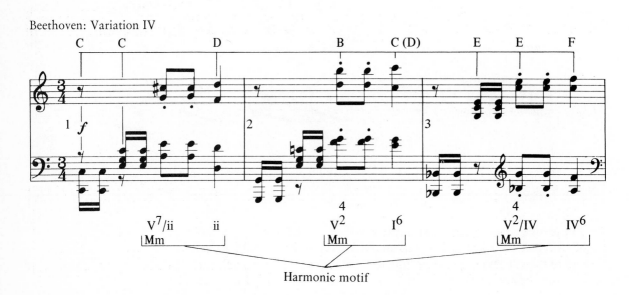

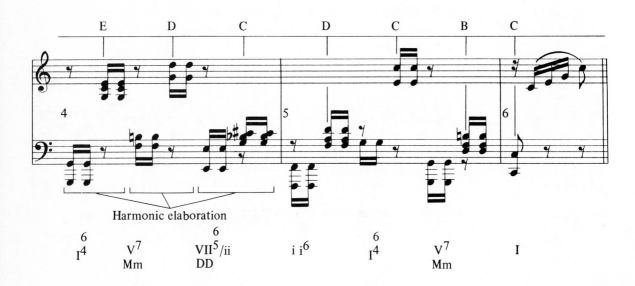

VARIATIONS BASED ON A MOTIF DERIVED FROM THE THEME

This example (not among those written by Beethoven) shows a motive (*motif* and *motive* are interchangeable) derived from the first four tones of the theme is used as the basis for an entire variation.

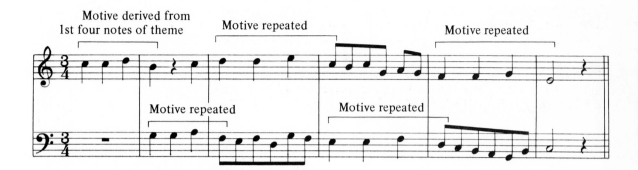

THEME PLACED IN ANOTHER VOICE

In this instance (not a variation by Beethoven) the melody is removed from its position in the upper voice (as with the theme) and becomes the bass voice.

To summarize the techniques of variation the following have been illustrated. It should be pointed out, however, that in similar and contrasting styles of music many other techniques are available to the composer. Those demonstrated here are but a few. A summary of variation techniques discussed in this chapter includes:

Embellished melodic line
Introduction of a rhythmic figure
Change of meter
Change of mode
Introduction of Alberti Bass figure
Change of harmony
Change of tempo
Change of mood

Harmonic elaboration
Use of harmonic motif
*Melody tones that change register
    from tone to tone*
*Variation based on a motif derived
    from the theme (entire melody
    not used)*
Theme placed in another voice

ASSIGNMENT 1   These two themes constitute the basis for compositions in theme and variation
                       form.

Theme No. 1

Theme No. 2

1   Using the first theme write a set of five variations using the following techniques:

    A   Embellished melodic line.
    B   Introduction of an Alberti Bass figure.
    C   Theme placed in another voice.
    D   Change of meter.
    E   Change of mode.

2   Using the second theme write a set of five variations using the following techniques.

    A   Introduction of a rhythmic figure.
    B   Change of harmony.
    C   Variation based on a motif derived from the theme.
    D   Change of tempo.
    E   Harmonic elaboration.

3   Write either composition for any medium you wish so long as the composition can be performed in class by class members.

ASSIGNMENT 2   Write a composition in continuous variation form.

1   Select an ostinato of four measures length.
2   Plan the composition so that the ostinato is repeated eight times.
3   Sketch ideas for each new ostinato repetition.
4   Plan a final cadence (authentic) at the end of the eighth repetition.
5   Make the earlier variations on the ostinato simpler and of thinner texture.
6   Plan a gradual crescendo from the 3rd or 4th repetition of the ostinato to the final (8th) repetition. Climax with thick texture and increased dynamics.
7   If you have difficulty composing an ostinato theme of your own you may use one of these:

1.

2.

3.

ASSIGNMENT 3 ·   Printed here is a complete theme and excerpts from twenty-four variations by Beethoven.

Indicate in detail the technique used in each variation. Some variations contain more than one technique.

Beethoven: 24 Variations on the Theme "Venni Amore" by V. Righini

Var. II

Var. III

Var. IV

Assignment 3 (continued)

Var. V

Var. VI

Var. VII

Var. VIII

Assignment 3 (continued)

Var. IX

Var. X

Var. XI

Var. XII

Assignment 3 (continued)

Var. XIII

Var. XIV

Assignment 3 (continued)

Var. XVII

Var. XVIII

Var. XIX

Var. XX

Scherzando

Var. XXI

Assignment 3 (continued)

Var. XXII

Var. XXIII

Adagio sostenuto

Var. XXIV

Allegro

2
The Period of Romanticism

Music history for the most part is marked by the alternation of two different creative attitudes. The first is exemplified by the conservative approach and features compositions that are carefully controlled, well-balanced, formal in nature, and restrained through an emphasis on the mastery of technical and compositional devices. The second attitude tends to accentuate the impulsive aspect of a composer's makeup, and stresses the new, the curious, the adventurous, the impetuous, and the passionate as uncensored by the controlled world of symmetry, balance, order, and proportion.

The balance, symmetry, and control that governed the Classical period (1750 to 1825) in all the arts were subdued or discarded almost entirely in favor of freedom, impulsiveness, and individuality of expression. This change during the first quarter of the nineteenth century ushered in the period of Romanticism in music. The people of the time experienced a need to identify themselves with the new and unusual, the exotic and mysterious elements they were beginning to discover. This curiosity manifested itself in the form of subjective expression where the individual tried to express his own personal reaction to his surroundings and environment.

Although much of the harmonic language of the Romantic period had already been crystalized and was used to a certain extent in earlier periods, the intensity and concentration of such vocabulary as altered chords (chords not conforming to the diatonic system) was a trademark and an undeniable ingredient of the Romantic style.

The ensuing six chapters are devoted to such dissonant or altered chords (nondominant Seventh Chords, Borrowed Chords, Secondary Dominant Chords, Neapolitan Sixth Chords, Augmented Sixth Chords, and Chromatic Mediants). Examples of all the above mentioned chords can be found in standard literature of both the Baroque and Classical period as can be seen from the quoted excerpts. However, the steadily increasing use of such chords through the Baroque, Classical, and Romantic periods culminated in the final quarter of the Romantic period with such composers as Wagner (1813–1883), Liszt (1811–1896), Franck (1822–1890), and Brahms (1833–1897). Here is a chart that compares the general stylistic characteristics of music written during the periods indicated. The chart shows only the broad comprehensive propensities and does not manifest smaller, less inclusive trends.

STYLE PERIOD COMPARISONS

BAROQUE STYLE	CLASSICAL STYLE	ROMANTIC STYLE
Basso continuo is one of the characteristic sounds of the period.	Basso continuo is virtually abandoned in favor of "written out" accompaniment.	Basso continuo is not used.
Concept of major and minor tonalities emerges.	Major and minor tonalities continued with little change.	Major and minor tonalities expanded to the point of extreme chromaticism.
Polyphonic texture is prominent and common in this period.	Shift from polyphonic to homophonic texture although polyphony still remains in many compositions.	Homophonic style is still favored to a considerable degree.
Tendency to monothematic compositions.	Polythematic compositions become most popular. Employment of contrast between vigorous melodies of instrumental nature and smooth lyric phrases.	Polythematic composition continued.
Melodic phrases generally not clearly defined with tendency to more continuous motion employing weakened cadences through which melodic line moves with little or no hesitation.	Phrases are apt to be short and composed of melodic formulas of a few notes that reach frequent caesuras and cadences. Cadences more defined melodically than in Baroque.	Dominated by lyric melody. Melody less formal and symmetric than in Classical period. Wide and angular leaps become more common than in Classical period. The age of sentimentality.
Tendency to provide elaborate decoration of melodies (ornaments, trills, mordents, etc.).	Ornaments continued but are not an integral part of the style.	Ornaments (especially the trill) continued but are greatly reduced in use. Upswing in use of unprepared dissonance (Appogg.)
Considerable use of the sequence. This device first became common during the Baroque period.	Use of sequence continued and is expanded.	Somewhat lessened use of sequence although still quite common. Tendency toward modulating or chromatic sequences.
"Functional" harmony developed in the Baroque.	"Functional" harmony continued and tends to be simple as in the Baroque with considerable emphasis I—IV—V.	"Functional" harmony continued in the Romantic period but became more rich, complex, dissonant, and chromatic. Tendency toward "coloristic" chords.
Basic triads and inversions are most common, but 7th chords also became a part of the style. 9th, 11th, and 13th chords much less common.	Triads and 7th chords continue much the same as in the Baroque. Ninth, 11th, and 13th chords gain little in frequency.	A wide spectrum of 7th, 9th, 11th, and 13th chords are used culminating in the late Romantic period.

STYLE PERIOD COMPARISONS (Continued)

BAROQUE STYLE	CLASSICAL STYLE	ROMANTIC STYLE
Harmonic color (sound quality of a particular aggregation of tones exploited for its own sake) is *not* a common practice of this period.	Harmonic color not an intrinsic part of the style.	Especially in the middle and late Romantic period this device became quite popular.
Metric beats are usually very strict in tempo with a minimum variance except for ritardandos, rallentandos, and an occasional accelerando. Tempo rubato is not a part of Baroque style.	Following the Classical ideal of balance and control, a particular tempo is seldom speeded or retarded. Tempo rubato is not a part of Classical style.	Much emphasis on tempo rubato employed. Used more often by solo performers than by groups in ensembles.
Emphasis on continuity of flow, repetition of rhythmic patterns, and prominence of the metric pulse.	Reiteration and emphasis on metric pulse is varied and somewhat lessened. Occasional pauses and rhythmic rest-points are common. Metric pulse is more likely to be lightly and quietly present (but not emphasized).	Tempos within a composition tend to be more radically varied in keeping with the trend to rubato. Tendency to more frequent changes of tempo. Some compositions of this period have a rather indistinct tempo and are inclined to flow amorphously.
Ensemble size is usually quite small. Choirs of 12 to 25 not uncommon. Instrumental groups also abbreviated in number. Inclination to contrast large sounds against small sounds (concerto grosso).	Ensembles grow both in size and variety, but are still quite small compared to those of the present day. Cautious addition of a few instruments to the orchestra.	During this period orchestras are expanded in all choirs. Strings are increased in number to balance the full complement of brass, wind, and percussion instruments. By late Romantic period the orchestra is the size of the present day ensemble. Exploitation of the orchestra for its varying coloristic effects is common.
Step dynamics (sudden shift in dynamics as opposed to gradual shift such as crescendo and decrescendo) are an integral part of the style and vital to interpretation.	Some change from the Baroque style. Beethoven is an early user of the "orchestral crescendo."	Increased use of dynamic contrast within the phrase rather than between phrases. More use of *gradual* change as with crescendo and decrescendo.

3
Borrowed Chords

In Major:	ii^{o6}	II^7	iv	$\flat VI$	VII^7	In Minor:	I (picardy)
		Dm			DD		

DEFINITION

Chords that are literally borrowed from parallel major and minor keys. Since there are three forms of the minor scale (natural, harmonic, and melodic) and one form of the major scale, there are a total of sixteen different possible triads and nineteen different 7th chords for any particular diatonic system of major and parallel minor keys.

Triad types for all diatonic forms of the key of C:

C Major: I   ii   iii   IV   V   vi   vii°

C minor: i   ii°   III   iv   v   VI   VII
(natural)

C minor: i   ii°   III⁺   iv   V   VI   vii°
(harmonic)

C minor: i   ii   III⁺   IV   V   vi°   vii°
(melodic)

Total triad types for the key of C including the major and all three forms of the parallel minor:

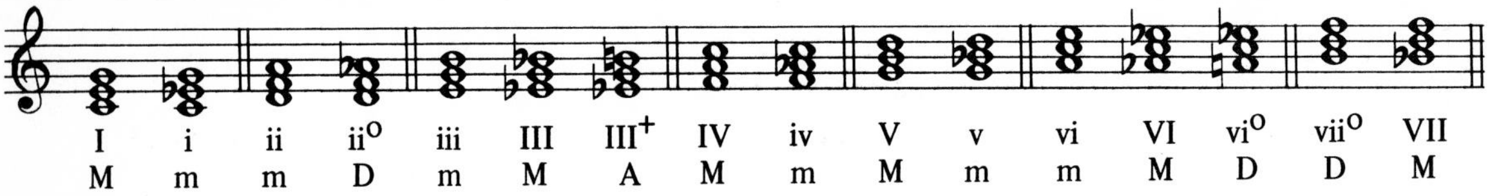
I i ii ii° iii III III+ IV iv V v vi VI vi° vii° VII
M m m D m M A M m M m m M D D M

BORROWED CHORDS IN MAJOR KEYS

Since the minor key with its three forms provide a wide variety of triad colors, there is more use of triads (and 7th chords) borrowed from the minor key for use in the major than vice versa. The major key with its one form lacks variety and demands enrichment from the parallel minor key. The most common borrowed chords in the major key are:

Most common borrowed (from the minor) chords in the major key:

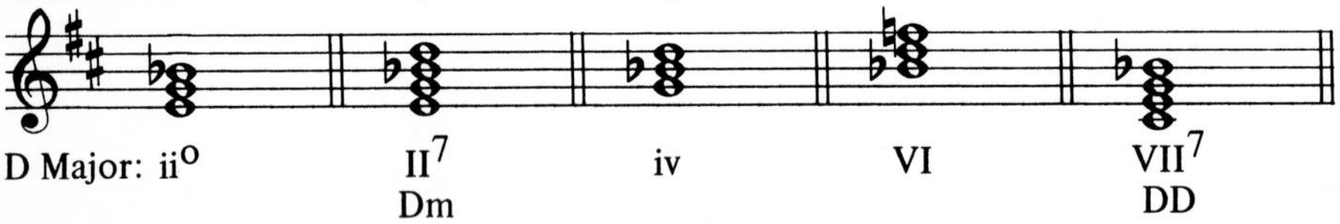
D Major: ii°
II7
Dm
iv
VI
VII7
DD

BORROWED CHORDS IN MINOR KEYS

The most common borrowed chord in the minor key is:

Picardy Third

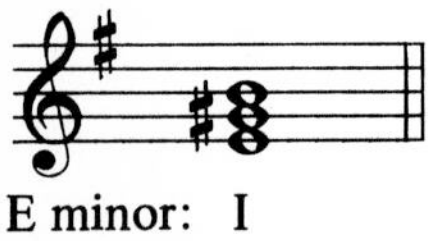
E minor: I

Bach: Jesu, Meine Freude

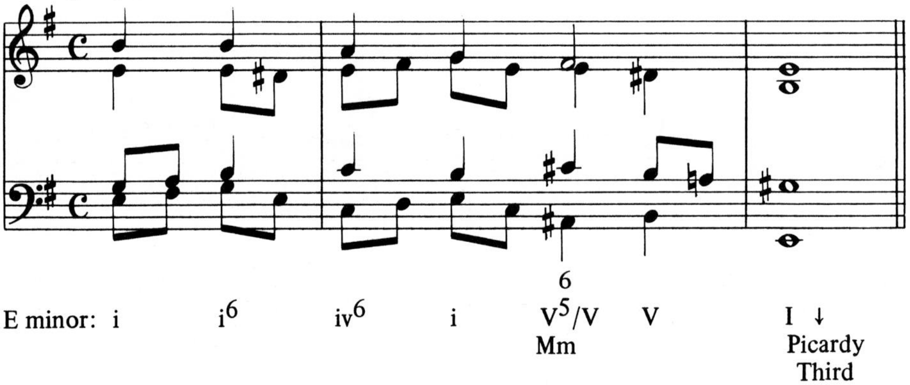
6
E minor: i i6 iv6 i V5/V V I ↓
Mm
Picardy
Third

Here are illustrations showing the use of borrowed chords in music literature:

Schubert: *Wanderers Nachtlied,* Op. 96, No. 3

peace,   on all   the   peaks you hard - ly can   see   a cloud

Bb Major: I   IV⁶ I⁴⁶ (VII³₄) I⁶ (II⁵₆)   VII⁷/V   V
                              DD   Dm   DD

Borrowed chords

Schubert: *Das Wirtshaus*

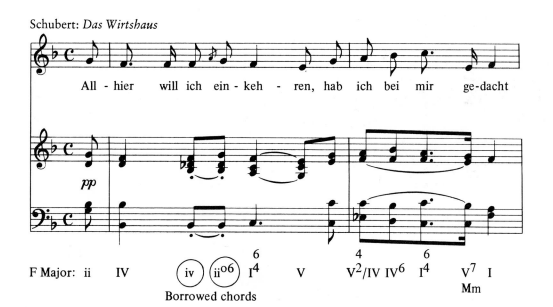

All - hier   will ich ein - keh - ren, hab ich bei mir ge-dacht

pp

F Major: ii   IV   (iv) (ii°⁶) I⁴⁶   V   V²/IV IV⁶ I⁴⁶ V⁷ I
                                                              Mm
          Borrowed chords

Bach: *Vater unser im Himmelreich*

F Major: V^6 I   vi $II^{\substack{6\\5}}$ V   (VI)
                              mm
                                   Borrowed chord

BORROWED CHORDS AS "COLOR" CHORDS

Borrowed chords are almost universally used as "color" chords, that is, they are employed mainly to achieve variety and offset the comparatively limited number of diatonic chords. Although the illustrations shown here provide only the most common usage, there are an almost infinite number of ways in which borrowed triads and 7th chords can be utilized.

PROGRESSIONS FROM BORROWED CHORDS IN MAJOR KEYS

Borrowed chords may be used as a substitute for diatonic chords, and with few exceptions follow the general principles employed for the same chords when unaltered. Here are some guidelines for writing and analyzing the *five most common* borrowed chords (from the minor) in the major keys.

II^{o6} in Major—Borrowed from Minor

The supertonic triad whether borrowed or diatonic usually proceeds to the V chord. The root of the V chord is a P4th above the root of the supertonic.

When this chord is borrowed from the minor key it becomes a diminished triad, is usually found in first inversion, and progresses on to the V chord as does its diatonic counterpart.

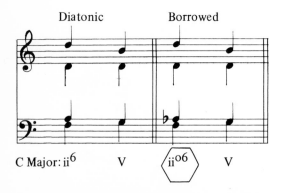

C Major: ii^6 V $\langle ii^{o6}\rangle$ V

II⁷ in Major—Borrowed from Minor
Dm

The II⁷ also progresses to the V chord. Dm7th chords when found as
    Dm
leading tone 7ths progress to the tonic (root of the tonic is one-half step
above that of the Dm7th), but no such convenient resolution is available
in the harmonic or melodic minor scales for the II⁷ since the III triad is
                                                   Dm
augmented and does not provide the stability furnished by the tonic.

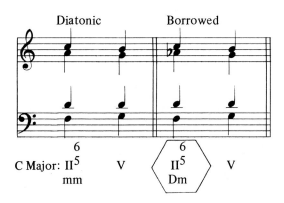

IV in Major—Borrowed from Minor

*The subdominant triad whether borrowed or diatonic progresses
most often to the V chord.* Usually the strongest progression for a triad occurs when its root lies a P4th below that of the succeeding chord:

TRIAD	STRONGEST ROOT PROGRESSION	IS TO
ii	Up a P4th (down a P5th)	V
iii	Up a P4th (down a P5th)	vi
V	Up a P4th (down a P5th)	I
vi	Up a P4th (down a P5th)	ii

However, since the 4th above the subdominant in the major and harmonic or melodic minor forms is an A4 rather than P4 the IV or iv triad is
prevented from following the same pattern to vii⁰. In addition the leading
tone triad is diminished and thus does not form the same strong relationships as in the case of the ii, iii, V, and vi triads (shown above).

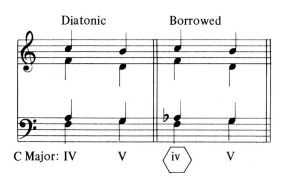

♭VI IN MAJOR—BORROWED FROM MINOR

The diatonic vi triad progresses normally to the ii, but when the triad is borrowed from the minor, its root is lowered one-half step, and the interval between the two roots is an A4 rather than a P4. This prevents the borrowed VI from progressing in that manner, *so it is usually followed by V or the borrowed iv.*

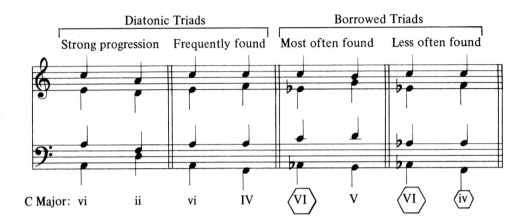

VII⁷ in Major—Borrowed from Minor
DD

The VII⁷ resolves to the tonic routinely whether as a diatonic or borrowed chord. In this resolution the roots of the two chords lie one-half step apart.

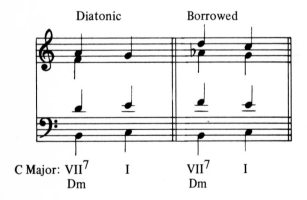

Here are some additional illustrations showing the use of borrowed chords.

Illustrates use of borrowed chords:
Borrowed Chords

Same except for diatonic chords:
Diatonic Chords

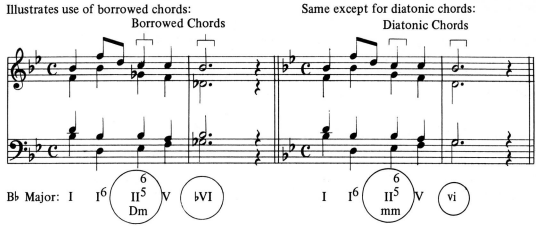

Handled in same manner as diatonic chords

Borrowed chords are not generally approached or left by chromatic progression in styles up to the Mid-Romantic period:

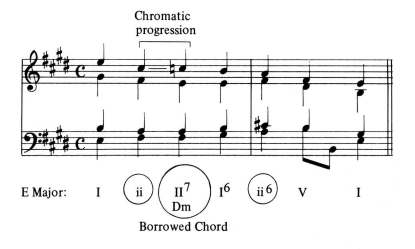

STYLISTIC USE OF BORROWED CHORDS

Baroque Period

Borrowed chords are found often in this period and are considered a part of the general style.

Classical Period

Stylistic considerations include borrowed chords in this period as well, and their frequency and use is little changed from that of the Baroque.

Romantic Period

This period saw a freer use including chromatic approach to and from the borrowed chord.

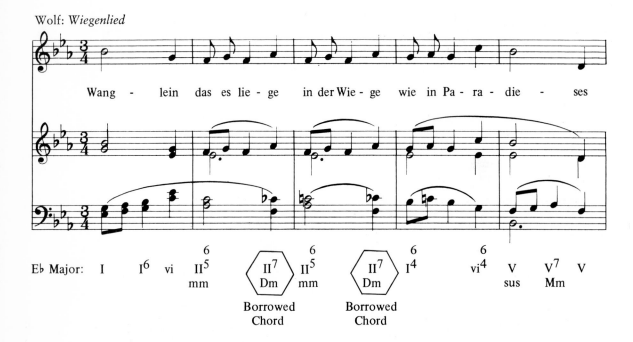

Wolf: *Wiegenlied*

Post-Romantic and Impressionistic Period

With the increased mixing of the modes, and the gradual decline in emphasis on dominant-tonic relationships, the borrowed chord becomes indistinguishable as a separate entity.

Here is an illustration of a borrowed chord (VII⁷) that appears among a group of other 7th chords and is not resolved in the traditional nineteenth-century manner (to a chord whose root lies a half step above).

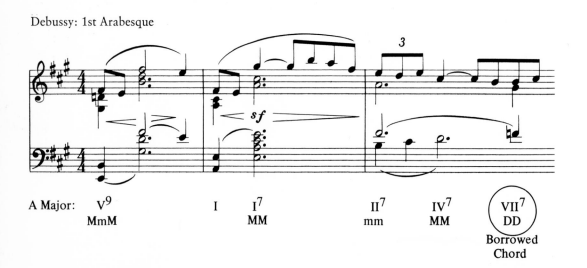

Debussy: 1st Arabesque

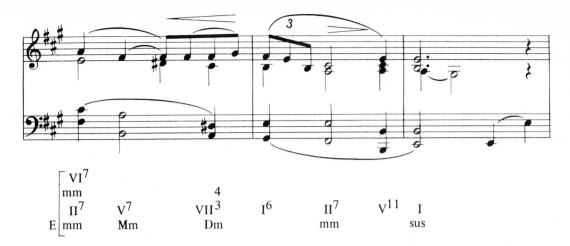

The following is another illustration showing a modal treatment (common in Impressionism) of what appear to be borrowed chords. Actually the use of the Lydian mode combined with chromatic mediants negates the traditional effect of borrowed chords entirely.

Debussy: *Pelleas et Melisande*

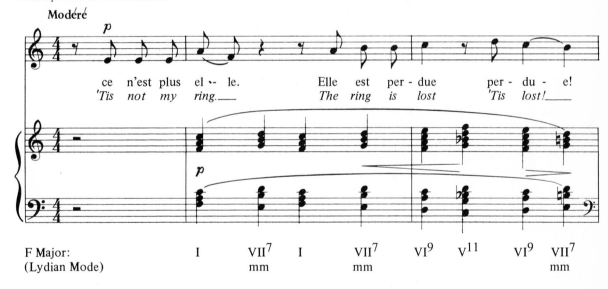

ASSIGNMENT 1   1   Write each requested chord in four-part harmony on the staves provided.
                    2   Then, write the chord that most conventionally follows it.
                    3   Analyze both chords.
                    4   The example illustrates correct procedure.

1. VII$^6_5$ IN D MAJOR (EXAMPLE)   4. ii^{o6} IN A-FLAT MAJOR
    DD
                                           5. VI   IN B MAJOR
2. II$^6_5$ IN F MAJOR
    Dm

3. iv^6 IN A MAJOR   6. II$^4_2$ IN G-FLAT MAJOR
                                               Dm

7. iv⁶   IN E MAJOR   9. ii⁰⁶   IN F-SHARP MAJOR

8. VII⁷ IN D-FLAT MAJOR   10. VII$_3^4$ IN G MAJOR
    DD   DD

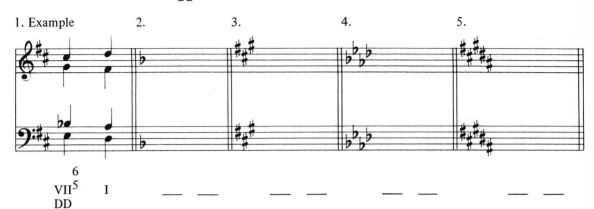

$$\begin{matrix}6\\ \text{VII}^5 \qquad \text{I}\\ \text{DD}\end{matrix}$$

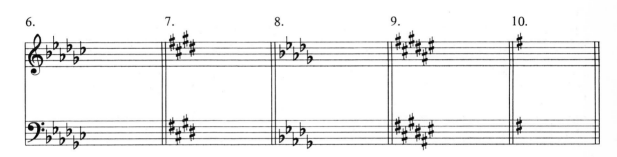

ASSIGNMENT 2
1 Add the tenor and alto voices to the phrases below.
2 Analyze each chord.
3 Add appropriate nonharmonic tones.
4 Divide the class into four sections (soprano, alto, tenor, and bass) and sing the phrases.
5 Arrange the phrases for a quartet of instruments.

1.

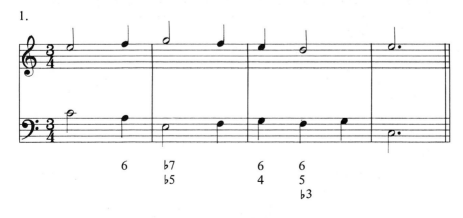

Assignment 2 (continued)

2.

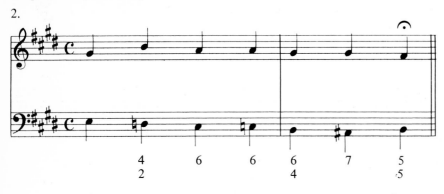

3.

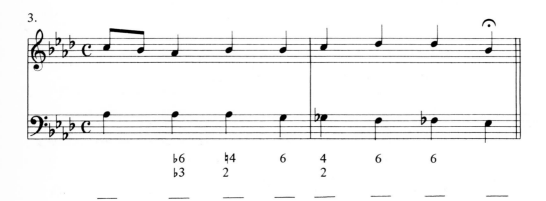

4.

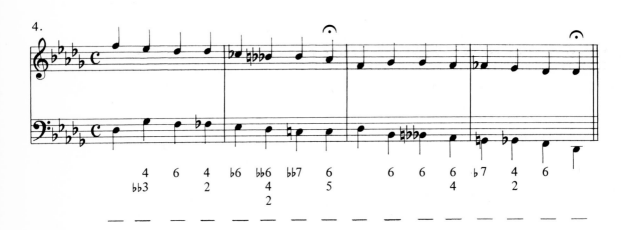

ASSIGNMENT 3   Below is a phrase from a chorale melody. Answer the following questions concerning harmonization of the melody.

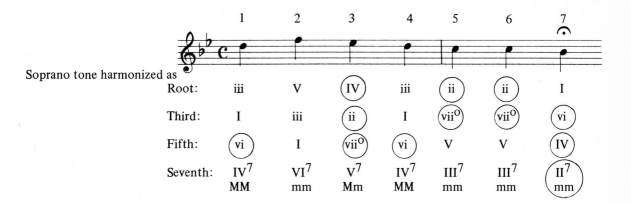

Soprano tone harmonized as

	1	2	3	4	5	6	7
Root:	iii	V	(IV)	iii	(ii)	(ii)	I
Third:	I	iii	(ii)	I	(vii°)	(vii°)	(vi)
Fifth:	(vi)	I	(vii°)	(vi)	V	V	(IV)
Seventh:	IV⁷	VI⁷	V⁷	IV⁷	III⁷	III⁷	(II⁷)
	MM	mm	Mm	MM	mm	mm	(mm)

1   For the harmonization of melody tone No. 3, how many of the circled chord symbols can be converted to borrowed chords?

2   For the harmonization of melody tone No. 1, can the circled chord be converted to a borrowed chord?

3   For the harmonization of melody tones No. 6 and 7, two of the circled chord symbols can be converted to borrowed chords in cadence formulas. Name the two chords and indicate two different cadence types in which borrowed chords could be included.

4   In the harmonization of melody tone No. 4, explain why the circled chord symbol could not be converted to a borrowed chord.

5   Connect by straight lines all possible descending P5th (ascending P4th) chord progressions.

ASSIGNMENT 4   Below is a complete chorale melody.

Chorale Melody: Wo Gott zum Haus nicht gibt sein Gunst
                 (If God does not give his blessings)

1   Harmonize the melody on a separate sheet of score paper.
2   Use a harmonic rhythm of one chord per quarter note.
3   Write out all possible harmonies as described in previous chapters; then, select a suitable harmonization and write the block chords beneath the melody tones. Be sure to include at least two or three borrowed chords.
4   Convert the block chords to four-part harmony with special emphasis on an interesting bass line.
5   Add appropriate nonharmonic tones.
6   Perform the compositions in class using a quartet of students each singing one of the four parts (soprano, alto, tenor, and bass).

ASSIGNMENT 5   Convert the above chorale harmonization to an instrumental composition (Chorale Prelude) retaining the basic melody tones and harmony. Among the possibilities are: change the meter, elaborate (decorate) the melody, arpeggiate the harmony, create new and interesting rhythms, etc.

The beginning of the composition as submitted by a student will help to illustrate the procedure.

Melody Tones of the Chorale

etc.

Basic harmony used in harmonizing the chorale melody:

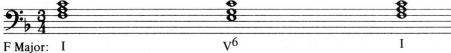

F Major: I   V⁶   I

ASSIGNMENT 6   Write a composition of approximately sixteen to twenty-four measures in length.

1 Plan the composition in three-part form.
2 Four to six four-measure phrases.
3 Plot the harmonic progressions first in block chords.
4 Then, add an appropriate melody.
5 Convert the block chords to the idiomatic style of the medium you choose.
   As an example if you write for a group of stringed instruments arrange the
   harmony to accommodate the peculiarities of the instruments involved.
6 Be sure to include at least three or four borrowed chords. Remember that
   borrowed chords can generally substitute for their diatonic counterparts.

ASSIGNMENT 7   The following excerpts contain borrowed chords.

1 Extract the chords and write them in simple position on the blank staff beneath each score.
2 Analyze each chord.
3 Discuss and compare the harmonic vocabulary in each excerpt.
4 Perform the excerpts in class.

Schumann: Papillons (Butterflies), Op. 2, No. 5.

Assignment 7 (continued)

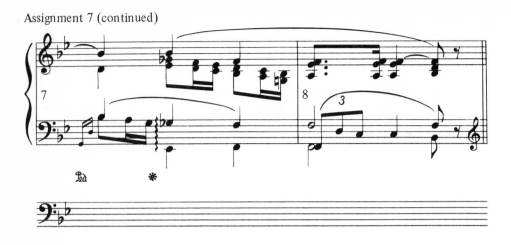

Schumann: *Ich Grolle Nicht* (from Dichterliebe) Op. 48

Lieb,   e - wig ver - lor' - nes Lieb!_____   ich

6   7   8

Faure: Lydia

mes   a - mours,   Mon âme   en bais - ers   m'est ra - vi - e!

1   2   3

Assignment 7 (continued)

O Ly - di - a, rends - moi _____ la vi - e,

Que je puis - se mou - rir, mou - rir tou - jours!

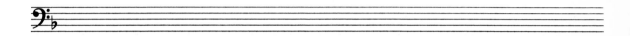

Chopin: Mazurka in A♭ Major, Op. 24, No. 3

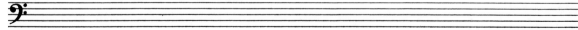

Assignment 7 (continued)

4
9th, 11th, and 13th Chords

V^9 V^9 V^{11} V^{11} V^{13}

MmM   *Mmm*   *aug*[11]

Other 9th, 11th, and 13th chords

9TH CHORDS

Definition

A superposition (placed above, one upon another) of four 3rds (one 3rd above the 7th chord). Chords are named from the interval between the root and the highest factor above it—the 9th.

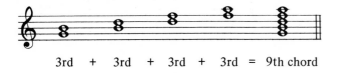

3rd   +   3rd   +   3rd   +   3rd   =   9th chord

History

The interval of a 9th can be found in early polyphony (around the twelfth or thirteenth century) as soon as the distance between the voices became wide enough to accommodate it.

Je cuidoie—Se j'ai—Solem

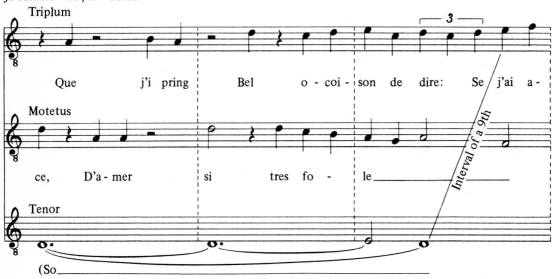

In subsequent centuries and styles the 9th continued as an important dissonant interval, but was relegated to the role of a passing tone or some other nonharmonic device. By the time of the Baroque period there were isolated instances where the 9th was frozen or made of sufficient strength that it achieved the importance of a chord tone. In the Classical period it appeared even more often as a possible chord factor. The following excerpt is an example of a possible 9th chord written by Schubert (circa 1812):

Schubert: *Rastlose Liebe* (Restless Love), Op. 5, No. 1

Chords reduced to simple position:

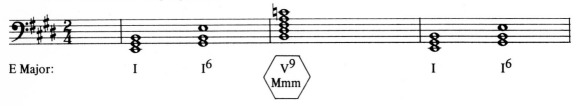

In the Baroque and Classical periods the 9th was resolved as a dissonance no matter whether it was considered as a part of the chord or was analyzed as a nonharmonic tone. Such careful treatment of dissonance dates
back even to style periods before chords were considered as such. Unquestionably the decision to analyze a 9th as a chord factor or as a
nonharmonic tone is moot, and the disposition of such tones and their
degree of solidarity will in the end have to remain with the particular
analyst. So long as consistency is maintained it makes little difference since
under both conditions (the 9th as a chord factor or as a nonharmonic
tone) the treatment by the composer is the same.

It was the Romantic period that eventually solidified the 9th as an in-
disputable chord factor. Here is an illustration showing its use by Wagner
in a composition written in 1859:

Wagner: *Tristan und Isolde* (voice part omitted)

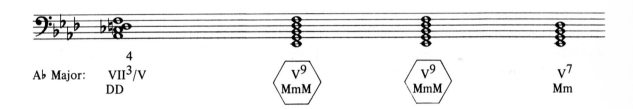

Note how even in the mid-nineteenth century the 9th of the chord is
still resolved one step down (as if it were simply a 9–8 suspension).

It was during the last quarter of the nineteenth century that the 9th
began to break from stylistic traditions of the past and became unresolved.
Composers following the Romantic tradition as well as those of the Post-
Romantic and Impressionistic bent adopted a style in which the 9th of the
9th chord did not follow the pattern of nonharmonic tones. Here is an
illustration showing its use by Franck in a composition written in 1886:

Franck: Sonata in A major for Violin and Piano

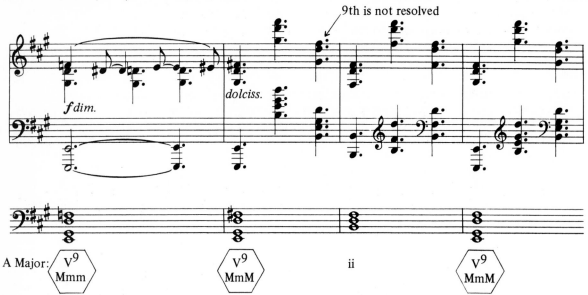

The greatest frequency of 9th chords occurred in the Post-Romantic and Impressionistic period (1875–1920). It was during this era that 9th chords were not only unresolved but were sometimes used successively. Such movement of all tones in parallel motion is called *planing* or *parallelism*.

Here is an illustration of planing from a composition written in 1899 by Maurice Ravel. Note the successive 9th chords and the nonresolution of the 9th in both.

Ravel: Pavane Pour une Infante défunte (Pavane for a Deceased Child)

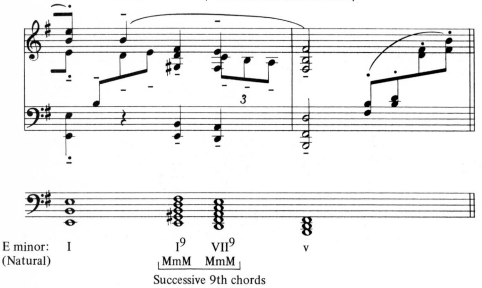

Here is an illustration from a composition written in 1901 by Scott Joplin. Although Joplin used most of the vocabulary of the late Romantic period (including secondary dominants, borrowed chords, augmented sixths, neapolitan sixths, and 7th chords) he used 9th chords sparsely.

Joplin: The Augustan Club Waltz

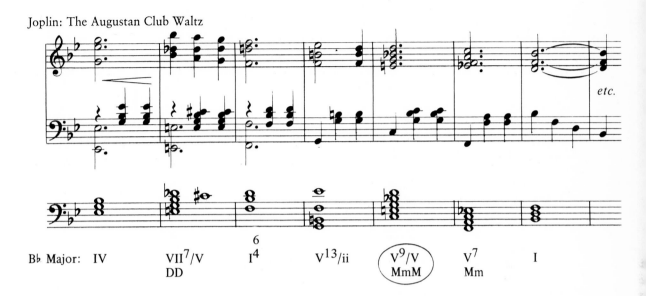

B♭ Major: IV   VII^7/V   I$^6_4$ V^{13}/ii   V^9/V   V^7 I
                      DD   MmM   Mm

In subsequent jazz styles the 9th chord became very prevalent and was used regularly in a full and sonorous harmonic style that made almost every chord into a 7th, 9th, 11th, 13th, or added tone chord. Here is an illustration of a typical cadence found in music of the 1950s. Note the absence of triads and the fact that the composition ends on a 9th chord.

Jazz of the 1950s

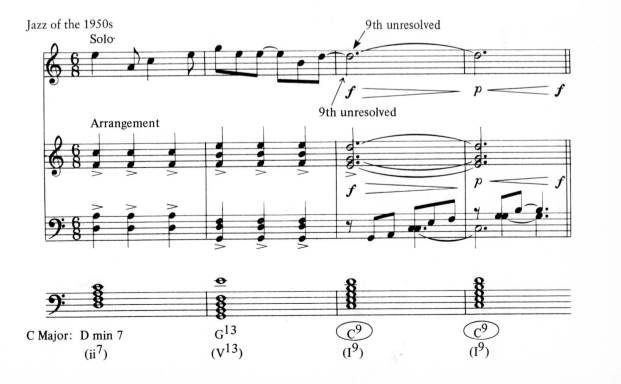

C Major: D min 7   G^{13} C^9 C^9
           (ii^7)   (V^{13})   (I^9)   (I^9)

Treatment of the 9th Chord

A   The 9th chord can be found on any step of the scale.

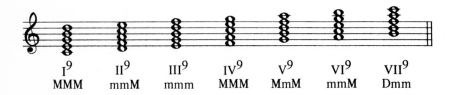

B   By far the most common of the 9th chords is the dominant. In major
keys it is MmM (Major triad, minor 7th, Major 9th) and in the minor
keys it is Mmm.

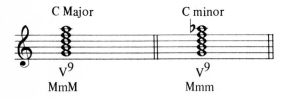

C   In piano, organ, small ensembles, orchestral settings, etc. all factors may
be present, but the dissonant factors (7th & 9th) are seldom doubled
since they are extremely active tones.

D   In four-part writing (chorale style) one factor must always be omitted
since the 9th chord contains five. The factor most often deleted is the
5th.

Chorale phrase showing 5th deleted in the 9th chord:

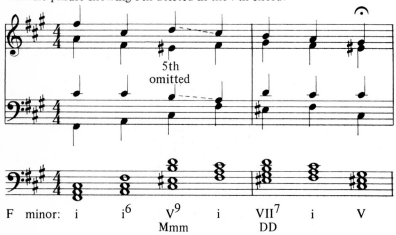

E   In four-part chorale writing the 9th and 7th factors should resolve
down one step to factors of the next chord as in the Classical to Mid-
Romantic style.

7ths and 9ths resolve down one step:

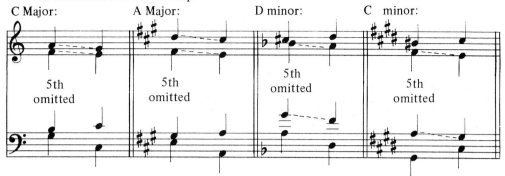

F   The 9th of the 9th chord is usually the highest sounding factor as can be seen from all previous examples from music literature in this chapter.

ASSIGNMENT 1   Write the requested 9th chord above each given tone. The example illustrates correct procedure.

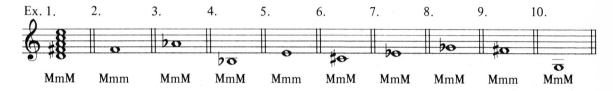

ASSIGNMENT 2   Add alto and tenor to the following phrases and analyze each chord. Follow these partwriting suggestions.

1   In four-voice writing delete the 5th factor of 9th chords.
2   Resolve both the 9th and 7th of 9th chords.
3   Observe all previous suggestions regarding doubling, spacing, voice order, and voice ranges.
4   Avoid large leaps (leaps larger than a P5th).

Assignment 2 (continued)

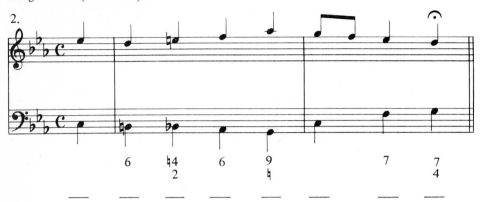

6   ♮4   6   9
     2   ♮

7   7
     4

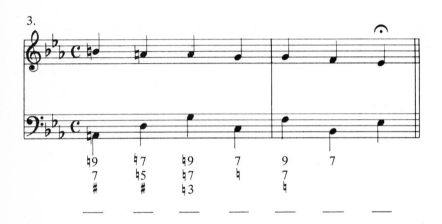

♮9   ♮7   ♮9   7   9   7
7   ♮5   ♮7   ♮   7
♮3   ♮

ASSIGNMENT 3   Complete the following excerpt to eight measures (two four-measure phrases).
Continue the accompaniment figure and general texture.

ASSIGNMENT 4   Printed below is an excerpt from "Pavane Pour une Infante defunte," written in 1899 by Ravel.

1 Make a complete harmonic analysis.
2 The key (or mode) is by no means clear.
3 Make a list of harmonic vocabulary (list the different chords found).
4 Indicate the types (MmM, Mmm, etc.) of 9th chords, whether resolved or not, and the chord that follows.
5 Transcribe the melody for a solo instrument and play the piano accompaniment as is.
6 Describe the types of chord progressions (descending P5ths, ascending P5ths, descending thirds, etc.) in the first five measures.

Ravel: Pavane pour une Infante défunte

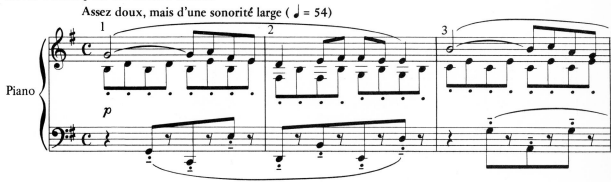

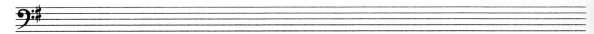

Assignment 4 (continued)

11TH CHORDS

Definition

A superposition of five 3rds—one 3rd above the 9th. Chord gets its name (11th chord) from the interval between the root and the highest factor —an 11th. An 11th is a compound interval composed of an octave and a 4th.

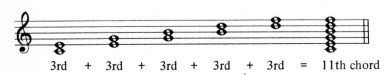

3rd   +   3rd   +   3rd   +   3rd   +   3rd   =   11th chord

HISTORY

Compared to 7th, 9th, and 13th chords, the 11th chord is rare in all periods. In *circle of descending 5ths (ascending 4ths)* progressions the 11th cannot resolve down one step to a triad since its resolution is not a factor. During the Baroque and Classical periods the 11th chord saw only occasional use.

During the late Romantic and Post-Romantic periods composers employed the 11th chord as part of the style, but it was always used sparingly and with some reserve.

Here is an illustration of an 11th chord used functionally by Debussy in one of his earliest works composed in 1888. Subsequently the style of Debussy involved less and less of functional harmony and developed the characteristics of parallel chords (chords moving from one to another in parallel motion—*parallelism* or *planing*).

Debussy: First Arabesque

Grieg: Vöglein (Little Bird) Op. 43, No. 4

Treatment of 11th Chords

A   The 11th chord can be found on any degree of the scale.

Diatonic 11th chords in C major:

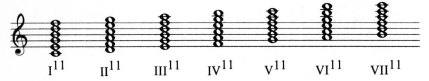

I^{11} II^{11} III^{11} IV^{11} V^{11} VI^{11} VII^{11}

B   The V^{11} chord is the most common.
C   All six factors are seldom found in the 11th chord. The 3rd is most often omitted, and if more than one factor is missing the 9th or the 5th is a frequent candidate.
D   In four-part chorale writing the 11th chord is quite rare, but when used it is usually missing the 3rd and either the 5th or 9th factor.
E   In *circle of descending 5ths (ascending 4ths)* progressions the 11th of the 11th chord cannot resolve to a triad since the resolution factor is not present. However, if the resolution chord is at least a 7th chord, the resolution is possible.

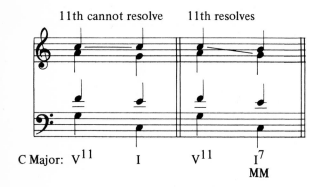

C Major: V^{11} I V^{11} I^7
MM

Four-part chorale phrase showing 11th chord with 3rd and 9th missing:

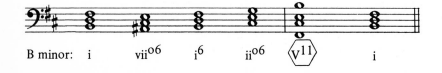

B minor: i vii^{o6} i^6 ii^{o6} ⟨V^{11}⟩   i

F   One final aspect of the 11th chord should be pointed out. It has within
its makeup two complete triads:

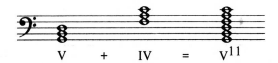

V   +   IV   =   V¹¹

Thus, an authentic cadence including a V^{11} chord has a definite dominant to tonic effect, but includes just the hint of a plagal cadence
intimated by the latent IV chord included in the total structure.

Ravel: Valses nobles et sentimentales (1911)—adapted. Copyright 1911, Editions
Durand et Cie. Used by permission of the publisher. Elkan-Vogel, Inc. sole
representative, United States.

C M: V¹¹   I

13TH CHORDS

Definition

*A superposition of six 3rds (three 3rds above the 7th chord). These
chords are named from the interval between the root and the highest
factor above it—a 13th. The interval of a 13th is a compound 6th (octave
and a 6th).*

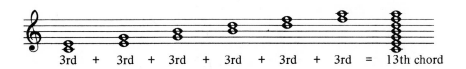

3rd + 3rd + 3rd + 3rd + 3rd + 3rd = 13th chord

History

13th chords, like the 9ths and 11ths, occurred in greatest frequency during the Post-Romantic and Impressionistic period (1875–1920), and like the
9th and 11th chords were used both as a functional chord (in chord
progressions) and in parallel movement (planing which is nonfunctional).

13th chords are quite rare in music up to the late Romantic period. Here is an isolated example written (1848) by Schumann in the Mid-Romantic period. The chord is used functionally as a V^{13} progressing normally to a I chord.

Schumann: Kleine Studie (Short Study) from Album for the Young (Op. 68)

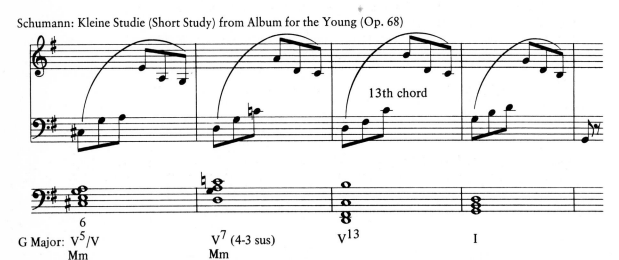

During the first decade of the twentieth century (1900–1910) the indigenous music of America, Ragtime, became quite popular. Composers such as Scott Joplin employed a variety of 7th, 9th, 11th, and 13th chords in a functional setting.

Here is an example of his use of the 13th chord. This composition was written in 1902. Note the very conservative approach (by step) to and from the 7th and 13th:

Joplin: A Breeze from Alabama

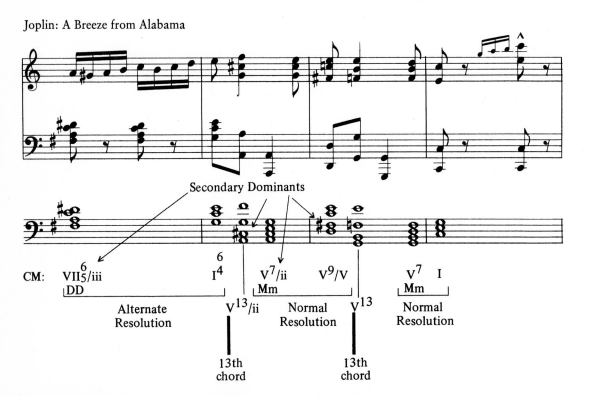

At nearly the same time the 13th chord was being used as functional harmony following the older traditional style of the Romantic period, Claude Debussy (1862–1918) utilized the same chord in quite a different manner. His 13th chords on occasion were both preceded and followed by other 13th chords in a parallel fashion. In this setting the chords no longer have harmonic function, but move about in a rigid way with each chord factor interlocked in a frozen arrangement that more approximates melody than harmony. This composition was written in 1905.

Debussy: Reflets dans l'Eau (Reflections in the Water) from Images (suite for piano)

Parallel movement of 13th chords

Some composers of the twentieth century maintained extensive ties with traditional harmonic styles relating back to the eighteenth and nineteenth centuries. One among these, Francis Poulenc, (1889–1963) was a member of the famous "Six" French composers who rebelled against the ideas and philosophy of the Romanticists. Although he employed functional harmony as a major stylistic quality his music is distinctively his own. His employment of 13th chords is very traditional, especially in view of the fact that this composition was written in 1962, one year before his death.

Poulenc: Sonata for piano and oboe. Copyright © 1962 by J&W Chester Edition Wilhelm Hansen, London Limited. Used by permission of the publisher.

Chords reduced to simple position:

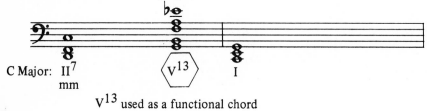

C Major: II⁷
          mm

V¹³ used as a functional chord

Treatment of 13th Chord

A   Seldom are all factors of the 13th chord present at the same time.

B   Because of the minor 9th interval between the 3rd and 11th factors, one or the other is generally missing in 13th chords.

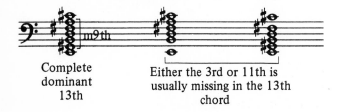

Complete   Either the 3rd or 11th is
dominant   usually missing in the 13th
13th   chord

C   The most smooth and euphonious arrangements of the 13th chord are obtained when dissonant factors (7th, 9th, 11th, 13th) are spread apart in the chord. For special effects and a more dissonant result the higher factors can be grouped together.

Arrangements of the 13th chord

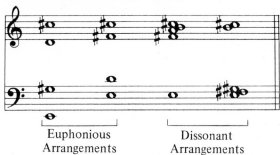

Euphonious Arrangements   Dissonant Arrangements

D   When the 13th chord is used functionally it is usually the V^{13} although it can be found on any scale degree.
E   In four-part writing the most common factors present are: the root, the 3rd, the 7th, the 9th, and 13th although a variety of combinations are possible so long as the 3rd and 11th are not present at the same time.

The dominant 13th chord in four-part harmony:

13th chord

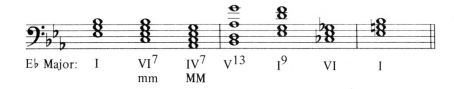

Eb Major: I   VI^7 IV^7 V^{13} I^9 VI   I
                   mm   MM

F   In many-voiced compositions such as orchestral, piano, and organ works the root may be doubled, but most often no doubling occurs.
G   Confusion between the added 6th chord and the 13th is quite possible since both contain either a 6th (in close position) or a 13th that is the compound (octave plus) equivalent of the 6th. In analysis, a good rule of thumb is to analyze as 13th chords only those that contain at least one other dissonant (7th, 9th, or 11th) factor besides the 13th itself. Thus, the chord that contains only triad factors plus the 13th is best analyzed as a chord of the added 6th.

Distinguishing between added 6th chord and 13th chord

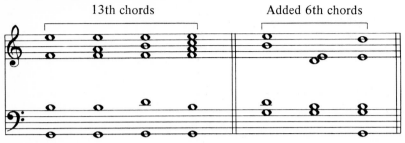

These contain at least one additional dissonant factor (7th, 9th, 11th) besides the 13th.

Added 6th chords contain only a triad plus the 6th.

H   The 13th of the 13th chord appears most often in the highest sounding voice as can be seen from all examples from music literature except one previously illustrated in this chapter.

ASSIGNMENT 5   Write the requested 11th and 13th chords. The first five are written in analysis symbols and the second five in popular music symbols.

ASSIGNMENT 6   Add alto and tenor to the following phrases and analyze each chord. Follow these partwriting suggestions:

1   Omit the 3rd in 11th chords. One other factor must be omitted also, and this is most often the 5th.
2   With 13th chords do not include the 3rd and 11th factors at the same time. Be sure, however, to include at least one other dissonant factor besides the 13th.
3   Resolve dissonant chord factors whenever possible, but such is not mandatory in these phrases.
4   All other previous suggestions regarding range, voice order, doubling, and spacing apply as well here.

1.

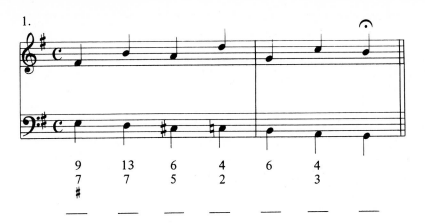

```
9    13    6    4    6    4
7    7     5    2         3
#
```

2.

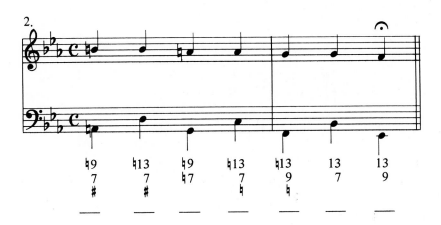

```
♮9   ♮13   ♮9    ♮13   ♮13   13   13
7    7     ♭7    7     9     7    9
#    #           ♮     ♮
```

3.

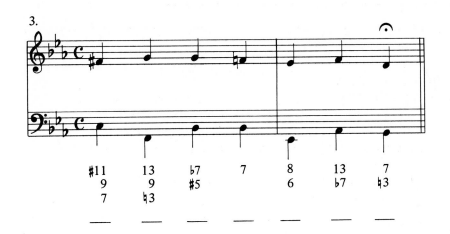

```
#11   13    ♭7    7    8    13    7
9     9     #5         6    ♭7    ♮3
7     ♮3
```

ASSIGNMENT 7

Write a short homophonic composition of about fourteen to twenty measures.

1   Use the harmonic progressions in No. 3 above (Assignment No. 6) and complete the composition with harmonic progressions of your own choosing.
2   4/4 meter and *C* minor.
3   Use one chord of the above for each measure of your composition (harmonic rhythm of one chord per measure)
4   Here is an illustration showing how the first two measures might be completed:

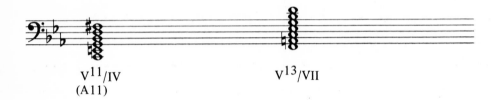

V^{11}/IV
(A11) V^{13}/VII

5   Write the composition for piano alone or for any combination of instruments or voices you wish.
6   Perform all compositions in class and have the students criticize each— favorably or unfavorably as the occasion demands.

ASSIGNMENT 8

Following is sixteen measures of a melody that is typical of a familiar popular style.

1   Copy the melody on a separate sheet of score paper and harmonize it first with block chords according to the popular music symbols given.
2   Arrange the block chords into a suitable piano accompaniment.
3   Chords may be inverted for better voicing.
4   Have one student play the melody on an instrument in class while another plays the accompaniment he has written.

ASSIGNMENT 9

1 Write a period (two four-measure phrases) of music.
2 Use the following harmonic progression:

MEASURES:	1	2	3	4	5	6	7	8
HARMONY:	I	VI^9	II^{13}	V^{13}	I	II^{13}	V^{13}	I

3 Compose a melody above the harmonic progression.
4 Use any meter and key signature you wish.
5 Write for any instrument or combination of instruments that are played by students in the class.

ASSIGNMENT 10

Write an original composition of approximately sixteen to twenty-four measures. Use whatever meter and key you wish, and write for any medium that interests you so long as it can be performed in class.

The composition should be predominantly 7th, 9th, 11th, and 13th chords.

ASSIGNMENT 11

Following is the 2nd movement of the Sonatine by Ravel.

1 Write the chords in simple position on the blank staff below each score of music.
2 Analyze each chord.
3 Discuss the use of 7th, 9th, 11th, and 13th chords—resolution of dissonant factors, types of progressions involving such chords, etc.
4 Discuss the general style and form. Compare this style with others analyzed earlier.

Assignment 11 (continued)

Mouvement de Menuet

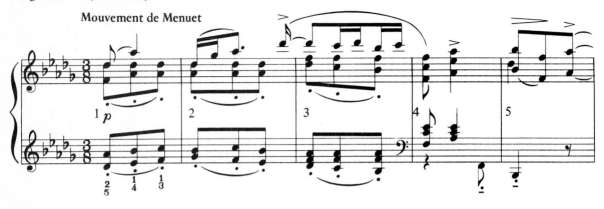

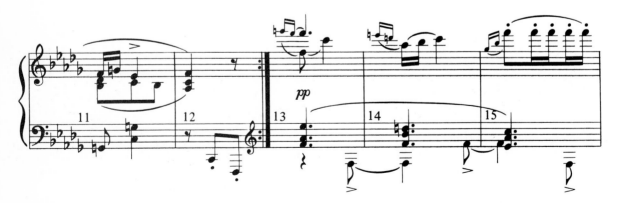

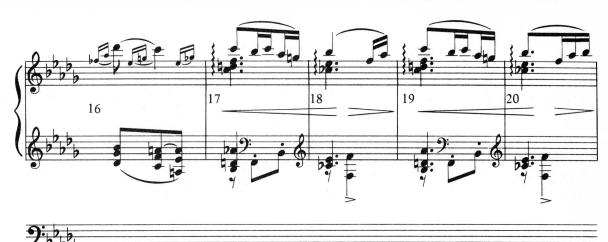

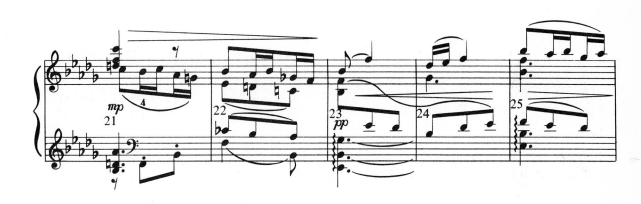

Assignment 11 (continued)

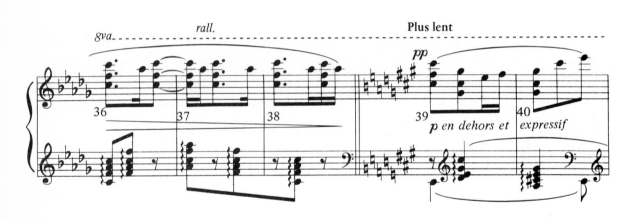

Assignment 11 (continued)

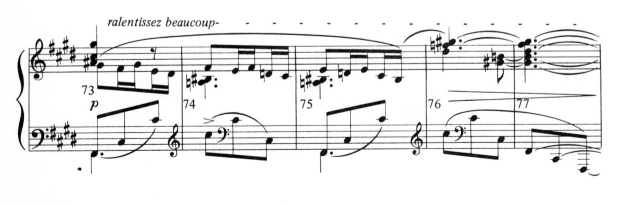

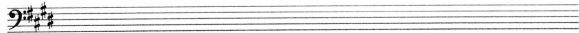

5
The Neapolitan
Sixth Chord

The Neapolitan 6th Chord in Major Keys: $\flat II^6 = N^6$
The Neapolitan 6th Chord in Minor Keys: $\flat II^6 = N^6$

DEFINITION

A major triad based on the lowered second degree of the major or minor scale.

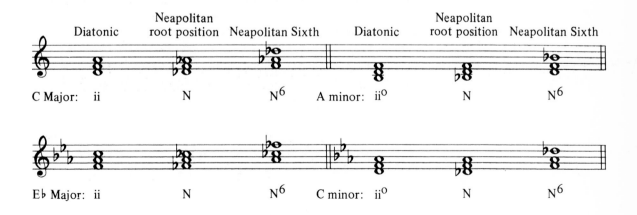

UTILIZATION OF THE NEAPOLITAN 6TH CHORD

A   The triad is generally found in 1st inversion—thus the name neapolitan "sixth." Tradition has permitted this name to extend even to the root position of the chord.

Mozart: Piano Sonata in D Major, K. 284

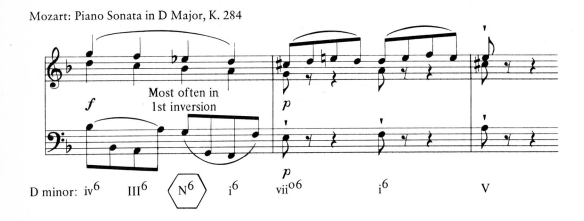

B   The neapolitan 6th chord is found more often in the minor than in the major mode.

N^6 in minor mode:
Beethoven: Sonata in C Minor, Op. 27, No. 2 (Moonlight)

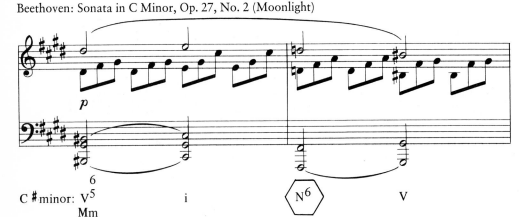

N^6 in major mode:
Schubert: G Major Mass

C   The neapolitan 6th chord produces a distinctive and colorful effect and customarily progresses (eventually) to the dominant chord—as does its diatonic counterpart. When it resolves directly the dominant is ordinarily a 7th chord with the fifth missing (to avoid cross-relation).

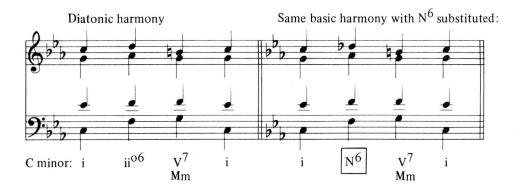

D   Although the eventual progression of the neapolitan is to the V, other chords are often interpolated between.

1. N^6 often progresses to either the VII^7/V or I^6_4 or both before reaching dominant harmony.

Some common resolutions of the Neapolitan 6th:

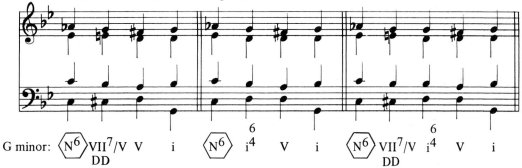

Here is an example from a Mozart composition of an N^6 progressing to a VII^7/V:
DD

Mozart: Fantasia, K. 397

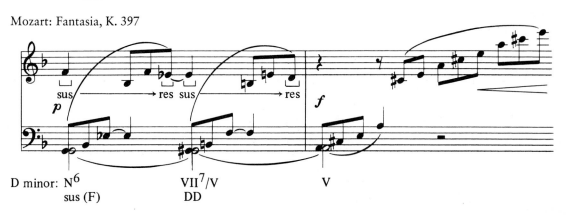

E   N⁶ may be preceded by any harmony used to precede the diatonic ii triad.

F   The reason for the title "neapolitan" is obscured in history and is unknown to us today.

G   Some theorists believe the neapolitan 6th derived from the Phrygian mode that contains a lowered 2nd (compared to natural minor). Whether such speculation is true or not there is a distinct suggestion of Phrygian flavor in the chord.

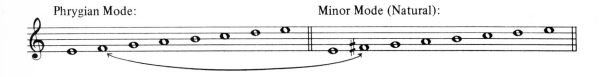

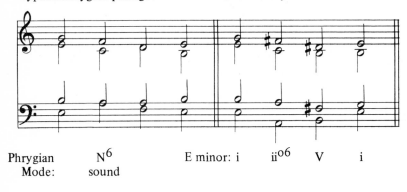

Phrygian   N⁶   E minor: i   ii°⁶   V   i
Mode: sound

HISTORY

Renaissance Period

Although there are examples of sonorities resembling the neapolitan in the Renaissance period, they are not treated as functioning chords and result generally from the use of the Phrygian mode.

Palestrina: Kyrie of the Mass: De Feria

Phrygian Mode:

Baroque Period

The neapolitan 6th is first found as a functioning chord in the Baroque period. It is used very sparingly in all periods including the Baroque. Conservative and conventional use is made generally of the N[6] in this period, and it is more often than not found near a cadence.

Bach: St. Matthew Passion

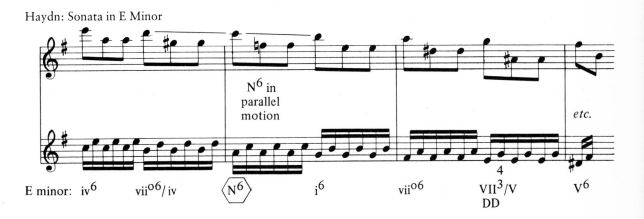

He was re-vil-ed al-so by the rob-bers, who with Him were cru-ci-fied

Neapolitan progresses directly to V

Neapolitan near a cadence

C minor: V^6 VII^7/V N^6 V   i
DD

Classical Period

The neapolitan 6th chord continued in use during this period in much the same manner as in the Baroque. On occasion it was used during the Classical period in a passage of extended parallel motion. Here is an illustration of this treatment:

Haydn: Sonata in E Minor

N^6 in parallel motion

etc.

E minor: iv^6 vii^{o6}/iv N^6 i^6 vii^{o6} VII^3_4/V V^6
DD

Romantic Period

The use of the N[6] increased in the Romantic period and the more pre-scribed treatment of earlier periods broadened considerably. Whereas the N[6] generally progressed to the V chord, several different alternatives developed during the Romantic period. Shown here are a few of the anomalous examples of N[6] use during this period.

Schubert: *Der Doppelgänger*

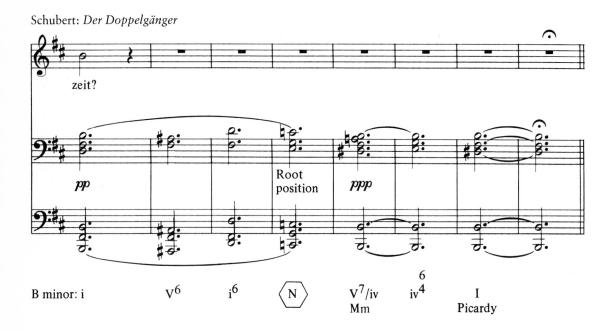

Rimsky–Korsakoff: *The Nightingale Charmed by the Rose,* Op. 2, No. 2

Post-Romantic and Impressionistic Period

Because it is strictly a device related to the harmonic idiom of the Baroque, Classical, and Romantic periods, its use in the Post-Romantic and

Impressionistic period was considerably diminished and eventually faded completely.

Here is an example of the use of a neapolitan chord in the works of Rachmaninoff. Note that it is not handled in the traditional manner since the N^6 does not resolve to the dominant but is treated in third relationship with the *E* triad that follows.

Rachmaninoff: Prelude, Op. 32, No. 10

B minor: i   N   iv vii^6 iv vii^6 iv   vii^6 iv i iv iv$^6_4$
(Phrygian:

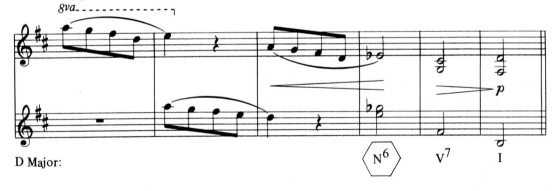

D Major: N^6 V^7 I

PARTWRITING THE NEAPOLITAN 6TH

1   N^6 *resolves to the V chord whether immediately or delayed by the* I^6_4
    and/or the VII^7/V.
            DD

2   *The bass note (3rd of the triad) is generally doubled.* The 5th of the triad may be doubled only if circumstances of voice leading require it. The root (lowered 2nd scale degree) is an active tone and should be avoided in doubling.

3   *The chord is found in root position on occasion, but here too the 3rd of the triad is most often doubled.*

4   *All previous practices regarding avoidance of parallel 5ths, good spacing, range of voices, etc. are to be observed.*

5   *The cross relation that occurs when the N⁶ resolves immediately to V is not always avoided by composers.* Some will add a 7th and remove the 5th of the V triad, but others seem to savor the astringent effect of the cross relation itself.

Both are found in literature

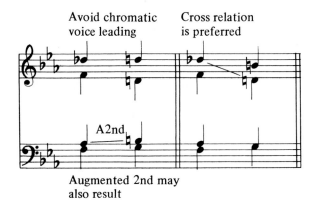

6   *If the neapolitan 6th is to be taken to the V triad, actual practice dictates that the root (lowered 2nd scale degree) does not usually proceed on in the same voice to the diatonic supertonic.* To do so creates an augmented 2nd in another voice.

7 *In certain arrangements of the chord (when the 5th is above the root)*
   partwriting is extremely difficult without crossing voices, which may be
   done under the circumstances.

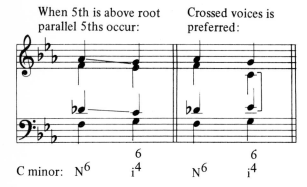

When 5th is above root   Crossed voices is
parallel 5ths occur: preferred:

C minor: N⁶   i⁴   N⁶   i⁴
                    6   6

ASSIGNMENT 1   Each given triad in four-part harmony below is the V chord in a MINOR key.

1 Determine the key (*minor* key) and write it in the blank between the staves.
2 Determine the neapolitan 6th chord in this key and write it in four-part harmony so that it leads smoothly to the V triad.
3 Place the analysis in the blanks beneath each chord.

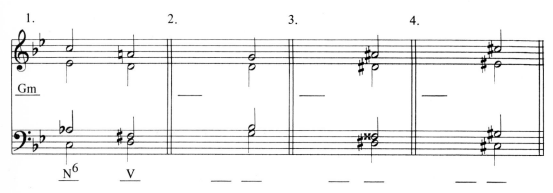

ASSIGNMENT 2   Below are four-part chorale phrases:

1   Add alto and tenor according to the figured bass symbols.
2   Provide a complete harmonic analysis:

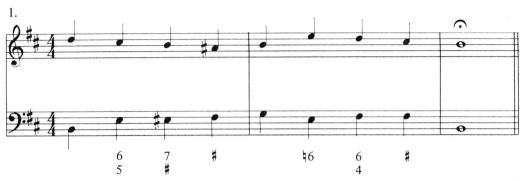

Analysis: ___   ___   ___   ___   ___   ___   ___   ___

Analysis: ___   ___   ___   ___   ___   ___   ___   ___   ___

THE NEAPOLITAN 6TH IN CHORD PROGRESSIONS

It is often difficult to incorporate a newly learned harmony in the context of music just as a newly acquired word does not feel comfortable in the vocabulary until it has been assimilated sufficiently. Thus, until a natural feel is developed for harmonizing a melody using the neapolitan 6th the following step-by-step procedure may be used.

Although the neapolitan 6th is not always followed by the V chord (either immediately or delayed) the progression to the dominant is the most conventional and should take priority in the studies below.

1   The melody to be harmonized is:

2   For the purpose of the moment each beat will be considered as a new
    harmony although when a selection is made, harmony may be repeated
    from one beat to the next.
        The possible diatonic triads that can be used with each melody tone
    are:

Melody tone as root:	i	vii^o	i	III$^+$	III$^+$	iv	ii^o	i
Melody tone as third:	VI	V	VI	i	i	ii^o	vii^o	VI
Melody tone as fifth:	iv	III$^+$	iv	VI	VI	vii^o	V	iv

3   To obtain a sufficient number of strong progressions (descending 5ths)
    and an appropriate balance of primary triads (I, IV, and V) both are
    marked—the strong progressions with a line from one chord to the next,
    and the primary triads are circled.

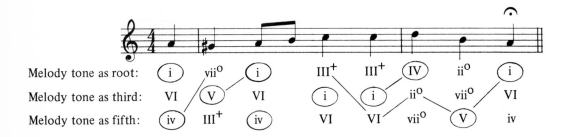

Melody tone as root:	i	vii^o	i	III$^+$	III$^+$	IV	ii^o	i
Melody tone as third:	VI	V	VI	i	i	ii^o	vii^o	VI
Melody tone as fifth:	iv	III$^+$	iv	VI	VI	vii^o	V	iv

4   Selecting from among all possible harmonizations, the following four are
    chosen as candidates. Since this melody is a phrase from a chorale it is
    appropriate to harmonize it simply.

Version 1:

Using only primary triads: i   V——i   i   i——iv   V——i   lacks variety

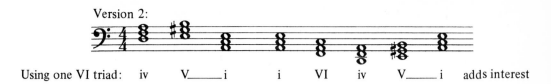

Using one VI triad: iv   V___i   i   VI   iv   V___i   adds interest

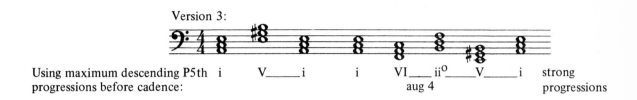

Using maximum descending P5th   i   V___i   i   VI___ii°___V___i   strong
progressions before cadence: aug 4   progressions

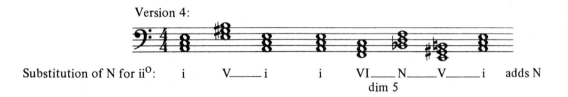

Substitution of N for ii°:   i   V___i   i   VI___N___V___i   adds N
                                            dim 5

5   The final version (No. 4) is chosen for harmonization and a bass line is
     sketched in. This bass line is acceptable because it provides sufficient
     contrary motion with the given melody and at the same time is direc-
     tional (proceeds in a single direction long enough to provide shape).

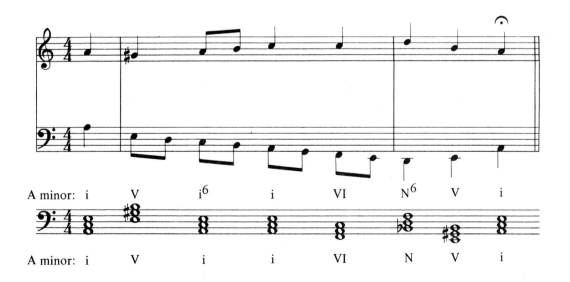

A minor: i   V   i⁶   i   VI   N⁶   V   i

A minor: i   V   i   i   VI   N   V   i

6   The inner voices are added and the phrase becomes complete:

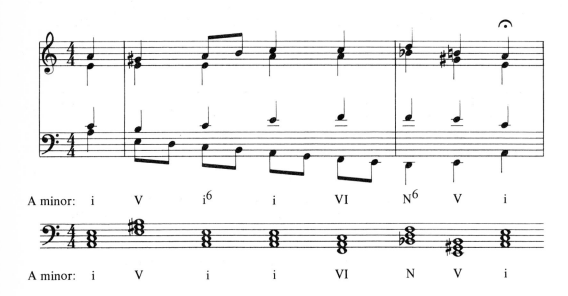

A minor: i   V   i⁶   i   VI   N⁶   V   i

A minor: i   V   i   i   VI   N   V   i

ASSIGNMENT 3   Following are melodies to be harmonized.

1   Using the procedures outlined above harmonize each of the two soprano lines using four-part harmony.
2   Include at least one neapolitan 6th chord in each.
3   Provide a harmonic analysis of each chord.
4   Use a harmonic rhythm of one chord per quarter note except at the cadence. On occasion the repetition of a chord may be desirable.

1.

G minor

2.

A minor

ASSIGNMENT 4   Following is a melody to be harmonized.

1   Using the procedures outlined above, harmonize the melody.
2   Use a harmonic rhythm of two chords per measure (dotted quarter per harmony).
3   Arrange the chords in a typical piano style, or if you are an instrumentalist, arrange the chords for at least three or four instruments with which you are familiar.

ASSIGNMENT 5   Write two phrases (in succession) of music:

1   Make the phrases parallel in relationship.
2   Use 3/4 meter and B minor
3   Make the harmonic scheme:

	PHRASE 1				PHRASE 2			
MEASURES:	1	2	3	4	5	6	7	8
HARMONY:	i	VI	VII⁷/V DD	V	i	VI	N⁶	V	i

(HARMONY row, aligned under measures: i | VI | VII⁷/V DD | V || i | VI | N⁶ | V | i)

4   Use homophonic texture (single line of melody with chordal accompaniment).
5   Write for any instrument or group of instruments familiar to you. Be sure to make the harmonic elaboration fit the instrument you choose.
6   Be sure to add all interpretation markings, phrasings, etc.

ASSIGNMENT 6   For the following composition:

1   Make a complete harmonic analysis in the same manner as is shown in the first measure (example).
2   Discuss:
   a   The key scheme
   b   The form
   c   The number of phrases
   d   The cadence formulas
   e   Compositional devices such as sequences, repetition, elongation, etc.
   f   Harmonic rhythm
   g   Any other significant points regarding this composition

Beethoven (1770–1827), *Variations on "God Save the King"*

C minor: i   ii°⁶

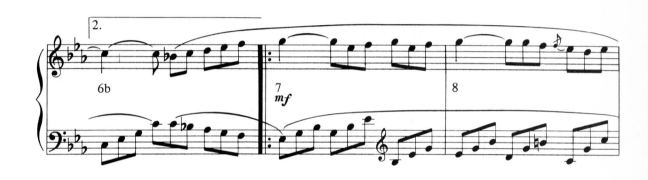

Assignment 6 (continued)

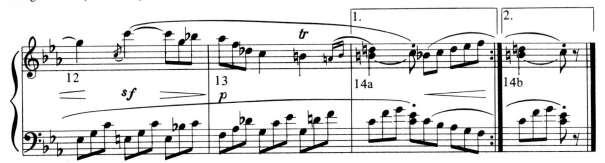

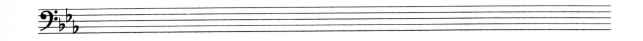

6
Augmented
Sixth Chord

Italian: $It^6 = IV^{6\sharp}$

German: $Gr^6 = IV\ \begin{smallmatrix}6\sharp\\5\\3\end{smallmatrix}$ *French:* $Fr^6 = II\ \begin{smallmatrix}6\sharp\\4\\3\end{smallmatrix}$

German: $Gr^6 = IV\ \begin{smallmatrix}6\sharp\\4\sharp\\3\end{smallmatrix}$

DEFINITION

A type of altered chord that contains the interval of an augmented 6th between the lowest sounding tone and another above it. Traditionally the chord maintains its name (augmented 6th chord) even when the augmented sixth is inverted to a diminished 3rd.

THE THREE TYPES

Italian — M3rd + A6th above the lowest sounding tone.

German — M3rd + A6th + P5th above the lowest sounding tone.

German — M3rd + A6th + AA4th above the lowest sounding tone.

French — M3rd + A6th + A4th above the lowest sounding tone.

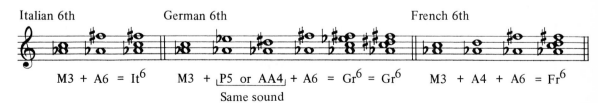

Italian 6th   German 6th   French 6th

M3 + A6 = It^6 M3 + ⌊P5 or AA4⌋ + A6 = Gr^6 = Gr^6 M3 + A4 + A6 = Fr^6

                     Same sound

Note that the *German Augmented 6th chord* has two possible spellings (same sound):

Two spellings for the German augmented 6th:

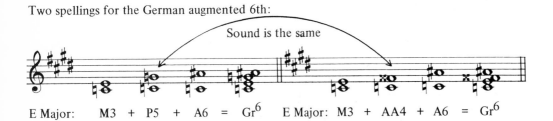

E Major: M3 + P5 + A6 = Gr^6 E Major: M3 + AA4 + A6 = Gr^6

German augmented 6th spelled with:

The tone a M3rd below the tonic is generally the lowest sounding tone for all three types in either major or minor keys:

Lowest sounding tone of augmented 6th chord is a major 3rd below the tonic:

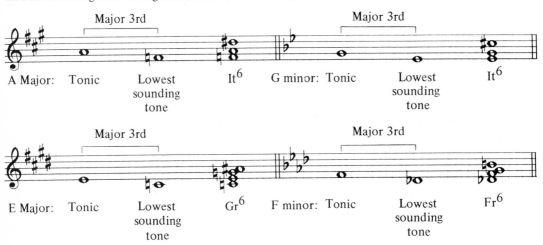

Found much less often is an augmented 6th chord whose lowest sounding tone is a m2nd above the tonic:

Lowest sounding tone of augmented 6th chord is (less often) a minor 2nd above the tonic:

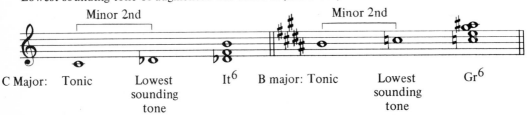

TREATMENT OF AUGMENTED 6TH CHORDS

Although augmented 6th chords bear little relationship in sound to their diatonic counterparts, they function in a very similar manner. Below are illustrations of diatonic chords followed by the same chords as augmented 6ths:

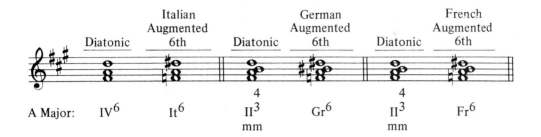

Diatonic chord progression: Same chord progression with augmented 6th:

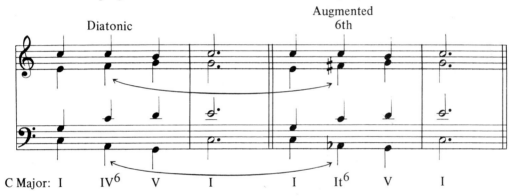

Mozart: Symphony in G Minor, K. 550

Diatonic chord progression
without altered chords used by Mozart   Same chord progression as Mozart composed it:

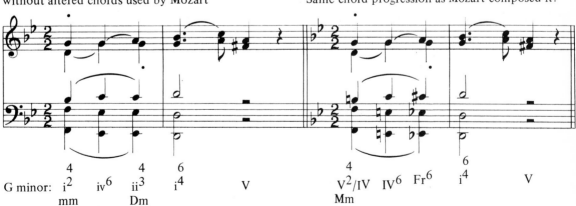

Augmented 6th chords whose lowest sounding tone is a M3rd below the tonic are followed by the V chord. The augmented 6th expands out to a perfect octave. Note that the German and French 6th is often followed by the tonic in second inversion in order to avoid parallel 5ths:

The interval of the augmented 6th expands out to a perfect octave:

Augmented 6th chords whose lowest sounding tone is a m2nd above the tonic are followed by the tonic chord. Note again that the German 6th requires special handling.

The interval of the augmented 6th expands out to a perfect octave:

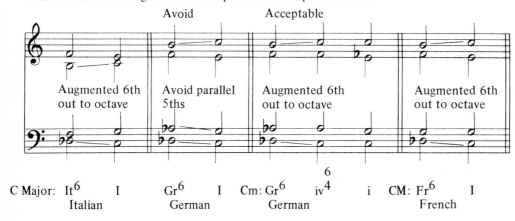

Although the great majority of augmented 6th chords occur on a tone an M3rd below the tonic, it is quite possible for an augmented 6th chord to be built on any diatonic or altered degree of the scale.

Rare use of augmented 6th chord:

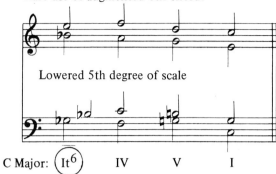

Lowered 5th degree of scale

C Major: (It^6)   IV   V   I

Altered tones of the augmented 6th chord are almost never doubled.
Factors of augmented 6th chords are not deleted.

The German augmented 6th chord with the P5th is used most often in minor keys while the same chord with the AA4th is used in major keys. Both chords are immediately followed by the tonic in second inversion before resolving to the V chord.

German augmented 6th chord spellings in major and minor keys:

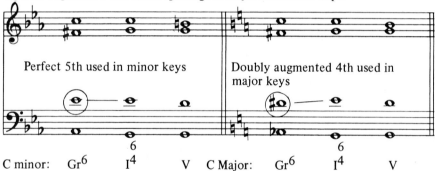

Perfect 5th used in minor keys   Doubly augmented 4th used in major keys

C minor: Gr^6 I$^6_4$ V   C Major: Gr^6 I$^6_4$ V

HISTORY

Baroque Period

The augmented 6th chord emerged in the Baroque period, but it was used very sparingly since this era tended more toward diatonic harmony.

Zipoli: Toccata

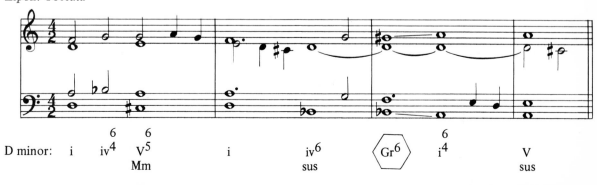

D minor: i   iv$^6_4$ V$^6_5$ i   iv^6 (Gr^6)   i$^6_4$ V
                          Mm   sus   sus

W. F. Bach: Polonaise No. 4

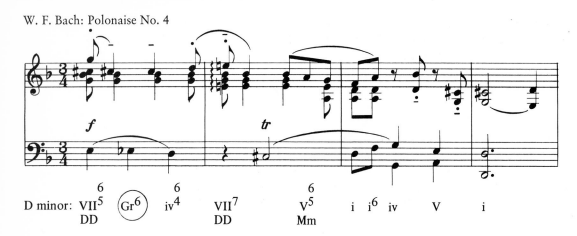

D minor: VII$^6_5$ (Gr^6) iv$^6_4$ VII^7 V$^6_5$ i i^6 iv V i
          DD   DD   Mm

Classical Period

This period saw increased use of the augmented 6th chords. Both Haydn and Mozart used such chords as did other composers. Stereotyped handling of the chords continued much as in the Baroque.

Mozart: *Das Veilchen*

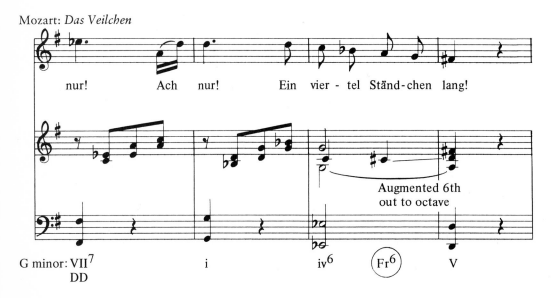

nur!   Ach   nur!   Ein vier - tel Ständ-chen lang!

Augmented 6th
out to octave

G minor: VII^7 i   iv^6 (Fr^6)   V
          DD

Haydn: Piano Sonata No. 52

Modulation from B♭
Major to C Major

B♭ Major: ⌈ I
CM: ⌊ ♭VII   It^6 V

Composers of the Classical period occasionally relaxed their strict handling of the Gr⁶ allowing it to resolve in parallel 5ths directly to the V triad. Those were dubiously termed *Mozart fifths*.

Romantic Period

As with most altered chords, augmented 6ths reached their zenith during the Romantic period. Use became more frequent, and handling of the chords became more free and unpredictable. Chord positions varied (not always in the conventional inversion), resolutions became less stereotyped, and augmented 6th chords were on occasion surrounded by other altered chords.

Chopin: Prelude No. 22

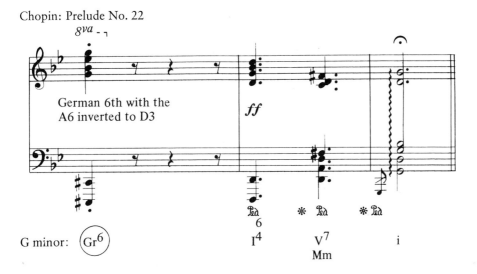

Schumann: *Frauen Lieben und Leben*

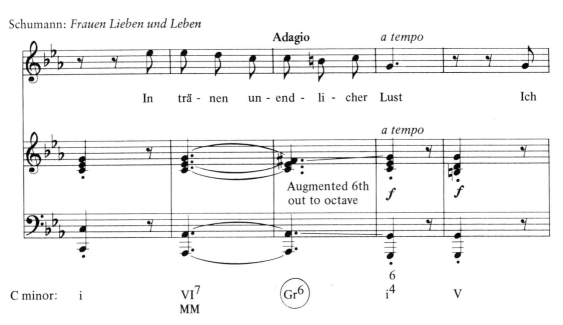

Chopin: Prelude No. 20

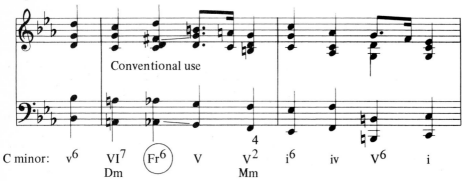

Sullivan: *Princess Ida*

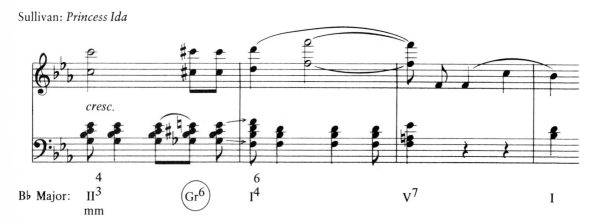

Post-Romantic and Impressionistic Period

While there are a number of examples of chords bearing the augmented 6th sound in this period, few would be considered true functioning augmented 6th chords. The type of motivating harmonic progression of the Romantic period gradually declined in the Post-Romantic and Impressionistic period. The advent of "floating" harmony (parallel chords, third relationship, and increased employment of ostinato and pedal tones) brought about an end to the dominant-tonic chord progression which was a trademark of the Baroque, Classical, and Romantic periods. The French augmented 6th sound continued into this later period as a *whole-tone chord* although its function seldom permitted it to expand to the perfect octave in the following chord. Except for rare instances the functioning augmented 6th chord ceased to exist in the Post-Romantic and Impressionistic period.

The following excerpt presents a German 6th sounding chord that progresses directly to the tonic chord thus eliding completely the expected V harmony and destroying the pronounced resolution of the A6th interval.

Ravel: Sonatine (1st movement)

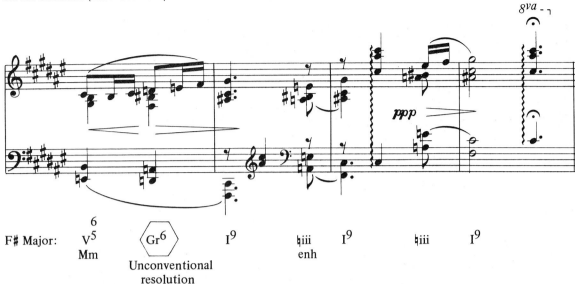

F♯ Major: V⁶₅   Gr⁶   I⁹   ♮iii   I⁹   ♮iii   I⁹
             Mm   enh

             Unconventional
             resolution

The excerpt below, written between 1892 and 1894 by Debussy, illustrates a sonority resembling that of a French augmented 6th chord. Here, as in many instances in the Impressionistic period, the chord retains the distinct sound, but its use in parallel chord construction is in direct contrast to earlier practice.

Debussy: Afternoon of a Faun

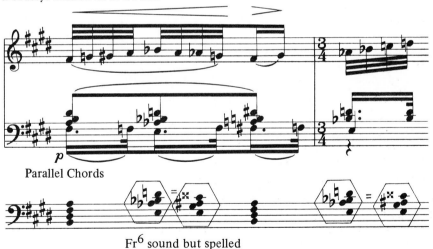

Parallel Chords

Fr⁶ sound but spelled
enharmonically

American Popular Music

While the later periods of *jazz* preferred highly adorned 7th, 9th, 11th, and 13th chords, and *rock* music favored the very simplest kind of basic triad harmony, the augmented 6th chord received some recognition especially in the early days of *ragtime*. Scott Joplin, one of the better known composers and performers of ragtime, includes a number of augmented 6th chords in his own compositions. Most of these followed the conventional treatment of the Baroque, Classical, or Romantic periods.

Joplin: Binks Waltz

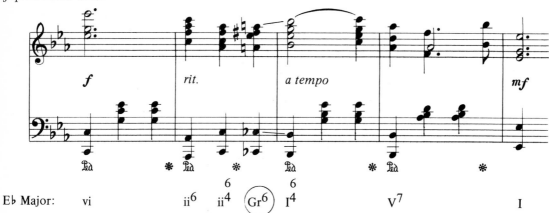

Joplin: The Cascades Rag

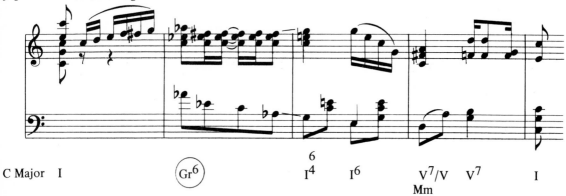

ASSIGNMENT 1

1   Write the requested chord in simple position on the staff.

2   Name the key. Each given tone is the *bass* note of the augmented 6th chord and is a major 3rd below the tonic of the key.

3   Note:

   a   Italian and French augmented 6th chords may resolve directly to V, and thus may be in either major or parallel minor mode.

   b   The German augmented 6th chord spelled with a P5th above the bass tone resolves to a tonic minor 6–4 chord and thus is used in minor mode only.

   c   The German augmented 6th chord spelled with an AA4th above the bass tone resolves to a tonic major 6–4 chord and thus is used in the major mode.

4   The example illustrates correct procedure.

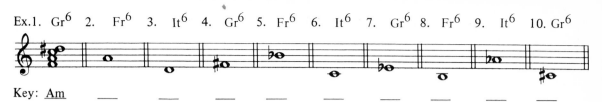

Ex.1. Gr⁶ 2. Fr⁶ 3. It⁶ 4. Gr⁶ 5. Fr⁶ 6. It⁶ 7. Gr⁶ 8. Fr⁶ 9. It⁶ 10. Gr⁶

Key: _Am_   ___   ___   ___   ___   ___   ___   ___   ___   ___   ___

ASSIGNMENT 2   In each exercise an augmented 6th chord in four-part harmony is given.

1 Write the *most conventional* resolution in four-part harmony.
2 Name the key in the blank provided. The bass tone of each given augmented 6th chord is a major 3rd below the tonic of the key.
3 Analyze both chords (the given chord and its resolution).
4 The example illustrates correct procedure.

Example

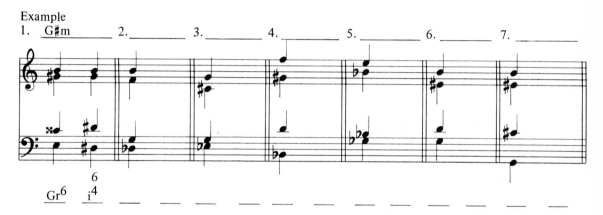

1. _G♯m_   2._____ 3._____ 4._____ 5._____ 6._____ 7._____

Gr⁶ i⁶₄   ___   ___   ___   ___   ___   ___

8._____ 9._____ 10._____ 11._____ 12._____ 13._____ 14._____

HARMONIZING MELODIES USING AUGMENTED 6TH CHORDS

To illustrate the harmonization of melodies with augmented 6th chords, the following melody will represent a model phrase:

A minor:

Melody tone harmonized as

	1	2	3	4	5	6	7
	i	III⁺	III⁺	(ii⁰)	i	(ii⁰)	vii⁰
	VI	i	i	vii⁰	VI	vii⁰	V
	(iv)	VI	VI	V	(iv)	V	III⁺
	(II⁷ Dm)	(IV⁷ mm)	(IV⁷ mm)	III⁷ AM	(II⁷ Dm)	III⁷ AM	I⁷ mM

Any melody tone that can be harmonized with diatonic ii, ii⁰, II⁷, iv, IV, or IV⁷ chords may support an augmented 6th chord as well. These chords are circled in the illustration above. Such diatonic chords can be converted to augmented 6th chords in the following way:

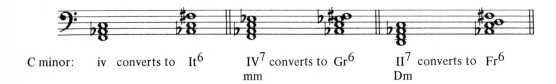

C minor: iv converts to It⁶   IV⁷ converts to Gr⁶   II⁷ converts to Fr⁶
                                          mm   Dm

Whether the augmented 6th chord can actually be substituted for any particular circled chord depends upon:

1 Whether the melody tone is one of the altered factors of the augmented 6th chord or not. If the diatonic melody tone is one of the factors that would necessarily be altered to form the augmented 6th chord it of course cannot be substituted.

2 Whether the melody tone following the augmented 6th harmony supports a resolution. For the Italian and French 6ths either tonic 6–4 or dominant harmony can be utilized, but with the German augmented 6th only tonic 6–4 is available due to the parallel P5ths that are unavoidable when resolving directly to V. Later composers (of the middle and late Romantic period) concerned themselves less with strict-voice leading and permitted the P5ths to exist. However, as a discipline, these should be avoided for the present.

In this particular phrase, all melody tones except the final will support an augmented 6th chord, but an augmented 6th chord could not be written in all instances because conventional resolutions (as in No. 3 below) are not always possible.

Melody
Tones:

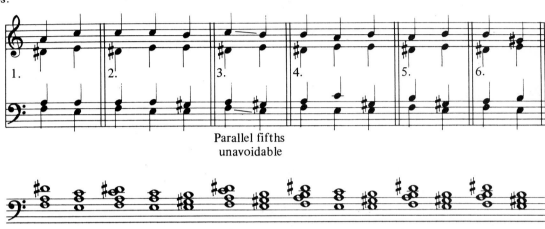

ASSIGNMENT 3

1 On a separate sheet of paper prepare a list of possible harmonies for the phrase below.

2 Circle all harmonies that could be converted to augmented 6th chords.

3 Determine (on separate score paper using four-part harmony) whether each possible augmented 6th chord can be conventionally treated. (See illustration above.)

4 Write a complete four-part harmonization of the phrase using at least one augmented 6th chord.

ASSIGNMENT 4   Following are two excerpts of melodies from instrumental music.

1   Make a complete harmonization of each on a separate sheet of score paper.
2   Write for any instrument or instruments you wish.
3   Decide first on the harmonic rhythm. Play or sing the melody over several
    times before making a final decision.
4   Then (as described in ''N.'' above) write out all possible harmonies for each
    area of harmonic rhythm.
5   Select the harmonic progressions you think will sound best. Write the block
    chords under the melody. Be sure to include at least one augmented 6th chord
    in each melody.
6   Using the block chords as a guide, sketch in a bass line, then the inner voices,
    searching at all times for opportunities to include imitation.
7   Perform the finished compositions in class and ask for student criticism.

ASSIGNMENT 5   Write an original composition of approximately thirty-two measures.

1   Instead of the usual four-measure phrase, experiment with unequal phrases (perhaps a three-measure and a five-measure phrase combining to form a period).
2   Plan the composition to be of incipient three-part form (a middle section that does not stand alone).
3   Include at least three or four augmented 6th chords as well as secondary dominants, borrowed chords, etc.
4   Make the "A" section modulate to a closely related key, then return to the tonic in the "B" section.
5   Write for any medium of your choice.
6   Perform the composition in class and ask the students to determine (from listening only) the following:
   a   The harmonic rhythm of the composition.
   b   The key to which the first section modulates.
   c   The number of phrases and the length of each phrase.
   d   The cadence types at the end of each phrase.
   e   Any compositional devices such as sequence, imitation, phrase extension, etc.

ASSIGNMENT 6   Analyze these excerpts from music literature.

1   Extract the chords and write them on the blank staff beneath each score.
2   Analyze each chord.
3   Analyze any compositional devices found in the excerpts.
4   Discuss the harmonic vocabulary of each excerpt and compare the styles represented here.
5   Perform the works in class and discuss performance practices.

Schubert: Allegro from Sonata for Piano in C Minor (1828)

Assignment 6 (continued)

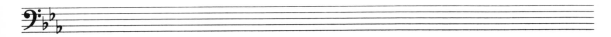

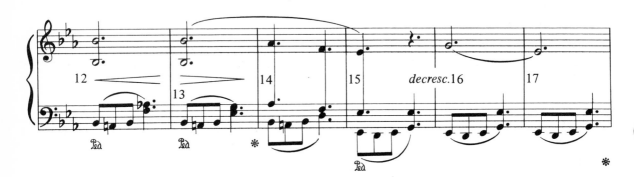

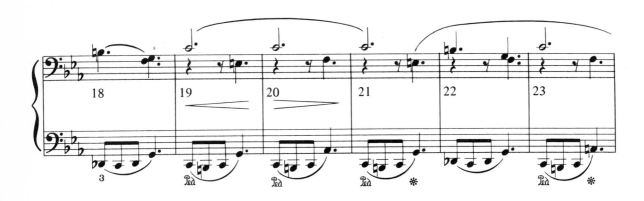

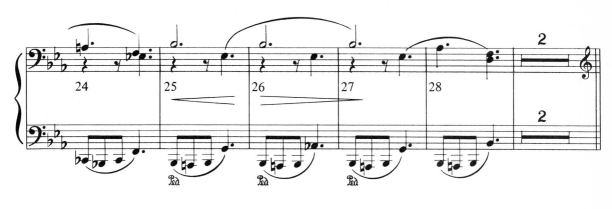

Beethoven: Piano Sonata No. 1 in F Minor, Op. 2, No. 1 (1st movement) (1795)

Assignment 6 (continued)

Beethoven: Piano Sonata, Op. 13 in C Minor (3rd movement) (1798–1799)

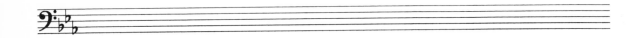

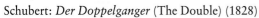

Schubert: *Der Doppelganger* (The Double) (1828)

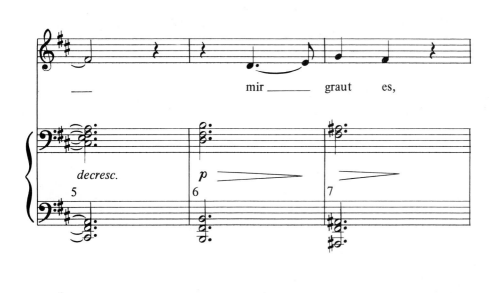

Assignment 6 (continued)

Tchaikovsky: Piano Concerto in B-flat Minor, Op. 23

7
Altered Dominants

$V+$ V^7 $V5\flat$ $V\ {}^7_{5\flat}$ V^7
        Am 3 3 Dm

$V+$ of V^7 of $V\ {}^{5\flat}_{3}$ of $V\ {}^7_{5\flat}$ of V^7 of
        Am 3 Dm

DEFINITION

Dominant triads or 7th chords that have been altered to heighten their tension and increase their need for resolution to the tonic chord. Although such chords appear in isolated instances prior to the Romantic period, their numbers increased considerably during the middle and late 1800s due to the desire on the part of composers to add more "color" to their harmony and to find alternatives to the highly structured diatonic authentic cadence.

HISTORY

Phrase interiors had seen much increase in chromaticism during the early Romantic period, but except for an occasional secondary dominant in a half cadence, the contagion had stopped just short of the final two chords.

The cadence is the single most important determining factor in key recognition, and up to the final half of the Romantic period the cadence had been kept relatively diatonic. Later in the nineteenth century, however, the gradual breakdown of the key systems overtook even the cadence, and altered dominants of one type or another became more prevalent.

TYPES OF ALTERED DOMINANTS

A   Dominant triad with the 5th raised one-half step (V$^+$).

B   Dominant 7th chord with the 5th raised one-half step (V^7).

                                              Am

C   Dominant triad with the 5th lowered one-half step (V$_3^{5\flat}$).

D   Dominant 7th chord with the 5th lowered one-half step (V$_3^{7\,5\flat}$).

E   On occasion other alterations of the dominant occur. One such is the dominant 7th chord with both the 5th and 3rd lowered one-half step. This produces a V^7.

                                        Dm

Each of the above is shown in the key of C major. Most can be employed in either major or minor mode, but the first two, V$^+$ and V^7, are

                                          Am

seldom found in the minor mode because the augmented 5th of the chords is enharmonically the same tone as the 3rd degree of the minor scale. Thus, the primary reason for the alteration (raising the 5th factor one-half step) is lost since the raised 5th cannot ascend one-half step in the minor mode.

C Major or minor:

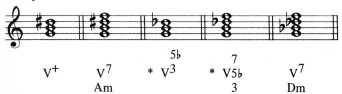

                                        5♭   7

    V$^+$ V^7 * V3   * V5♭   V^7

              Am   3   Dm

    * The usual method for analysis symbols cannot be used here since these sonorities do not conform to the usual major, minor, diminished, or augmented sounds. The "5♭" indicates that the 5th above the bass is lowered one-half step.

The V$_3^{7\,5\flat}$ in 2nd inversion is a duplicate of the French augmented 6th chord that resolves to the tonic:

Chorale with diatonic harmony:

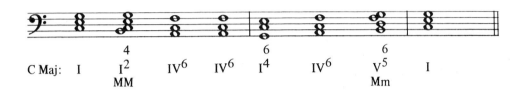

Same chorale with chromatic harmony and an altered dominant:

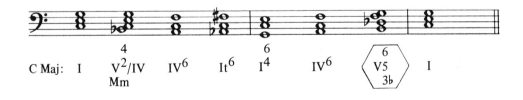

These excerpts from music literature demonstrate the use of altered dominants:

Wolf: *Das verlassene Mägdlein* (The Forsaken Maiden)

Franck: Chorale from Prelude, Chorale, and Fugue for Piano

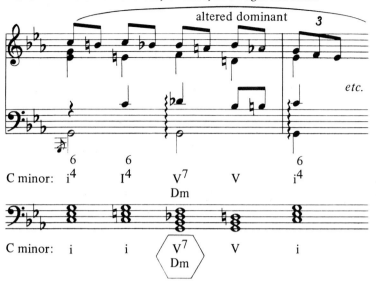

Grieg: Das Kind der Berge (The Mountain Child)

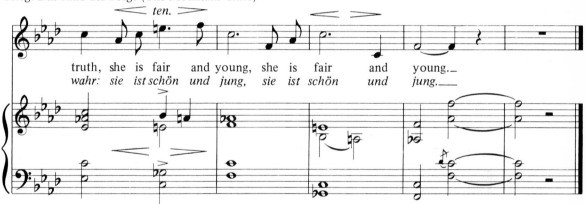

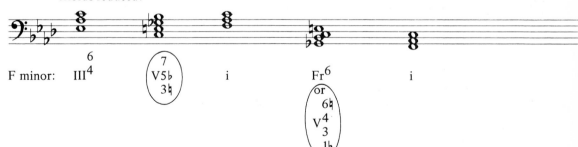

THE TREATMENT OF ALTERED DOMINANTS

A   *Altered dominants function the same as their diatonic counterparts.* In the late Romantic period altered dominants may be found anywhere a diatonic dominant would normally be located.

B   *The altered tones in altered dominants proceed in the direction of their alteration:*

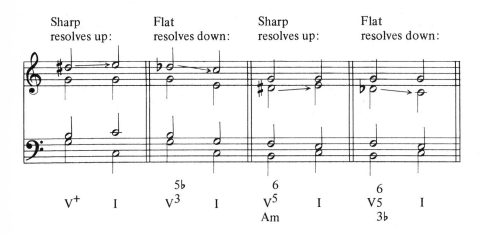

C   *Altered tones are seldom doubled.*

ALTERED DOMINANTS AS SECONDARY DOMINANTS

Just as dominant chords may be altered, these same dominant chords may be altered in the same way when they become secondary dominants. Thus, the *altered secondary dominants* constitute a wide array of chords employed especially by composers of popular music and jazz.

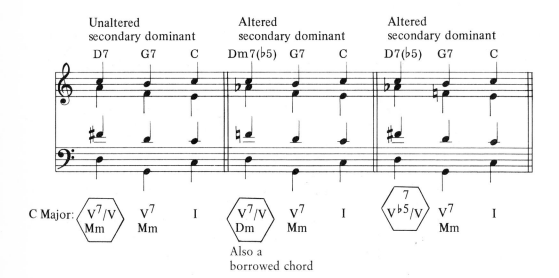

The example illustrated below provides some idea of the abundant use of *altered secondary dominants* in popular music and jazz.

Mercer and Arlen: My Shining Hour (1943). Copyright 1943 by Harwin Music Corp. Copyright renewed. All rights reserved. Used by permission of Edwin H. Morris & Co., Inc.

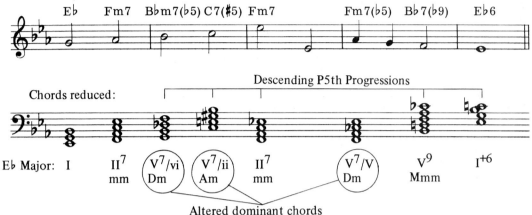

ASSIGNMENT 1   Write the requested chord above the given tone. Then, indicate the major key in which this chord is found. The example illustrates correct procedure.

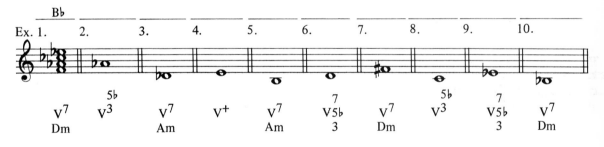

ASSIGNMENT 2

1   Add the alto and tenor voices to the phrases below. Follow these suggestions:
   A   Resolve the 7th of altered dominants that contain 7ths.
   B   Resolve dissonant factors of 9th, 11th, and 13th chords when possible. In some instances it is not possible to resolve all dissonant factors. As in previous assignments:
   C   Avoid parallel P5ths, P8, and P1.
   D   Avoid augmented 2nds, augmented 4ths, and diminished 5ths in the melodic line of any of the voices.
   E   Observe conventional doublings, voice ranges, spacing and voice order.
2   Analyze each chord.
3   Have some students place their assignments on the blackboard. Divide the class into four sections (soprano, alto, tenor, and bass) and sing them using a student conductor.

1.

	7	7		9	♮7		13	9		7
		♭5		7	♯5		7	♮7		
			♯3				♯3	3		

2.

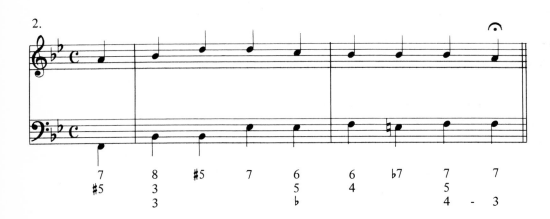

	7	8	♯5	7	6	6	♭7	7	7
	♯5	3			5	4		5	
		3			♭			4 - 3	

3.

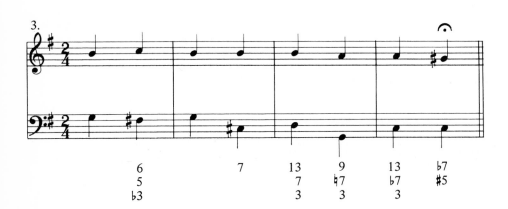

	6		7	13	9	13	♭7
	5			7	♮7	♭7	♯5
	♭3			3	3	3	

ASSIGNMENT 3   Following is a series of chords in simple position.

1 Analyze each chord first.
2 Use this set of harmonic progressions from chord No. 1 through 17 as a basis for a composition of approximately twenty to thirty measures.
3 The composition should be homophonic in texture.
4 Compose a suitable melody above the harmonic progressions.
5 Arrange the chords for any appropriate medium (piano, woodwind instruments, etc.).
6 Use any meter you wish.
7 Play the compositions in class and have students criticize.
8 The following illustration is one possible beginning:

Beginning of the composition using the first four chords: (Written for piano)

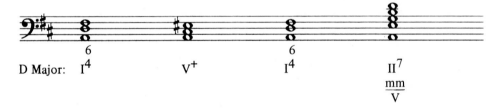

9 Be sure to include all interpretation and dynamic markings.

Harmonic progressions to be used as the basis for a composition:

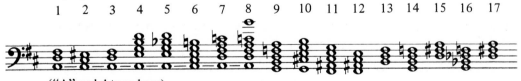

("A" pedal tone here)

Chord roots

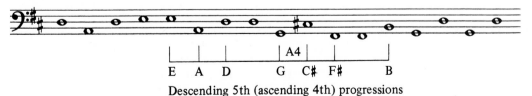

Descending 5th (ascending 4th) progressions

ASSIGNMENT 4   Write a composition of sixteen to twenty-four measures length.

1   Employ at least two altered dominants (altered dominants may be used in most instances where diatonic dominants are found).
2   Use several other altered chords (secondary dominants, borrowed chords, augmented sixth chords, etc.).
3   Plot the harmony first in block chords.
4   Then, add a suitable melody.
5   Convert the block chords to idiomatic use in any medium you wish.
6   Select your own meter and key signature (major keys will be easier and will afford more opportunities for altered dominants).
7   Play the completed compositions in class and ask students to criticize.

ASSIGNMENT 5   The following excerpt is from an Impromptu, Op. 31, No. 2 by Gabriel Fauré, a late Romantic period composer.

1   Place the chords in simple position on the blank staff beneath each score.
2   Analyze each chord.
3   Discuss the harmonic vocabulary found in this composition.
4   Discuss the use of any prominent nonharmonic devices.
5   Have one of the pianist members of the class play the excerpt.

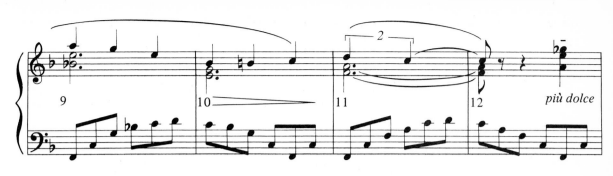

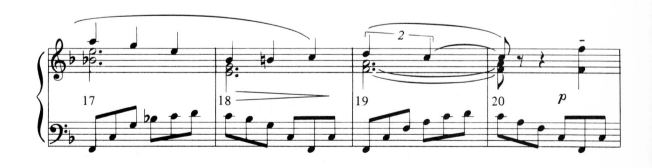

Assignment 5 (continued)

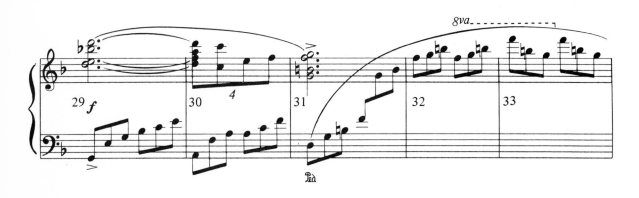

8
Chromatic Mediants

Chromatic Mediants in Major Keys: *VI, ♭VI or ♮VI, and ♭vi or ♮vi*
                                            III, ♭III or ♮III, and ♭iii or ♮iii
Chromatic Mediants in Minor Keys: *vi, ♯VI or ♮VI, and ♯vi or ♮vi*
                                            iii, ♯III or ♮III, and ♯iii or ♮iii

DEFINITION

The altered mediant and submediant triads (and 7th chords on occasion).

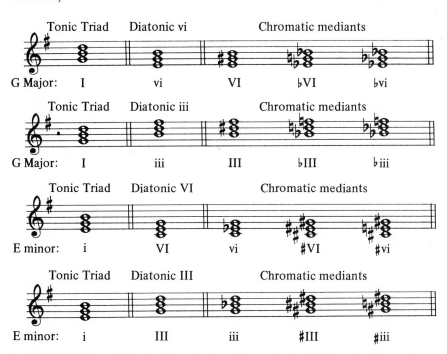

THE UTILIZATION OF CHROMATIC MEDIANTS

A   Chromatic mediants are used to provide unusual color and interest and
are generally chosen as substitutes for the diatonic mediants.

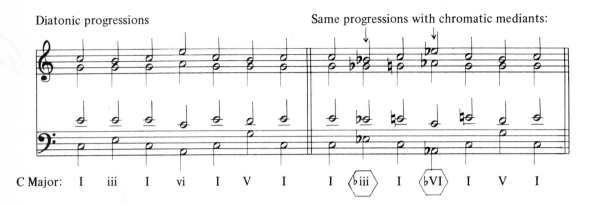

B   Since diminished and augmented triads have need for specific resolutions, only major and minor triads are usually employed as chromatic
mediants.
C   Harmonic progressions utilizing chromatic mediants most often emphasize the third relationship with the tonic and are frequently preceded or
followed by the tonic chord.

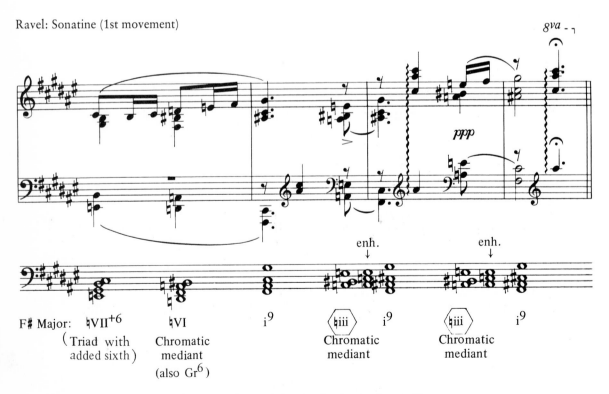

Ravel: Sonatine (1st movement)

D   Chromatic mediants are but one phase of the third relationship (adjacent chords whose roots lie a third apart) device that became an

integral part of Post-Romantic and Impressionistic harmony. As harmonic progressions emphasizing dominant-tonic relationships began to decrease in use during the late Romantic period, third relationships became more and more the practice. Here was a way in which a style could maintain tertian harmony (chords constructed in thirds) and preserve the basic ideas of harmonic progression, but at the same time reduce the tonic-dominant polarity to a point where tonality would still be present but not nearly so preponderant.

E   Chromatic mediants may be found at any point in a phrase and are often used in cadences to substitute for the dominant.

Chromatic mediant used as a substitute for the dominant in a cadence

Shostakovich: No. 3 of Three Fantastic Dances

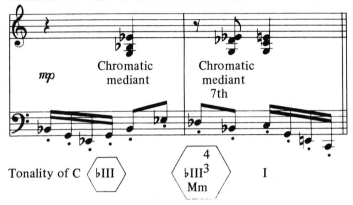

F   Cross relations frequently occur in the use of the chromatic mediant. Sometimes cross relations are carefully avoided, but frequently the cross relation is exploited for the sake of unusual and novel sound.

G   Some chromatic mediants can be analyzed in more than one way. The following illustration shows the similarity between a chromatic mediant and a dominant of the submediant.

Double analysis for some chromatic mediants

d'Indy: The Song of the Heath

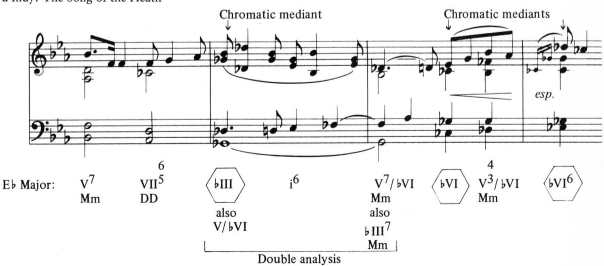

If a chord functions as a chromatic mediant (exploits third relation-ship with the tonic or dominant) it should be analyzed as such. If it functions as a secondary dominant (progresses on to a tonicized chord) it should be analyzed in that manner.

Basically all chords with a double analysis potential should be classi-fied according to function. Chords that function as chromatic mediants should be analyzed as chromatic mediants; chords that function as secondary dominants, borrowed chords, and so on should be so analyzed.

H   Dominant harmony (V) can also support chromatic mediants (III and VII). Less often even subdominant harmony (IV) may be surrounded by chromatic mediants (II and VI).

HISTORY

Renaissance Period

Except for a few composers like Gesualdo, chromatic harmony, much less chromatic mediants, is practically nonexistent.

Baroque Period

Chromatic mediants are certainly not a part of the general style of this period, although some rare instances exist.

Classical Period

Although the Classical period also finds the chromatic mediant a rarity, there are examples such as the following that illustrate a change of key through the root relationships of a major third. In this example, the tonic in D major follows the dominant in B minor, and the relationship is that of a chromatic mediant.

Mozart: Fantasia in C Minor, K. 475

B minor: V   i⁶   i   V   i⁶   i   V

Modulation by
Chromatic mediant

D Major: I _____ V / I   I

Romantic Period

Chromatic mediants, although not found as often as other altered chords, came into use during the Romantic period. Most examples are found in music relating to the later portion of the style period.

Examples of chromatic mediants in the Romantic period

Dvorak: Symphony No. 5 in E minor, Op. 95

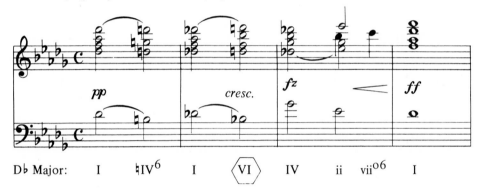

D♭ Major: I   ♮IV⁶   I   ⟨VI⟩   IV   ii   vii°⁶   I

Brahms: Symphony No. 3 in F Major, Op. 90

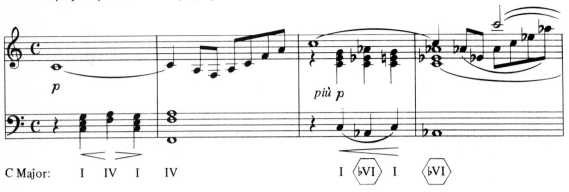

C Major: I   IV   I   IV   I ⟨♭VI⟩ I ⟨♭VI⟩

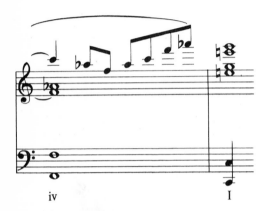

iv   I

The contributions of Richard Wagner (1813–1883) from the middle through the late Romantic period influenced music everywhere. The search for the universal and all-embracing that characterized the Romantic movement had a counterpart in Wagner's theory of music drama that sought to embrace all the arts in one complete art work striving for a common dramatic end. Certainly his greatest endowments to the world of culture were the operas he composed.

His mature style of writing may be capsulized thus:

a   Extremely chromatic.
b   Uses tertian harmony (chords built in thirds).
c   Avoids the tonic for long periods.
d   Frequently uses 7th, 9th, 11th, and 13th chords.
e   Uses many altered chords such as the neapolitan, augmented 6ths, etc.
f   Style gives the effect of constant modulation thus weakening tonality and placing greater emphasis on the resolution of the chords themselves.
g   Resolution of dissonant chords is often unconventional.

The following example demonstrates his use of the chromatic mediant. It differs from the more common practice of associating the chromatic mediant with the tonic and tends to set up small islands of chromaticism in which the chromatic mediant is the focal point.

Wagner: *Tristan und Isolde* (Act II, accompaniment only)

Post-Romantic and Impressionistic Period

Third relationship abounds in this period, and chromatic mediants become even more prominent than in the Romantic Period. Strict dominant-tonic relationships break down considerably and are replaced by chromatic mediants in many instances.

Chromatic mediants are often found in sections that are tonally very ambiguous. Thus, straying far afield from the tonic becomes a primary stylistic trait of this period, and chromatic mediants are often employed in the procedure.

Ravel: Pavane Pour une Infante Défunte

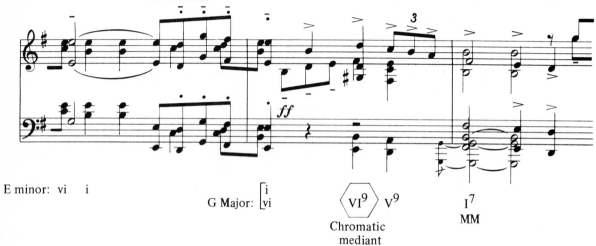

Since planing is a dominant feature in the style of the Post-Romantic and Impressionistic periods, it is possible to find many planed chords that have the spelling of chromatic mediants. Although such chords have lost the functional quality originally designed for them in the Romantic period, they still maintain some of the chromatic flavor that colors their use.

Ravel: Sonatine (3rd movement)

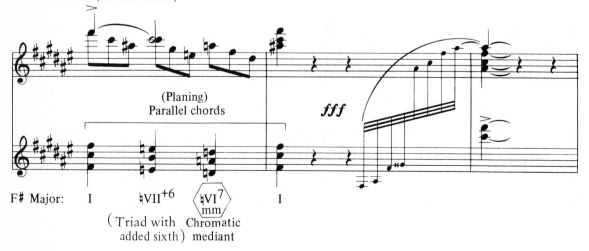

The Twentieth Century

Since this is a period of many styles and divergent forms, the use of chromatic mediants is at best spotty. Those styles that developed gradually from the Romantic period and maintained basically a triadic context (examples: Prokofieff, R. Strauss, Vaughan Williams, Rachmaninoff, etc.) contain chromatic mediants treated generally in a very free and unconventional manner.

Following is an example of a chromatic mediant that is embedded in the context of parallel chord construction:

Starer, Bright Orange from "Sketches in Color." © Copyright 1964 by MCA Music, a division of MCA, Inc. Used by permission. All rights reserved.

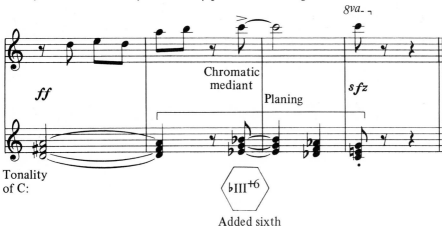

This excerpt illustrates a chromatic mediant that is also a 7th chord with both a M3rd and m3rd:

Grainger: Spoon River

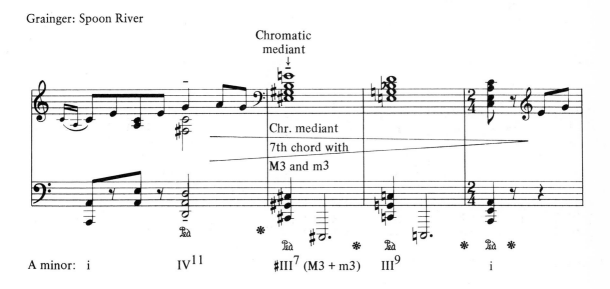

ASSIGNMENT 1   Write the three chromatic submediants and three chromatic mediants for each
                      of the following keys:

                      1   D MAJOR (EXAMPLE)
                      2   B HARMONIC MINOR
                      3   G HARMONIC MINOR
                      4   A MAJOR

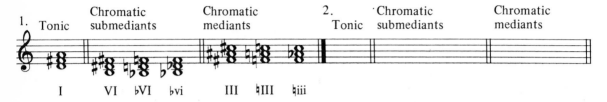

3.   4.

ASSIGNMENT 2   1   Instead of the usual figured bass, popular music symbols are given above the
                          soprano tones.
                      2   The bass melody is given and should not be altered. The placement of the
                          bass tones may indicate an *inversion* of the chord described by the popular
                          music symbol.
                      3   Add alto and tenor voices.
                      4   All previous suggestions and recommendations concerning four-part writing
                          apply here.
                      5   Dissonant chord factors can be resolved in most instances.
                      6   A few unconventional doublings will be necessary in the phrases below.
                      7   Analyze each chord.
                      8   Be prepared (if the instructor requests) to categorize each chord—whether
                          secondary dominant, altered dominant, borrowed chord, chromatic mediant,
                          diatonic triad, diatonic 7th chord, etc. A few chords might fall into two
                          categories.
                      9   To refresh the memory regarding the symbols used the following will be
                          helpful:
                          a   A letter (like "A") with no other marks indicates a major triad.
                          b   7th chords unless otherwise indicated refer to major-minor 7ths
                              (C^7 = C E G B♭)
                          c   The dominant sounding 13th chord in minor requires a flatted 13th.

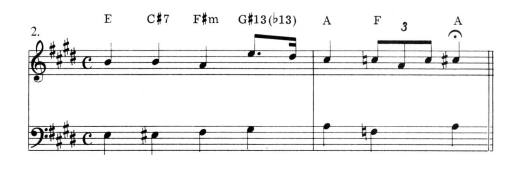

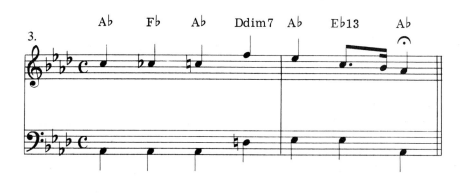

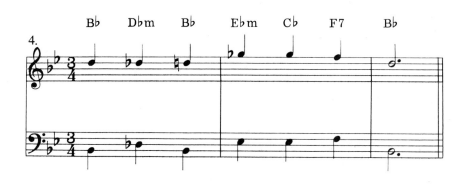

ASSIGNMENT 3   1   Analyze each chord in the following set of harmonic progressions.

2   Compose two phrases of music using the preceding set of progressions as a basis.
3   Write the composition in homophonic texture.
4   Use whatever meter signature you wish.
5   Compose a melody above the set of progressions.
6   Convert the block chords to a suitable idiomatic style for whatever medium (piano, strings, woodwinds, percussion, voices, etc.) you select.
7   Perform the composition in class and have other students criticize.
8   To illustrate the procedure, the following beginning is excerpted from a student composition. This particular one is for piano.

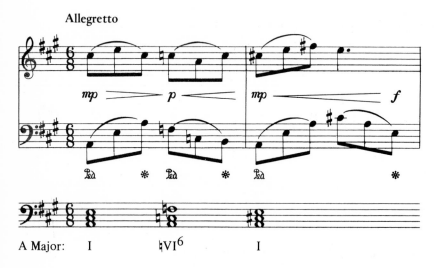

A Major: I   ♮VI⁶   I

ASSIGNMENT 4   Using the set of harmonic progressions in Assignment 3 above, add three more periods (about 24 measures) to complete a longer composition. Compose the additional harmonic progressions yourself. As a suggestion:

Chromatic mediants generally sound well if preceded and followed by tonic harmony, but they are also preceded *or* followed (not both) by the dominant with good results.

Chromatic mediants used in music literature are most often found in a harmonic style that includes generous use of other altered chords such as secondary dominants, borrowed chords, augmented 6th chords, and altered dominants as well as diatonic 7th, 9th, 11th, and 13th chords.

ASSIGNMENT 5

1 The excerpt below is from the opera "Tristan und Isolde," which was completed by Wagner in the year 1859.
2 Extract the chords and write them in simple position on the blank staff provided.
3 Place a circle around each chromatic mediant.
4 Discuss the general style of the music. Indicate salient features that make
  this style distinctive. Compare with other styles studied so far.
5 Perform the work in class with piano accompaniment. Have the men sing the
  part of Tristan (some may have to sing an octave lower than written) and the
  women the part of Isolde.
6 Listen to this excerpt from recordings.
7 Become familiar with the plot of the opera.

9

Analysis: Chorale from Chorale, Prelude, and Fugue by Cesar Franck

An important composer of the late Romantic period is the Belgian, César Franck. Along with Liszt and Wagner, his style of writing was a capstone of the period and represented the quintessence of the Romantic ideal, a fitting climax to the melodic and harmonic style that was soon to become outdated by the compositional characteristics and techniques of the twentieth-century composers.

Franck was primarily an organist and by 1853 had climbed the ladder of church positions in Paris to become choirmaster at St. Clotilde, a position he held until his death in 1890. He was appointed as the teacher of organ at the Paris Conservatoire in 1872, but contrary to the wishes of the administration he managed to teach more composition than organ. During his lifetime he was not taken seriously as a composer and was considered a maverick by his contemporaries.

In his entire lifetime Franck composed only about ninety works of which less than twenty are still being published. These consist mainly of a symphony (which is *cyclic*—same theme appears throughout the various movements), some secular choral music, and compositions for the organ and piano. Almost all of the works remaining in the repertory today were written during the last fifteen years of Franck's life. He was known as an excellent improviser, and many of his compositions reflect this influence.

Although Franck adopted more or less conventional forms from the past, the compositions themselves show that he developed a kind of theme transformation (metamorphosis) rather than the usual theme development. Here are some of the more common characteristics of his style:

1 Adopted the *cyclic* device as a compositional technique.
2 Tendency to squarecut and balanced phrases with conventional cadences that are highly chromaticized.

3   Melodic phrases are often no more than a decoration of a central tone from which he departs and returns to regularly.

4   Favors *third relationship* (chord progressions in which the roots of adjacent chords are a third apart).

5   Prefers restless and constant modulation (often in third relationship as well). Was described by one of his contemporaries as "the modulating machine."

6   Both his melody and harmony indulge in considerable chromaticism.

7   Harmonic vocabulary utilizes the favorite chords of the late Romantic period: borrowed chords, nondominant sevenths, secondary dominants, augmented sixth chords, chromatic mediants, altered dominants, and 9th, 11th and 13th chords.

8   Much use of sequence and quite often in conjunction with chromatic modulations.

9   Preferred thematic transformation to thematic development.

10   Rhythmic interest is seldom a feature of his style.

The excerpt analyzed here is taken from the *Prelude, Chorale, and Fugue,* written in 1884, six years before his death. This piano composition is typical of his harmonic and melodic style. As is typical with Franck, there is no pause between movements of this work, and the *Chorale* is approached from the *Prelude* through third relationship (a long-held major-minor 7th chord on "B" melts into the opening of the *Chorale,* which begins on an *E-flat* triad rather than an *E* major triad that would form a more conventional dominant-tonic relationship).

Franck: From Prelude, Chorale, and Fugue for Piano

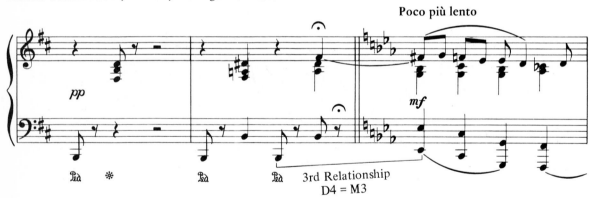

Franck: From Prelude, Chorale, and Fugue for Piano

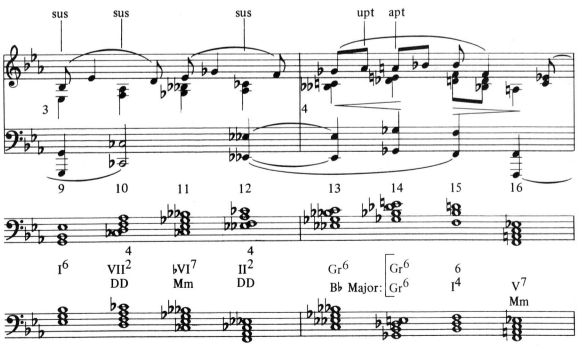

KEY

E-flat major from chord   1 through 14
B-flat major from chord 15 through 24
C minor   from   chord 25 through 42

MELODY

Phrases

Phrase A = Chords   1 through 18
Phrase B = Chords 19 through 40
Since this section is based on a chorale, Franck does not follow his usual four-measure balanced phrasing.

Sequences

A   Measures 1 and 2 are in sequence (2 legs) with measure 2 being an exact and modulatory leg.

B   Of much less importance is the short (sometimes only two tones) se-
    quences of the type in measure 9:

Measure 9:

Seq. 1   Seq. 2

Repetition

Measure 6 is a repetition of measure 5.

Structure

A   Melody is extremely conjunct with forty-two stepwise movements and
    only eight leaps.
B   A majority of the *structural* and *secondary* tones of the melody outline
    the tonic triad of the key including the keys of *B-flat* major and C
    minor (to which the composition modulates). This phenomenon, not
    found in most melodies, illustrates a strengthening of tonality in a style
    where the harmonic vocabulary makes tonality less evident.

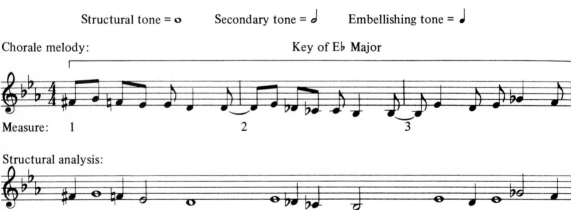

Chorale melody: Key of E♭ Major

Measure: 1   2   3

Structural analysis:

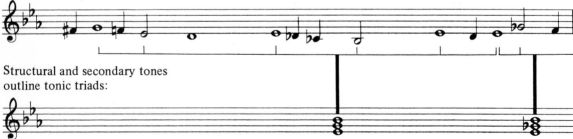

Structural and secondary tones
outline tonic triads:

HARMONY

Harmonic Vocabulary

CHORD NUMBER	HARMONIC ANALYSIS	CHORD TYPE	KEY	REMARKS:
1	I	Diatonic triad	E-*flat* maj.	
2	vi	Diatonic triad	E-*flat* maj.	
3	iii	Diatonic triad	E-*flat* maj.	
4	VII^6_5 DD	Borrowed chord	E-*flat* maj.	The "C-*flat*" is borrowed from the parallel minor.
5	$\flat VI^6$	Chromatic mediant	E-*flat* maj.	Major triad A major third below the tonic.
6	GR^6	Augmented sixth chord	E-*flat* maj.	Doubly augmented sixth chord in root position.
7	I^6	Diatonic triad	E-*flat* maj.	
8	V^4_2 Mm	Dominant 7th chord	E-*flat* maj.	
9	I^6	Diatonic triad	E-*flat* maj.	
10	VII^4_2 DD	Borrowed chord	E-*flat* maj.	Similar to chord no. 4.
11	$\flat VI^7$ Mm	Chromatic mediant	E-*flat* maj.	Same as chord no. 5 with an added 7th.
12	II^4_2 DD	*Functions* as a borrowed chord	E-*flat* maj.	Enharmonic equivalent of chord no. 4 (has same sound but is spelled differently.)
13	GR^6	Augmented sixth chord	E-*flat* maj.	Not the usual place for an augmented sixth chord in E-*flat* major.
14	GR^6	Augmented sixth chord	E-*flat* maj. and B-*flat* maj.	Pivot chord in modulation to B-*flat* major.
15	I^6_4	Diatonic triad	B-*flat* maj.	
16	V^7 Mm	Dominant 7th chord	B-*flat* maj.	
17, 18 19, 20	I	Diatonic triad	B-*flat* maj.	
21	V^6_5 Dm	Altered dominant	B-*flat* maj.	A dominant 7th chord with two tones altered to make it sound diminished-minor.

CHORD NUMBER	HARMONIC ANALYSIS	CHORD TYPE	KEY	REMARKS:
22	$VII^{\overset{4}{3}}/IV$ DD	Secondary dominant	*B-flat* maj.	Has the same sound as chord no. 4 & 12.
23	I	Diatonic triad	*B-flat* maj.	
24	$V^{\overset{6}{5}}$ Dm	Altered dominant	*B-flat* maj.	Same chord as no. 21.
25	V^7 Mm	Dominant 7th chord	C minor	
26	$V^{\overset{4}{2}}$ Mm	Dominant 7th chord	C minor	
27	III^+	Diatonic augmented triad	C minor	
28	$V^9 \, (\overset{4}{3})$	Dominant 7th chord with added minor 9th	C minor	
29	i	Diatonic triad	C minor	
30	$I^{\overset{4}{2}}$ mm	Nondominant 7th chord	C minor	
31	$V^{\overset{4}{3}}/V$ Mm	Secondary dominant	C minor	
32	GR^6	Augmented sixth chord	C minor	Augmented sixth chord treated conventionally.
33	$i^{\overset{6}{4}}$	Diatonic triad	C minor	
34	$I^{\overset{6}{4}}$	Borrowed chord (from major)	C minor	
35	V^7 Dm	Altered dominant	C minor	Same type and function as chords no. 21 & 24.
36	V	Diatonic triad	C minor	
37	$i^{\overset{6}{4}}$	Diatonic triad	C minor	
38	$IV^{\overset{6}{5}}$ mm	Nondominant 7th chord	C minor	
39	$i^{\overset{6}{4}}$	Diatonic triad	C minor	
40	enh IV^7 Dm	Altered subdominant 7th chord	C minor	This is a plagal cadence with an altered subdominant. Similar to no. 21, 24, and 35 except that this is plagal while the others were authentic (V)
41 & 42	i	Diatonic triad	C minor	

ALTERED CHORDS

ALTERED CHORD TYPE	FOUND AT CHORD NUMBERS:
Borrowed chord	4, 10, 12, and 34
Augmented sixth chord	6, 13, 14, and 32
Altered dominant	21, 24, 35, and 40 (subdominant)
Chromatic mediant	5 and 11

DIATONIC CHORD TYPE	FOUND AT CHORD NUMBERS:
Diatonic triad	1, 2, 3, 7, 9, 15, 17, 18, 19, 20, 23, 27, 29, 33, 36, 37, 39, 41, 42
Dominant 7th chord	8, 16, 25, and 26
Nondominant 7th chord	30 and 38
Ninth chord	28

TOTAL NUMBER OF ALTERED CHORDS: 16
TOTAL NUMBER OF DIATONIC CHORDS: 26

DEDUCTIONS CONCERNING USE OF ALTERED CHORDS

A   Of the four German augmented sixth chords that appear in this excerpt, two (no. 14 & 32) are treated conventionally with resolutions to the I_4^6 chord, and two (no. 6 & 13) demonstrate highly irregular use, one being in root position (inverting the augmented 6th to a diminished 3rd) and the other (no. 13) is followed immediately by another augmented sixth chord!

B   Of the two secondary dominant chords, the first (no. 22) does not reach its tonicized resolution at all while the second (no. 31) must wait through five successive chords for its resolution!

C   The dominant 7th chords fare somewhat better. All eventually find normal resolution although no. 25 & 26 are extended through the III$^+$ and a V^9 before finally arriving at a conventional tonic chord.

D   The altered dominants (including the one altered subdominant, no. 40) all contain a diminished triad plus minor seventh. Since there are four such chords (no. 21, 24, 35, and 40) their presence is certainly a factor in setting the harmonic style of this short excerpt.

E   Franck's harmonic vocabulary in this composition contains nearly all of the altered chords common to the late Romantic period.

F   His use of these chords is often unconventional and unorthodox, which accounts for the particular harmonic flavor of most of his compositions.

G   Thus, it is not primarily the chords themselves that account for his individual harmonic style, but the way in which he manipulates them.

H   The very high ratio (38%) of altered chords is typical of late Romantic period compositions, and reflects the culmination of the gradual shift away from the diatonic harmony that had been taking place during the entire Romantic period.

Nonharmonic Tones

FREQUENCY

NONHARMONIC TONE TYPE	NUMBER OF OCCURRENCES
SUS (suspensions)	6
UPT (unaccented passing tones)	6
APT (accented passing tones)	5
RETARD (retardations)	2
ANT (anticipation)	2
LNT (lower neighboring tone)	2
APP (appoggiatura)	1

Because of the highly conjunct nature of the melody (primarily step-wise) most of the nonharmonic tones are of the stepwise type (few leaps such as those found in appoggiatura or escape tones).

Cadences

A   At chords 16–18 = imperfect authentic cadence (unaltered)
B   At chords 40–42 = plagal cadence with an altered IV (IV⁷)

$$\text{Dm}$$

The alteration of both the V and the IV chords (at no.'s 21, 24, 35, and 40) indicate a definite characteristic at least as it regards this particular composition. In each instance the chord is altered so it will sound diminished-minor.

Harmonic Rhythm

Extremely simple (as with most chorales) frequency of one chord per metric beat except in a few instances.

RHYTHM

This chorale is essentially metric with little rhythmic emphasis.

TEXTURE

Essentially homophonic (melody line in upper voice with supporting harmony beneath).

FORM

Since this is but a short excerpt of a longer work the form cannot be discussed.

10
Sonata Allegro Form

Sonata
Sonata Allegro Form
Exposition
Development

Recapitulation
1st Theme
1st Theme Group
2nd Theme

2nd Theme Group
3rd Theme
Codetta
Coda

Transition
Retransition
Bridge
Bridge Passage

DEFINITION

A name given to the structure that is used in the first movement, and at times other movements, of a symphony, sonata, quartet, trio, overture, and so on. The form itself contains three main sections, an exposition, development and recapitulation.

DESCRIPTION

Sonata allegro form is sometimes called simply sonata form, but the longer term is used here to distinguish the form from the title of three- or four-movement works that are known as sonatas. Thus, sonata allegro form or sonata form refers to a single movement of one of these multi-movement compositions while the term sonata (minus "allegro" and "form") refers to the entire work including all its movements.

Although the term sonata was used in a variety of ways prior to 1750, this chapter deals with the form as it emerged in the mid-eighteenth century.

Sonata allegro developed from binary form in which the exposition was part 1 and the development and recapitulation were part 2. The process of maturation was slow indeed, and although the binary form of the Baroque period (1600–1750) contained all the necessary ingredients for sonata allegro form, the actual culmination did not take place until the mid-eighteenth century. The form was perfected and brought to popularity during the Classical period, which saw its most concentrated application.

A feature of sonata allegro form that must be well understood before details are undertaken is that the term includes a variety of alternatives to the set pattern. The outline of the form as shown below is simply a point of departure—few actual sonatas adhere to this structure rigidly. As each section of sonata allegro form is discussed in detail, the alternatives and deviations from the norm will be noted so that misconceptions will not develop.

The form as a whole is represented thus:

SECTION	KEY
Exposition	
1st theme or theme group	Tonic
Transition	Modulates
2nd theme or theme group	Dominant or relative major (if in minor key)
3rd theme or theme group	Dominant or relative major (if in minor key)
Development	
No standard design, but development of one or more themes from the exposition takes place.	Various keys—usually more than one
Recapitulation	
1st theme or theme group	Tonic
Transition	No modulation
2nd theme or theme group	Tonic
3rd theme or theme group	Tonic
Coda	Tonic

Exposition

The first main section of sonata allegro form containing at least contrasting key relationships and more often contrasting themes set apart by transitions.

THEME 1

This is usually in the tonic key giving the listener stability and a frame of reference for the ensuing sections. Sometimes in a movement of considerable length the first theme may embrace more than one musical idea in which case it is labeled a first theme group. Since first theme material is traditionally in the tonic key, confusion is avoided in reference to form—a modulation will herald an ensuing section. Example: Beethoven, Piano Sonata, Op. 2, No. 2, 1st movement.

TRANSITION

Sometimes called a bridge or bridge passage, the transition prepares for the next theme and performs the following functions:

A Positioned between themes 1 and 2 the transition provides a vital modulation from the tonic key to the new key of the second theme.

B The transition may contain elements of the first theme such as a motive, a particular harmonic progression, or an inherent rhythmic figure. Example: Beethoven, Piano Sonata, Op. 2, No. 1, 1st movement.

C The transition may be entirely different melodically and rhythmically from either the first or second theme. Example: Beethoven, Piano Sonata, Op. 22, 1st movement.

D In the earlier sonatas of the very late Baroque or early Classical period the transition does not modulate at all but gives the effect by ending on the dominant chord of the tonic key. Then, the second theme achieves the modulation quickly by simply beginning in the new key. Example: Mozart, String Quartet in *D*, K. 575, 1st movement.

THEME 2

A Most often the second theme (or 2nd theme group if it is multithematic) is in contrast to the first. If the first is assertive and bombastic the second is conventionally quiet and lyric. Example: Haydn, Symphony No. 86, 1st movement.

B Some sonatas, especially the early sonatas (circa 1750) are monothematic (contain only one theme). The earlier concept of sonata allegro form placed considerable emphasis on the contrast of keys rather than themes, and as a result the second theme was simply the first in a new key. Thus, these emerging sonatas were more compact and less complex than those that evolved later. Example: Haydn, Piano Sonata, Hob. 49, 1st movement.

C If the movement itself is in a major key the second theme is likely to be in the dominant major. Example: Haydn, Symphony No. 93, 1st movement.

D If the movement is in a minor key the second theme may be either in the dominant minor or relative major. Example: Haydn, Symphony No. 95 in C minor, 1st movement.

E During the early Classical period the above characteristics were less often abrogated than in the late Classical and Romantic periods where much greater freedom was expressed, and second themes were more often found as second theme groups with one or more groups in other keys than those prescribed above. Example: Beethoven, Piano Sonata, Op. 2, No. 3, 1st movement.

THEME 3 (CLOSING THEME)

A Many sonatas, in particular those of abbreviated length, contain no third theme. Example: Haydn, Symphony No. 103, 1st movement.

B When it appears, the third theme may be of any character—contrasting with both theme 1 and 2 or supplementing either.

C This is the weakest theme of the three in the exposition and is not an essential feature of the form.

D   The third theme is sometimes followed by a codetta (small coda) that uses first theme material.

E   Since the entire exposition was often repeated, a transition at the end of this section was sometimes used to lead back to the beginning of the exposition and then again at the end of the repeat to the development.

Development

A   *The main function of the development is to provide an opportunity for treating one or more of the themes from the exposition in a novel and different way.* Instead of simply presenting the theme, the development should provide the musical equivalent of a commentary or editorial in which the many aspects or viewpoints regarding the theme may be investigated. One small portion of it may be scrutinized carefully with five or six versions or variants, or as the composer chooses, the techniques of sequence, modulation, augmentation, diminution, counterpoint, fragmentation, change of mode, and so forth, may be explored.

B   Although developments are highly structured, the nature of this organization varies greatly from one composition to the next. Even within the works of one composer there are few distinguishing marks in the organization of developments that could be said to apply universally to his works.

C   Most developments are divided into clearly defined sections, each of which treats a particular aspect of the exposition.

D   Not always are the main themes developed, and there are many examples where an obscure transition passage from the exposition is given significant treatment in the development. Example: Mozart, Piano Sonata in *D* Major, K. 576, 1st movement.

E   By its very nature the development section tends to restlessness, key change, fragmentation, agitation, and impetuosity.

F   The final section of the development is often called a *retransition,* a term that identifies the preparation for the recapitulation to follow shortly. Frequently the retransition anticipates the return through fragmentation and sequence of the first theme, thus leading smoothly and logically to the beginning of the recapitulation.

Recapitulation

The recapitulation provides the necessary return to tonic that is portended in the flight from tonic early in the exposition. Both the exposition and development digress from stability and tonal constancy, but the recapitulation furnishes the necessary component that permits the composition to close with appropriate equilibrium.

RETURN OF THEME 1

A   The first theme is traditionally returned in the tonic key.

B   Exceptions are few, but they do occur. Example: Tchaikovsky, Symphony No. 4 in *F* Minor, 1st movement.

C   Theme 1 is sometimes shortened and may be altered slightly, but it is unmistakably the first theme and is one of the easiest manifestations of the form to recognize when listening. Example: Haydn, Symphony No. 103 in *E-flat* Major, 1st movement.

TRANSITION

In the recapitulation the transition of the exposition must be refashioned in order that it not modulate since all themes in the recapitulation are in the tonic key.

RETURN OF THEME 2

A   Appears in the tonic key.

B   When the composition is in a minor key and the second theme is in the relative major (in the exposition), it will often be found in the parallel major of the original key in the recapitulation. Example: Beethoven: Symphony No. 5 in C Minor, Op. 67, 1st movement.

C   Theme 2 also may be shortened or rearranged in the recapitulation.

RETURN OF THEME 3

Appears in the tonic key and like the second theme may be found in parallel major when it appears in the exposition in the relative major.

RETURN OF CODETTA

Frequently this is simply a restatement of the codetta from the exposition but in the tonic key.

CODA

A   Many compositions in sonata allegro form contain no coda whatsoever, or in some cases a very brief one. Example: Haydn, Symphony No. 94, in *G* Major (Drum Roll), 1st movement.

B   However, some movements incorporate codas of such magnitude that they compare favorably in size and interest with the exposition development, and recapitulation. Example: Beethoven: Symphony No. 3 in *E-flat* Major (*Eroica*), 1st movement.

C   Some codas assume the behavior of a development section, and continue the shaping of themes from the exposition. Example: Beethoven, String Quartet, Op. 18, No. 3, fourth movement.

D   It is not unusual at all in extensive codas to find a new theme introduced. Example: Beethoven, Symphony No. 5, Op. 67, 1st movement.

11

Analysis: Symphony No. 5, Op. 67, First Movement by Beethoven (1770-1827)

ABOUT THE COMPOSER

In 1808 at the age of thirty-eight Beethoven sold his Fifth Symphony along with the Sixth Symphony, two trios, and a cello sonata to the publisher Breitkopf & Härtel for 100 ducats in gold.

In the years from approximately 1800 to 1808 Beethoven wrote six of his nine symphonies, a period of considerable activity as well as musical growth for him. Although the Fifth Symphony does not fall into his most mature period, it represents a middle era during which he composed many of his more conventional but highly creative and original works.

Anton Schindler, a lawyer, musician, and secretary to Beethoven, wrote a biography of him that was published in 1840. In a later edition (1860) he stated, "What a life of poetry this work unfolds before our senses, allowing us to see into its depths! The composer himself provided the key to those depths when one day, in the author's presence, he pointed to the beginning of the first movement and expressed in these words the fundamental idea of his work, 'Thus Fate knocks at the door!' "

The authenticity of Schindler's recollection is highly questionable since he frequently was fanciful regarding small details of the past; nonetheless, the quote has remained to this day, fantacized, enlarged, and a welcome item for the writers of record jacket notes.

Beethoven: Symphony No. 5, Op. 67 (1st movement). Arranged for piano, two hands, by Otto Singer (Edition Peters No. 196a). Copyright © 1936 by C. F. Peters. Reprint permission granted by the publisher.

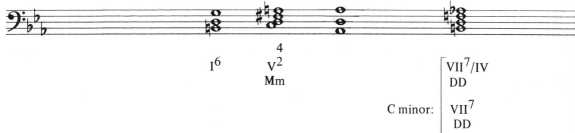

$$\text{I}^6 \qquad \text{V}^{\scriptsize\begin{array}{c}4\\2\end{array}}$$

Mm

$$\text{C minor:} \left[\begin{array}{l}\text{VII}^7\text{/IV}\\\text{DD}\\[1em]\text{VII}^7\\\text{DD}\end{array}\right.$$

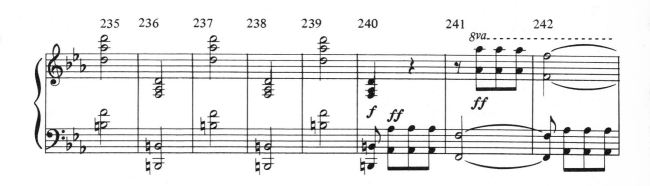

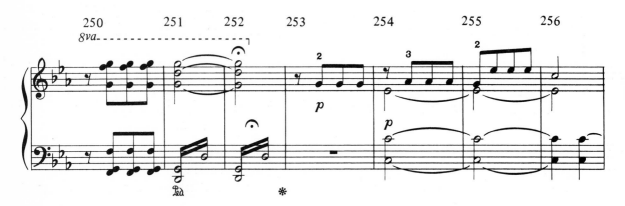

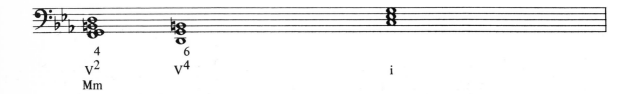

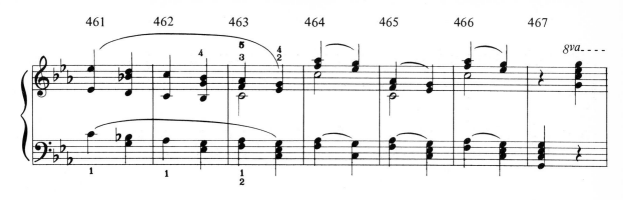

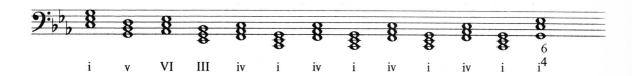

i   v   VI   III   iv   i   iv   i   iv   i   iv   i   i$^6_4$

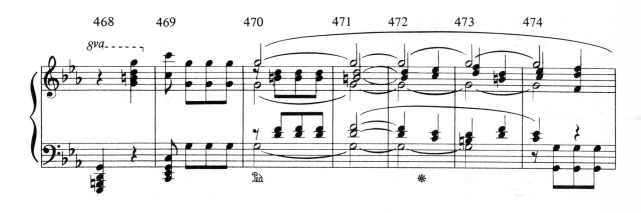

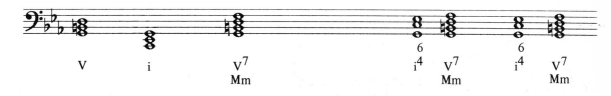

V   i   V^7 i$^6_4$ V^7 i$^6_4$ V^7
      Mm   Mm   Mm

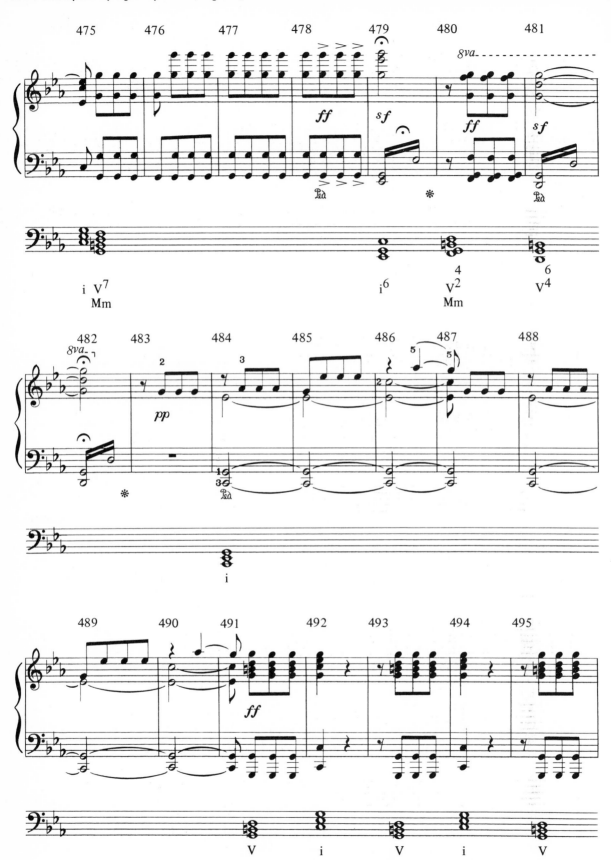

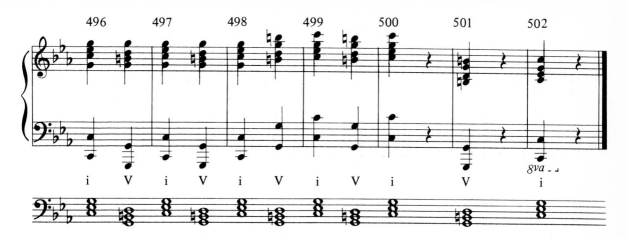

SYMPHONY NO. 5, OP. 67, 1ST MOVEMENT
BEETHOVEN
ANALYSIS

KEY

MEASURES	KEY	RELATIONSHIP	TYPE
1–51	C minor	Original key	
52–128	E-flat major	Relative major	Closely related
129–140	F minor	Subdominant minor	Closely related
141–148	C minor	Original key	
149–193	G minor	Dominant minor	Closely related
194–203	F minor	Subdominant minor	Closely related
204–209	B-flat minor	Subtonic minor	Closely related via subtonic major (B-flat major)
210–219	F-sharp minor	Tritone relationship	Foreign key
220–231	G major	Dominant major	Closely related via dominant minor (G minor)
232–306	C minor	Original key	
307–375	C major	Parallel major	Parallel major
376–502	C minor	Original key	

Melody

FORMAL STRUCTURE OF THE MOVEMENT AS A WHOLE

MEASURES	MATERIAL	KEY	DESCRIPTION
1–123	**Exposition**		
1–51	Theme 1	C minor	Based on motive derived from first 5 measures of the movement
52–58	Transition	C minor to E-flat major	Leads from theme 1 to theme 2
59–82	Theme 2	E-flat major	Contrasting theme laced with bits of the motive from theme 1

MEASURES	MATERIAL	KEY	DESCRIPTION
83–93	Transition	*E-flat* major	Leads from theme 2 to theme 3
94–108	Theme 3	*E-flat* major	Not an important constituent of the composition
109–124	Codetta	*E-flat* major	Derived from theme 1
124–246	**Development**	**Various**	
124–179	Development of theme 1	F minor C minor G minor	Development of the motive
179–239	Development of theme 2	G minor F minor *B-flat* minor *F-sharp* minor G major C minor	Development of the introductory notes to theme 2:
240–248	Development of theme 1	C minor	Serves as a transition to the recapitulation
248–375	**Recapitulation**		
248–295	Theme 1	C minor	Same as theme 1 of exposition
296–302	Transition	C minor	Leads from theme 1 to theme 2, but must avoid modulation.
303–330	Theme 2	C major	Theme 2 is in C major to parallel the *E-flat* major of the exposition. This is a common practice.
331–345	Transition	C major	Leads from theme 2 to theme 3
346–361	Theme 3	C major	Again, C major parallels the *E-flat* major of the exposition.
361–375	Codetta	C major	Repeats codetta of exposition
375–502	**Coda**	C minor	
375–422	Coda, part 1	C minor	Uses theme 1
423–469	Coda, part 2	C minor	Introduces new theme!
469–502	Coda, part 3	C minor	Uses theme 1

The Themes Themselves

THEME 1

Measures 1 — 5

This theme, one of the most famous in all of music, is a classic example of motivic development. The entire first theme section (measures 1 through 51) is made up entirely of derivatives of the above motive. The following excerpts show the motive transposed, inverted, and altered in intervallic relationships, but the rhythm is so pervasive that any ancillary form of it is instantly recognized.

Derivatives of the motive

Measures 7 — 8   Measures 29 — 31

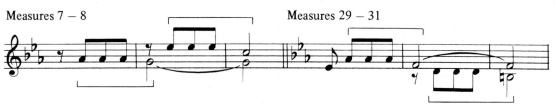

Measures 35 — 36   Measures 52 — 54

Measures 137 — 138   Measures 248 — 249

THEME 2

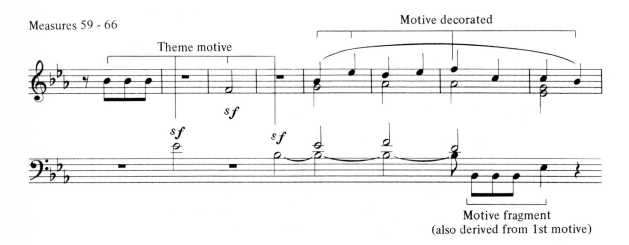

Measures 59 - 66

Theme motive

Motive decorated

Motive fragment
(also derived from 1st motive)

Providing a contrast to the driving quality of theme 1, this theme is melodious but contains some degree of anxious and restless longing that prevails throughout the movement. Beethoven treats this theme in a rather matter-of-fact manner in both the exposition and recapitulation, and selects only the motive itself (1st 4 measures) for inclusion in the development section. Furthermore, it is laced with the rhythm of the motive from theme 1.

THEME 3

Measures 94 – 99

Not all analysts consider this to be a separate theme and place it as part of "theme group 2." However, for purposes of detail it may well be considered separately since it is preceded by a section of definite transitional nature.

The Transitions

TRANSITION FROM THEME 1 TO THEME 2 (MEASURES 52–58)

Made up of the motive from theme 1, this transition is nearly indistinguishable from that section. The chord (VII^{6}_{5}/V in *E-flat* major) supporting the melody in the exposition has the same sound in the recapitulation, but it is spelled differently and progresses on to a V^6 in C major thus making it unnecessary to alter the transition when it appears in the recapitulation.

Enharmonic spelling of a diminished 7th chord in modulation to different keys

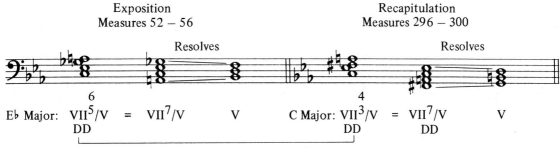

Exposition
Measures 52 – 56

Recapitulation
Measures 296 – 300

Eb Major: VII^5/V   =   VII^7/V   V   C Major: VII^3/V   =   VII^7/V   V

DD   DD   DD

These two chords have same sound

TRANSITION FROM THEME 2 TO THEME 3

Even though short passage does not modulate and normally transitions do not occur between themes 2 and 3, the nature of the harmonic progressions and the melodic constituents of these measures gives the effect of a transition.

TRANSITION IN EXPOSITION (MEAS. 83–93)

Key of *E-flat*
Borrows from *E-flat* minor
Does not modulate
Lasts eleven measures
Bass proceeds by half steps up

SAME TRANSITION IN RECAP. (MEAS. 331–345)

Key of *C*
Borrows from *C* minor
Does not modulate
Lasts fifteen measures
Bass enharmonically outlines a diminished triad.

Codetta

CODETTA OF EXPOSITION (MEAS. 109–124)

Key of *E-flat* major
No modulation
Uses motive from theme 1

CODETTA OF RECAPITULATION (MEAS. 361–375)

Key of *C* major
No modulation
Uses motive from theme 1, and is the exact duplicate (except for transposition) of the codetta in the exposition.

The Development Section

This is a fairly typical development section in that it:
A   Is very modulatory.
B   Develops theme 1 and theme 2.

The Coda (Following the Recapitulation)

This long and extended coda vies for equal importance with the exposition, development, and recapitulation if for no other reason than its length:

SECTION	NO. OF MEASURES
Exposition	124
Development	122
Recapitulation	128
Coda	128

However, the coda is significant musically for other reasons:

A   It introduces a new theme (measure 423).
B   It develops (without modulation) the first theme motive in a new way (measure 400).
C   Although present throughout the work, the element of sequence is emphasized considerably (measures 407–455).

HARMONY

Tonic and Dominant Harmony

Tonic and dominant harmony predominates throughout.

HARMONY	PERCENTAGE
Tonic and dominant	73%
Other	27%

The Descending P5th Progression

The descending P5th (ascending P4th) progression accounts for nearly half of all progressions in the composition.

TYPE OF PROGRESSION	PERCENTAGE OF USE
Descending P5th (ascending P4th)	48%
Ascending P5th (descending P4th)	27%
Ascending 2nd (descending 7th)	13%
Descending 3rd (ascending 6th)	7%
Descending 2nd (ascending 7th)	3%
Ascending 3rd (descending 6th)	2%

There are many instances of chord roots in the typical descending P5th pattern. One instance is illustrated here:

Typical descending P5th pattern

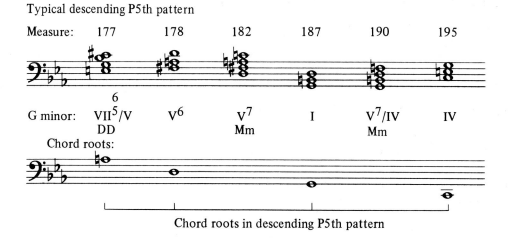

Chord roots in descending P5th pattern

Below is an illustration from the coda:

Typical descending 5th pattern

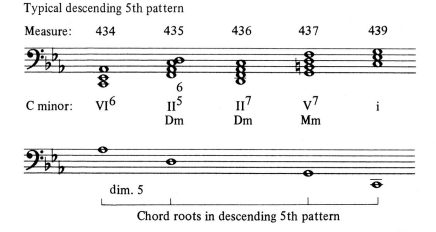

Chord roots in descending 5th pattern

Harmonic Vocabulary

The harmonic vocabulary consists of typical chords of the period:

A   Diatonic triads, 7th chords, and 9th chords.
B   Secondary dominants, both Mm and DD.
C   Neapolitan sixth chords.
D   Augmented sixth chords, both Italian and German.

Resolution and Progression

Most chords are treated according to conventional practice:

A   Most Mm secondary dominants resolve normally.
B   Most DD secondary dominants take an alternative analysis as is customary.
C   Two of the three neapolitan sixth chords appear at points of modulation and thus do not proceed to the V as usual.

Neapolitan Sixth chords as pivot chords in modulation

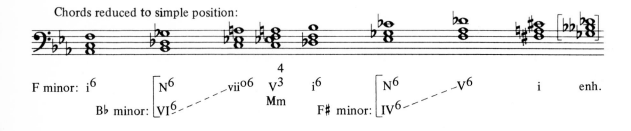

D   The two Italian augmented sixth chords resolve to V as expected, but the Gr^6 is delayed in resolution.

Delayed resolution of GR^6

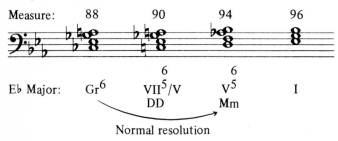

Normal resolution

Harmonic Rhythm

A   No one harmonic rhythm dominates the movement.

B   Perhaps the harmonic rhythm that occurs most often is that of one chord per measure.

Harmonic rhythm of one chord per measure

Meas: 348   349   350   351   352   353   354

Chords reduced to simple position:

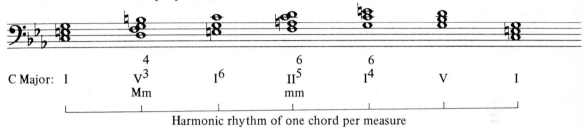

Harmonic rhythm of one chord per measure

C   Most harmonic changes are irregular and do not form consistent patterns.

RHYTHM

Rhythm is a most important factor in this composition. The ascendant figure: ♩♫ | 𝅗𝅥 or ♩ or ♪ is indelibly associated with the motive of the first theme and occurs no less than 193 times in the 502 measures of the movement!

This rhythm:

A   Is the basis for the first theme.

B   Is used repeatedly with the second theme.

C   Is the foundation for the coda at the end of the exposition.

D   Is reiterated often in the development.

E   Recurs regularly in the recapitulation.

F   Dominates the final coda.

ORCHESTRATION

Instruments

The list of instruments for the entire symphony (all movements) is as follows:

1	*Piccolo**	3	*Trombones**
2	Flutes	2	Timpani
2	Oboes		Violins I
2	Clarinets		Violins II
2	Bassoons		Viola
1	*Contrabassoon**		Cello
2	French Horns		String Bass
2	Trumpets		

* The instruments italicized above were not used in the first, second, or third movement. Beethoven wrote to Count Oppersdorff (whom he hoped would sponsor it) concerning the last movement: "The last movement of the symphony is with 3 trombones and piccolo—though not with 3 kettledrums, but will make more noise than 6 kettledrums and better noise at that."

Spacing and Doubling

Beethoven generally follows the same tenets of spacing and doubling as are found in most music of this period as well as those suggested for four-part writing in this book. An illustration of one typical tutti (all instruments playing) distribution is provided for analysis.

Typical tutti distribution

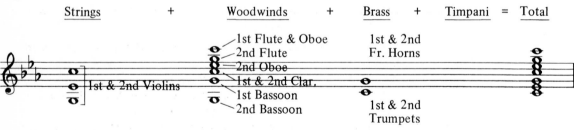

INSTRUMENTS PLAYING *C* (ROOT)	INSTRUMENTS PLAYING *E♭* (THIRD)	INSTRUMENTS PLAYING *G* (FIFTH)
1st flute	1st violins	2nd flute
1st oboe	2nd violins	1st bassoon
1st clarinet	2nd oboe	2nd bassoon
2nd clarinet		1st horn
1st trumpet		2nd horn
2nd trumpet		1st violins
1st violins		2nd violins
2nd violins		
Violas		
Cellos		
String basses		

Observations:

A   The root is most substantially reinforced.
B   The third receives the least proportion of sound.
C   The fifth is amply supported but not so much as the root.
D   The lowest third (E♭) is two octaves and a 3rd above the lowest root.
E   Below Middle C only the root and fifth are sounded.
F   Spacing is widest in the lower range.

Although space is not available for an exhaustive analysis of the orchestration suffice to say that in general the basic principles of balanced doubling and spacing as practiced throughout this period of musical writing are reflected in the orchestration of Beethoven.

ASSIGNMENT 1

Beethoven's Opus Two contains three piano sonatas that were the first such works of his. The first movement from the first sonata is printed here in its entirety. It was dedicated to Joseph Haydn.

1   Make a complete analysis of this movement using the approach illustrated in this chapter.
2   Invite a student to perform the work in class.
3   Discuss the movement in class and compare its form with that of the first movement of the Fifth Symphony analyzed in this chapter.
4   Invite a member of the piano faculty to the class and ask him to discuss performance practices in regard to this particular work.

Assignment 1 (continued)

Beethoven: Piano Sonata No. 1 in F Minor, Op. 2, No. 1 (1st movement)

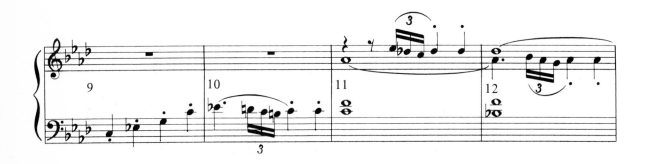

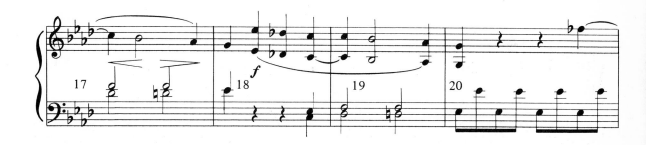

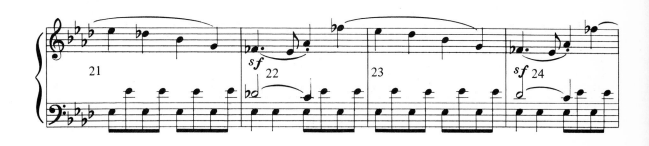

Assignment 1 (continued)

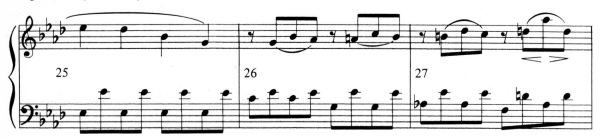

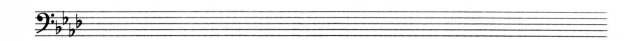

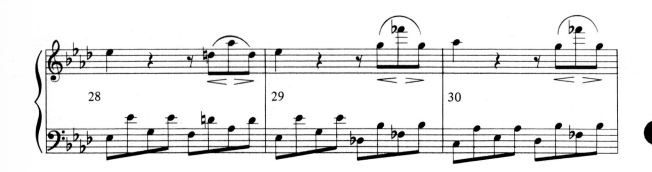

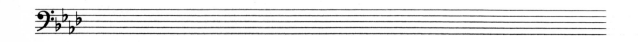

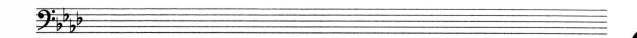

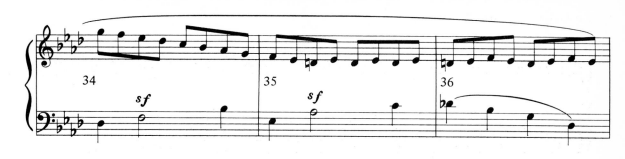

Assignment 1 (continued)

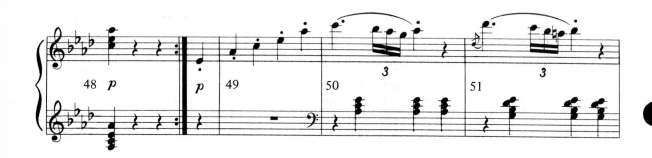

Assignment 1 (continued)

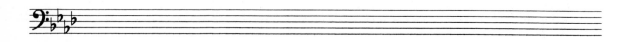

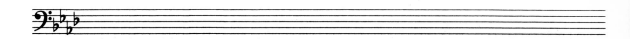
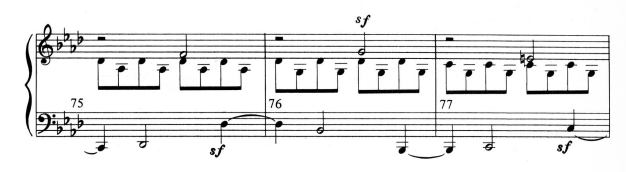

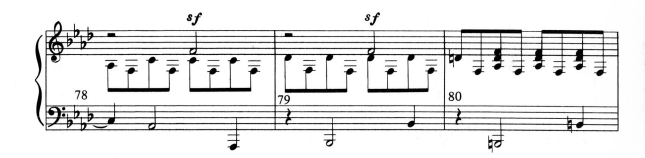

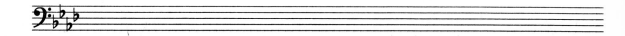

Assignment 1 (continued)

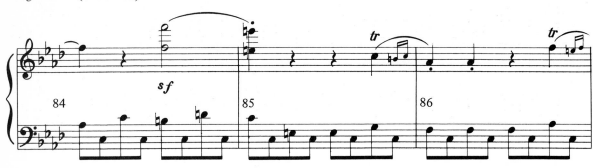

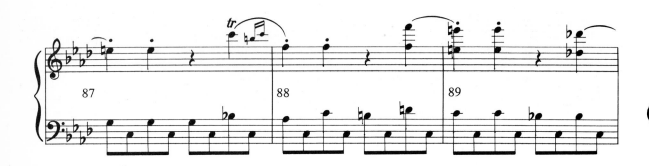

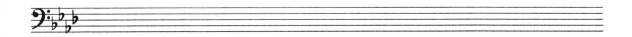

Assignment 1 (continued)

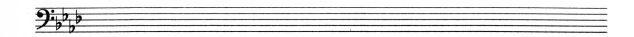

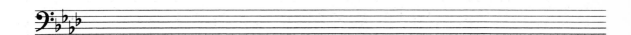

Assignment 1 (continued)

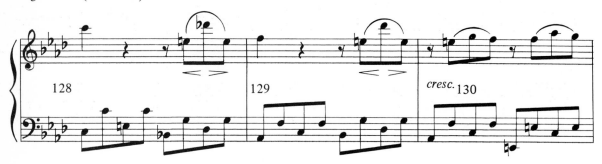

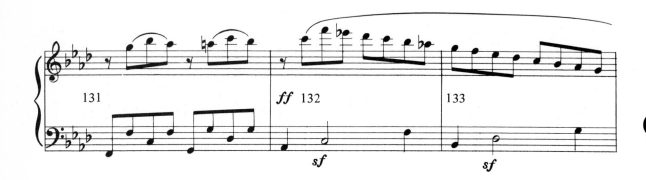

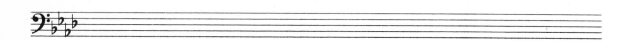

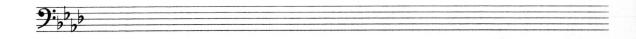

Assignment 1 (continued)

ASSIGNMENT 2

1. Write the exposition of a sonata allegro form.
2. Compose your own first and second theme. (Add a third theme if you wish).
3. Use the 1st movement of the Beethoven Piano Sonata, Op. 2 No. 1 (above) as a model for the form.
4. Place the first theme in *G* minor.
5. Place the second theme in *B-flat* major.
6. The transition will probably provide the greatest difficulty. Although not always recommended it may be wise to write the transition after composing the first and second themes. Plot harmonic progressions *backward* from the beginning of the second theme to insure that the transition will lead smoothly and logically.
7. Although using the 1st movement of the Beethoven Piano Sonata as a guide for *form,* write the composition for any instrument or combinations that interest you.
8. Perform the compositions in class.
9. Have members of the class identify the various sections of the exposition through listening only.

ASSIGNMENT 3

Continue the above composition (Assignment 2) through the development section.

ASSIGNMENT 4

Complete the movement (Assignment 2 and 3) by adding the recapitulation.

12
Rondo Form

GENERAL CHARACTERISTICS OF RONDO FORM

A One of the larger, more extended forms.
B Contains a regularly recurring section.
C The regularly recurring section customarily retains the same key or tonality.
D Different material is introduced between the sections that recur.
E Transition passages provide smoothness between the larger main sections.
F Rondos are primarily an instrumental form although developed from vocal forms.

TYPES OF RONDOS

A B A

Sometimes known as First Rondo or Three-Part Rondo form and distinguished from the more common sectional three-part form by its transitions. Often found in slow movements from sonatas and symphonies of the Classical period.

Examples: Beethoven, Piano Sonata, Op. 7, second movement
Haydn, Symphony No. 100, second movement

A B A C A or A B A B A

Known also as Second Rondo or Five-Part Rondo form. Occurs also in slow movements, but may in addition be found as last movements of sonatas and symphonies.

Examples: Mozart, Piano Sonata, K. 457, second movement
Beethoven, Piano Sonata, Op. 2, No. 3, second movement

A B A C A B A

Known as Third Rondo or Seven-Part Rondo form. Quite common. Characteristically the last movement of Classical symphonies, string quartets, and sonatas.

Examples: Beethoven, Piano Sonata, Op. 2, No. 2, fourth movement
Beethoven, Symphony No. 6, fifth movement

A B A Development A B′ A

Known as Sonata Rondo and differs from Third Rondo only in that a development similar to that in Sonata Allegro form replaces the normal "C" section. Appears in the final movement of symphonies, string quartets, and sonatas.

Examples: Beethoven, Piano Sonata, Op. 27, No. 1, fourth movement
Haydn, Symphony No. 94, fourth movement

Departures from Prescribed Form

While the above four types of Rondo form a large body of music literature, composers are not averse to the use of altered versions some of which are:

A B C A	Variant of Three-Part Rondo
A B A C	Variant of Three-Part Rondo
A B C A B A	Variant of Seven-Part Rondo
A B A C B A	Variant of Seven-Part Rondo
A B A DEVELOPMENT B A	Variant of Sonata Rondo Form

HISTORY

The rondo of the Classical period developed from a vocal form (Rondel) dating back to the medieval period (500–1450). The *Troubadors* of *Provence* employed a type of composition with a recurring section, and similar forms were maintained through the Renaissance (1450–1600). In the

Baroque period (1600–1750) the concept of rondo was utilized by Bach in some of his instrumental suites while other composers of the same period adapted the form in a similar manner.

The rondo forms discussed in this chapter are those of the Classical period (1750–1825), the era that developed and perfected the form. The earlier form is often designated by a different spelling: *rondeau*.

OTHER TERMS THAT RELATE TO RONDO FORM

Refrain   The recurring section that dominates rondo form. The "A" section.

Episode   The passages that occur between the recurring sections. The "B" "C" or "D" themes.

Couplet   Same as episode.

Transition   Material that leads from one section to the next. Connects a refrain to an episode.

Retransition Connects and leads from an episode back to a refrain.

ANALYSIS: HAYDN, PIANO SONATA IN D MAJOR, FINALE

Form

A B A C A, an example of five-part rondo form.

CHARACTERISTICS THAT ARE COMMON TO A MAJORITY OF FIVE-PART RONDO FORMS ARE:

A   Contains a regularly recurring section (section "A").
B   The "A" sections maintain the same tonality (D major).
C   The *Episodes*, "B" and "C" are respectively D minor and G major that contrast with the recurring D major of the "A" sections.
D   Each section of the rondo is in a small *binary* or *rounded binary (incipient three-part form)* form of its own.

CHARACTERISTICS THAT DEPART FROM A MAJORITY OF FIVE-PART RONDO FORMS ARE:

A   Transition passages from the "A" sections to the episodes are non-existent.
B   The "B" section contains no retransition back to the final "A" section.

Analysis Outline

PHRASE MEASURES	KEY	CADENCE	SMALL FORM	TYPE	OVERALL FORM
1–4	D major	Auth	a		
5–8	A major	Auth	b:		
9–12	D major	Half	c	Rounded binary	A
13–16	D major	Auth	a′		
17–20	D major	Auth	d:		
21–24	D minor	Half	e		
25–28	F major	Auth	ep:		
29–34	D minor	Half	ef	Binary	B
35–40	D minor	Auth	eg′		
41–44	D major	Auth	a		
45–48	A major	Auth	b:		
49–52	D major	Half	c	Rounded binary	A
53–56	D major	Auth	a′		
57–60	D major	Auth	d:		
61–64	G major	Half	h		
65–68	G major	Auth	hp:		
69–72	G major	Half	i	Rounded binary	C
73–76	G major	Half	h		
77–80	G major	Auth	hp:		
81–84	G major	Half	j	Retransition	
85–93	G major to D major	Half	k		
94–97	D major	Auth	a		
98–101	A major	Auth	b		
102–105	D major	Auth	a′		
106–109	A major	Auth	b′	Rounded binary	A
110–113	D major	Half	c′		
114–117	D major	Auth	a″		
118–122	D major	Auth	d′:		

The Themes

Theme "A"

Theme "B"

THEME "C"

Melody

SECONDARY TONES

The melody of both "A" and "C" sections is composed of a high proportion of secondary tones indicating more than normal arpeggiation and strong harmonic tendencies. The short excerpt from the "A" theme illustrates the harmonic tendencies inherent in the melody:

PHRASE LENGTHS

Of the 28 total phrases only four depart from the conventional four-measure length: 29–34, 35–40, 85–93, 118–122. All except the last (118–122) appear at the end of a section.

Harmony

A The composition reveals a heavy emphasis on tonic and dominant harmony. Sixty-eight percent of the prevailing harmony is either tonic or dominant.

B Descending P5th (ascending P4th) progressions predominate. The single descending P5th is the most common, but successions of three and two occur throughout the composition.

3 descending P5th progressions in succession

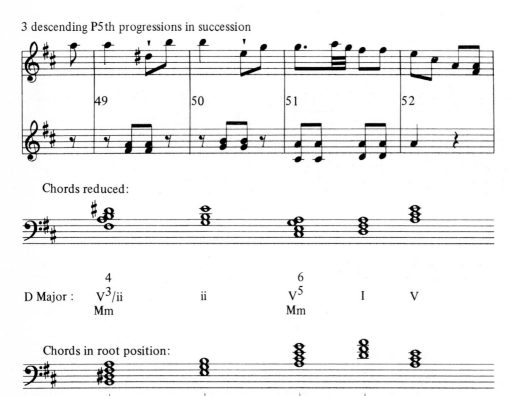

Descending P5th progressions
(Same as ascending P4th progressions)

Conventional cadence formula (2 successive descending P5th progressions)

Chords in root position:

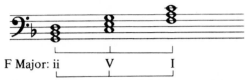

F Major: ii   V   I

2 successive descending P5th progressions

Harmonic Rhythm

Few surprises are in store for the listener in this composition.

A   A steady harmonic rhythm of one chord per measure predominates in every section except the first episode "B."

B   As is usual in this period the harmonic rhythm tends to increase at the approach to the cadence.

C   The regularity of the harmonic rhythm tends to support the square cut symmetrical effect accomplished in this composition.

SECTION	PREDOMINATING HARMONIC RHYTHM
A	80 percent of the harmonic rhythm is at the rate of one chord per measure.
B	75 percent of the harmonic rhythm is at the rate of two chords per measure.
C	70 percent of the harmonic rhythm is at the rate of one chord per measure.

Haydn: Piano Sonata in D Major, Finale

Presto, ma not troppo

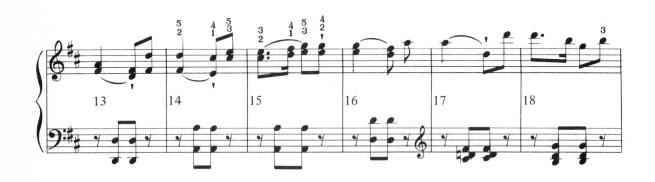

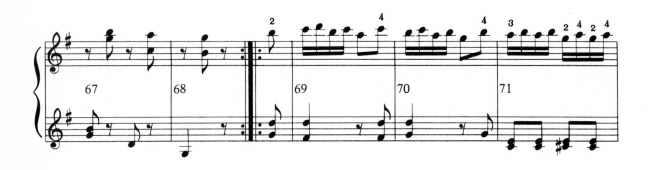

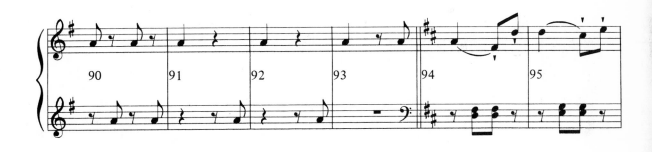

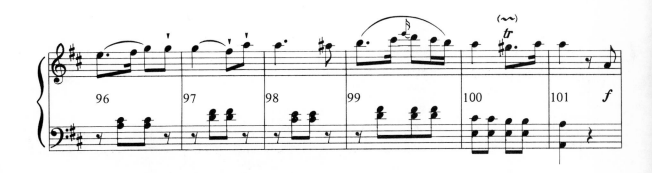

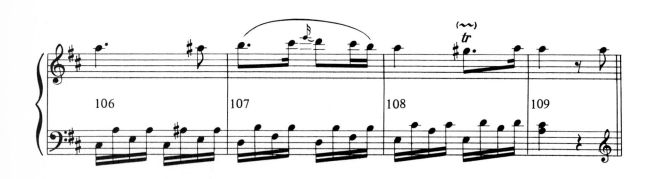

ASSIGNMENT 1

The following composition is in seven-part (A B A' C A' B' A') rondo form. Analyze it carefully, then fill in the following blanks:

1 The keys of the seven sections are:
   Section A: _____   Section C: _____   Section A': _____
   Section B: _____   Section A': _____
   Section A': _____   Section B': _____

2 The transition sections are:
   Section A to B: measures _____ through _____
   Section A to C: measures _____ through _____
   Section A to B': measures _____ through _____

3 The retransition sections are:
   Section B to A': measures _____ through _____
   Section C to A': measures _____ through _____
   Section B' to A': measures _____ through _____

4 The harmonic analysis of measures 44 through 50 is:

   _____ _____ _____ _____ _____ _____ _____
   MEAS. 44 MEAS. 45 MEAS. 46 MEAS. 47 MEAS. 48 MEAS. 49 MEAS. 50

5 Find the following devices or structural elements in the composition:
   A step progression lasting at least three full measures: measures _____ through _____.
   A succession of five descending 5th progressions: measures _____ through _____.
   A four-measure phrase comprised entirely of contrary motion between two voices: measures _____ through _____.
   Three consecutive four-measure phrases with the relationship a b b': measures _____ through _____.

Assignment 1 (continued)

Beethoven: Piano Sonata, Op. 13 (3rd [final] movement)

Allegro

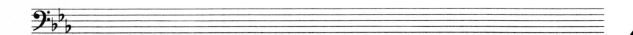

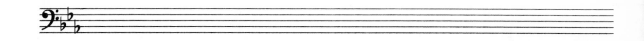

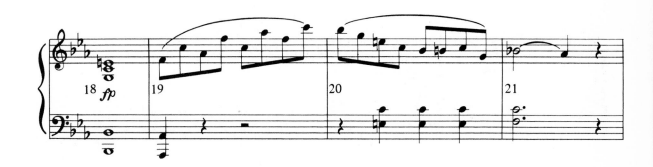

Assignment 1 (continued)

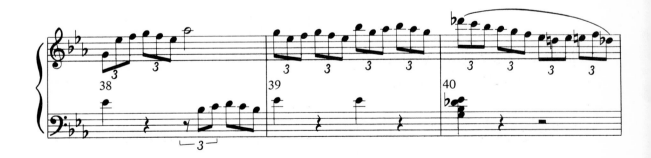

Assignment 1 (continued)

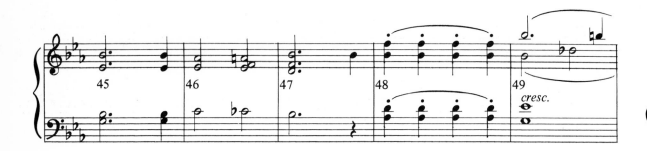

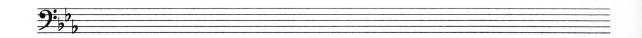

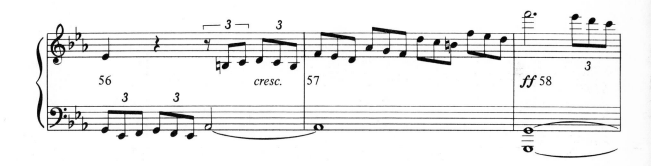

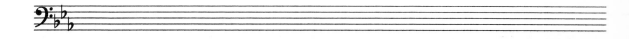

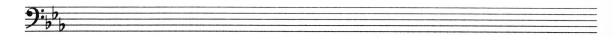

Assignment 1 (continued)

Assignment 1 (continued)

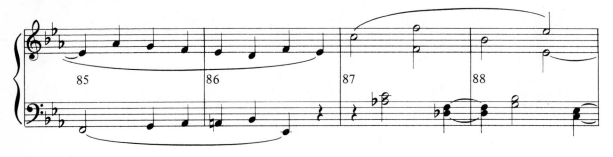

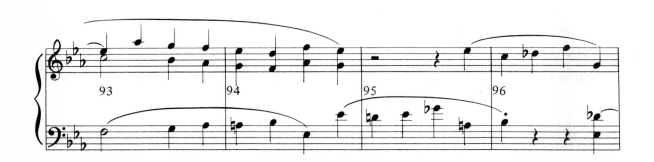

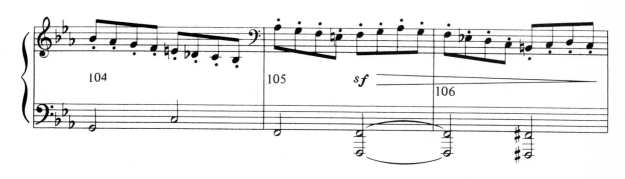

Assignment 1 (continued)

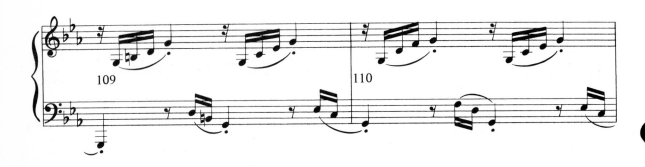

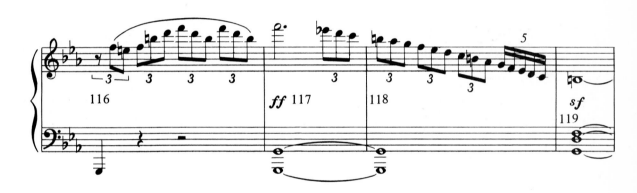

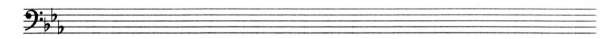

Assignment 1 (continued)

Assignment 1 (continued)

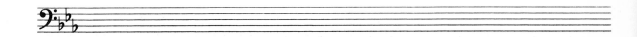

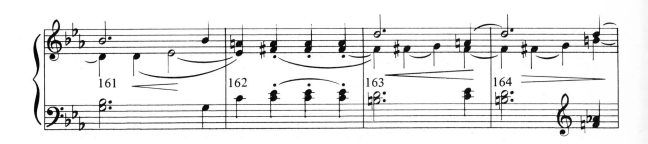

Assignment 1 (continued)

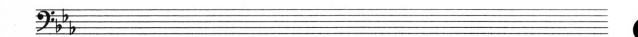

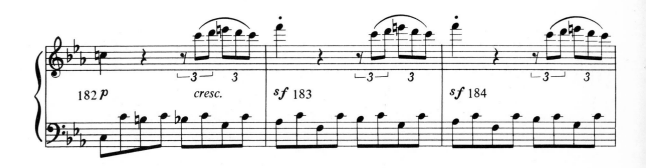

Assignment 1 (continued)

Assignment 1 (continued)

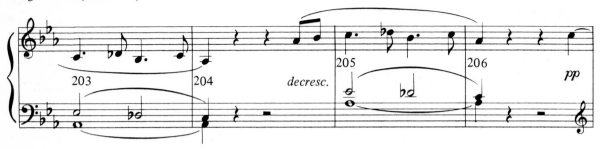

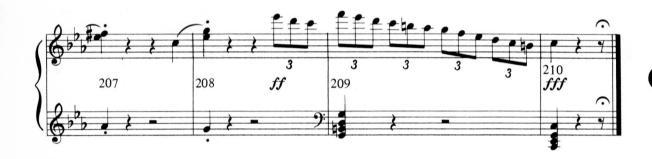

ASSIGNMENT 2   Write a composition in rondo form:

1   Observe the following compositional scheme:

Section	No. of Measures	Key	Use the Following Compositional Devices:
A	8	A major	Two four-measure phrases in parallel relationship.
Transition	4	To F♯ minor	Sequence of at least two legs
B	8	F♯ minor	Two four-measure phrases in contrasting relationship.
Retransition	4	To A major	Sequence of at least two legs
A′	8	A major	Same as first "A" with elaborated accompaniment.
Transition	4	To E major	Sequence or descending 5th progressions
C	8	E major	Two phrases in any relationship or length you wish
Retransition	4	To A major	Descending 5th progressions
A′	8–12	A major	Similar to first "A" but with different accompaniment figure.

2   Write for any combination of instruments played by class members.
3   Play the compositions live in class or record them for presentation in class.
4   As the compositions are played, the class members will indicate the form from listening only.

13

The Sixteenth Century: Late Renaissance Polyphony

Authentic Mode	Lydian Mode	Hocket
Plagal Mode	Mixolydian Mode	Macro-Rhythm
Musica Ficta	Aeolian Mode	Micro-Rhythm
Clausula Vera	Ionian Mode	Text Setting
Dorian Mode	Portamento	Agogic Accent
Phrygian Mode	Cambiata	Text Painting

The sixteenth century was busy with activity in almost every area of endeavor. Discovery of the New World, the development of modern nations, the birth of the Protestant movement, the Counter-Reformation designed to nullify it, and similar expressions of the human spirit in painting, literature, architecture, and music were all a part of the glorious Renaissance.

Some of the most famous composers of the sixteenth century wrote for the Catholic church service. Among them were Palestrina, Di Lasso, Byrd, Morales, Victoria, Andrea Gabrieli, and his nephew Giovanni. Their motets and masses were based on a combination of chordal and imitative polyphony handed down to them by earlier composers like Josquin Des Pres, but the general style was a bit more refined especially with regard to the vertical sonorities and the treatment of dissonance.

Polyphony of the sixteenth century differs considerably from that of the eighteenth, since the concept of harmonic progressions, invertible chords, and harmonic function that developed in the Baroque was not known or practiced at that time. Thus, sixteenth century polyphony displays perhaps the greatest independence of melodic line of any period in musical history.

MODAL TREATMENT

A   *The music is essentially modal.* No distinction is made between authentic and plagal modes.

B   *Accidentals were often added to the pure modes.* Such accidentals were
called *musica ficta* since they were not written in the manuscript but
were added automatically by singers. In modern editions, the accidentals
are indicated above the staff. Two important reasons exist for the use
of accidentals:

1   *For reasons of musical taste during the sixteenth century the melodic
tritone was not used.* Thus, *B-flats* were often added to avoid this tritone
(even between nonadjacent tones).

Melody without musica ficta: Same melody with musica ficta:

B♭ changes A4 to P4

2   *Composers of the period preferred a leading tone a half-step below
the final or tonic (as in our major and harmonic minor mode).* The
Dorian, Mixolydian, and Aeolian modes lack this leading-tone
quality, and thus accidentals were added to raise the pitch one-half
step at the cadence points.

3   The Phrygian mode is singularly different from other modes in that
a half step occurs between the first and second degrees. A
leading tone of sorts is produced naturally above the *final* (term
used to indicate the *tonic* of a mode).

Clausula vera without musica ficta: Clausula vera with musica ficta:

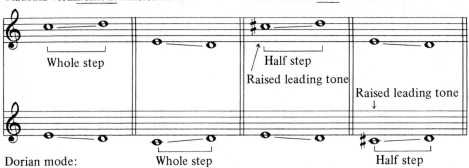

CONSONANCE

*Composers of the time did not think in terms of triads and other
chords, but organized their sonorities (vertical structures) according to inter-*

vals above the lowest sounding tone. Consonance is the basis of sixteenth century counterpoint.

CONSONANT INTERVALS
Perfect unison
Perfect 5th
Perfect octave
Major and minor 3rds
Major and minor 6ths

Intervals used in the sixteenth century to construct consonant vertical structures in three or more voices were in effect the same as our later root position and 1st inversion triads. Since sonorities are figured from the lowest sounding voice upward, and only consonances are used in this computation, the 2nd inversion triads and diminished triads in root position were not used. Second inversion triads contain a P4th with the lowest tone, and the root position diminished triad contains a diminished 5th up from the lowest tone.

Typical sonorities found in the strict 16th century choral style:

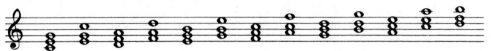

Sonorities <u>not</u> used (as consonances):

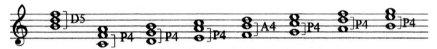

DISSONANCE

While consonance was the basic controlling force in sixteenth-century writing, *dissonance* occurred around the established sonorities much as in the harmonic style of the eighteenth century. With the stricter composers, such as Palestrina and Di Lasso, neighboring tones and many other nonharmonic tones are rare. Certain figures such as passing tones, suspensions, Nota Cambiata, and Portamenti (anticipations) were clichés of the period and are found frequently.

DISSONANCES FOUND MOST FREQUENTLY IN THE STRICT SIXTEENTH-CENTURY CHORAL STYLE

Accented passing tone	Suspension	Nota cambiata
Unaccented passing tone	Portamento (anticipation)	Neighboring tone (seldom in two voice writing)

Portamento

A common device of the sixteenth century resembling very much the anticipation found in harmonic counterpoint of the eighteenth century.

In 4/2 meter the portamento is usually of quarter note value. The portamento was most often used as a decoration for the resolution of suspensions, but less often the portamento tone itself was dissonant. The portamento figure consists of three successive tones, but the portamento tone itself is the second of the three:

Portamento figure as suspension decoration:

Dissonant portamento:

Nota Cambiata

A common melodic device of the sixteenth century generally comprising four tones. The second tone of the four is the cambiata itself. In effect it is a decoration of a descending melodic 3rd. The first and third tones are always consonant (with the lowest sounding tone) while the second and fourth may or may not be dissonant.

Nota cambiata:

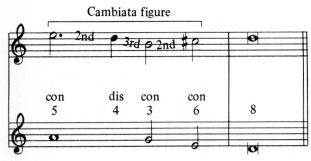

Unaccented Passing Tone

May occur in either half- or quarter-note values, but not in whole notes or breves.

Lasso: Justus cor sum tradet

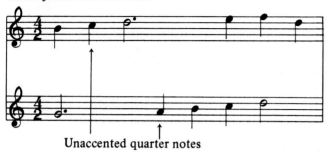

Unaccented quarter notes

Des Pres: Missa L'Homme Armé: Benedictus

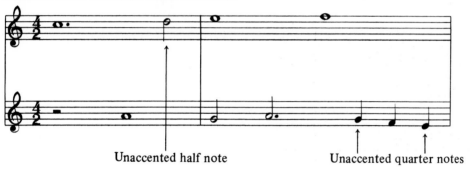

Unaccented half note   Unaccented quarter notes

Descending Accented Passing Tone

Occurs only in quarter-note values and on 1st portion of beats 2 and 4 (of 4/2 meter).

Lassus: Missa L'Homme Armé   Des Pres: Missa Da Pacem

Accented passing tone   Accented passing tone

Suspension

In two-voice writing only the 7–6 and 2–3 suspensions occur. Only half notes are suspended, and the suspensions are resolved on half-note values. Suspensions occur only on beats 1 and 3 of 4/2 meter.

Lassus: Sancti mei

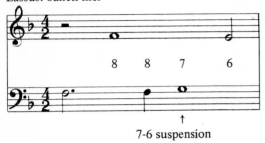

7-6 suspension

Lassus: Sancti mei

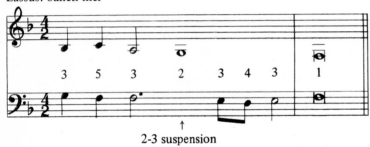

2-3 suspension

In three or more voices the 4–3, 9–8, and 2–1 suspensions are added:

4-3 suspension in 3 voice writing:

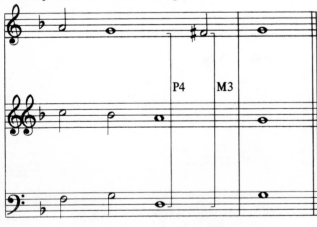

4-3 suspension

REGULATION OF DISSONANCE

Dissonance in the sixteenth century was highly regulated and occurred only in certain metric locations. Most editors of this music transcribed manuscript of the period into 4/2 or 3/1 meter, although other meters can be found. Dissonance, when placed in a framework of 4/2 meter, observes the following criterion.

Dissonance is found only as nonsonority tones. Passing tones, both accented and unaccented, suspensions, portamento tones, and cambiata tones account for nearly all of the dissonance in strict sixteenth-century choral writing.

The following chart indicates where dissonance falls in 4/2 meter:

NONSONORITY TYPE	IS FOUND WITH THIS NOTE VALUE	ATTACK MAY OCCUR ON THIS BEAT
Unaccented passing tone	Half note	2 or 4
	Quarter note	The 2nd portion of any beat
	Eighth note	The 2nd portion of any beat
Descending accented passing tone	Quarter note	The 1st portion of beats 2 or 4
Suspension	Half note (may be decorated)	1 or 3
Portamento tone	Quarter note	The 2nd portion of any beat
Cambiata tone	Quarter note	The 2nd portion of beats 2 & 4
Lower neighboring tone	Quarter note	The 2nd portion of any beat

The same information organized according to beats and portions thereof:

BEAT	TYPE OF DISSONANCE (ABOVE THE LOWEST SOUNDING TONE) THAT MAY BE USED IN 4/2 METER:
1	Half-note suspension
1½	Quarter-note passing tone Portamento tone Nota cambiata Eighth-note lower neighbor or passing tone
2	Half-note passing tone Quarter-note accented passing tone
2½	Quarter-note passing tone Portamento tone Nota cambiata Eighth-note lower neighbor or passing tone
3	Half-note suspension
3½	Quarter-note passing tone Portamento tone Nota cambiata Eighth-note lower neighbor or passing tone
4	Half-note passing tone Quarter-note accented passing tone

4½   Quarter-note passing tone
         Portamento tone
         Nota cambiata
         Eighth-note lower neighbor or passing tone

MELODIC ORGANIZATION

A   Melodic movement is predominantly stepwise.
B   Melodic leaps that are seldom if ever used include:

MELODY LEAPS SELDOM FOUND

Ascending M6ths
All descending 6ths
All 7ths
All diminished and augmented intervals
Leaps greater than an octave

C   Other leaps are common.
D   Triads are sometimes outlined in the melody.
E   Two successive leaps in the same direction that do not outline a triad
     are rare.
F   After a leap the melody usually returns in the direction of the leap.

**After leap the melody returns
in the direction of the leap**

G   Sequences, so common to the eighteenth century, are infrequent in the
     sixteenth century.
H   Melodic tritones are avoided.

BAR LINES

   Original manuscripts of the period did not contain bar lines. However,
since music without bar lines is difficult for present-day musicians to read,
scholars and editors have recopied the scores and added bar lines.

RHYTHM (ASSUMING 4/2 METER)

A   Note values consist of breves, whole notes, half notes, quarter notes,
     and eighth notes (in pairs) in 4/2 meter.
B   Tie note values to equal or shorter note values only. Also, tie note
     values only to adjacent note values.

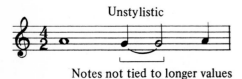

Notes not tied to longer values

Tie adjacent note values only

C   Quarter rests are not used at all, and half rests are found only on beats
1 and 3.

Unstylistic

Quarter rests not found

Unstylistic

Half rest on beats 1 and 3 only

D   Eighth notes occur only on afterbeats (2nd portion of a beat).

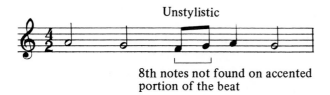

Unstylistic

8th notes not found on accented
portion of the beat

E   Certain other rhythms were usually avoided. An example is a single
quarter-note pair on beats 1 and 3 unless followed by a 𝅗𝅥. or 𝅝.

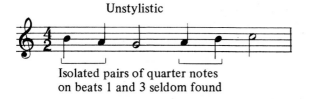

Unstylistic

Isolated pairs of quarter notes
on beats 1 and 3 seldom found

F   Compositions generally begin with at least a dotted half note. More
often the value is a whole note or breve.
G   The composition ends with at least the value of a whole note, but most
often the value is that of a breve.

Macro-Rhythm

Rhythm that works within or coincides with the metric beat. A rhythm
that reinforces the meter. Given the term macro- because it accentuates the
meter of the composition or section.

Micro-Rhythm

*Rhythms that work at odds with the metric beat. A kind of cross-
rhythm that denies the pervading meter and in some instances sets up a*

meter of its own that is different from the meter signature. Given the term micro- because of its short duration in relation to the entire composition or section.

Micro-rhythm

Palestrina: Offertory, Exaltabo Te

As written:

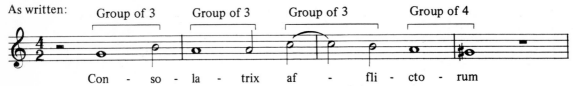

Rewritten to show rhythmic groupings more clearly:

CADENCES

Clausula Vera

The *Clausula Vera cadence* is most common in two voices. The voices either expand out to an octave (from a 6th) or contract to a unison (from a third). Differing from the eighteenth-century concept in which cadences are formed by two chords, the clausula vera is, strictly speaking, a linear cadence (formed by converging or diverging lines). Clausula vera cadences end on either the octave or the unison.

Clausula vera cadences:

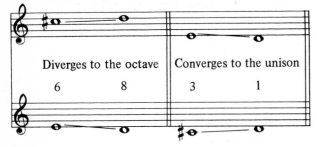

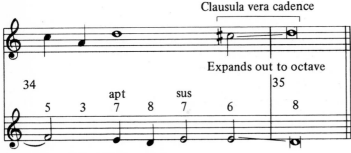

apt = Accented Passing Tone
sus = Suspension

Plagal Cadence

Less often found is the *plagal cadence* that (in two voices) contains the leap of a P5th up or a P4th down in the lower voice.

Plagal cadences:

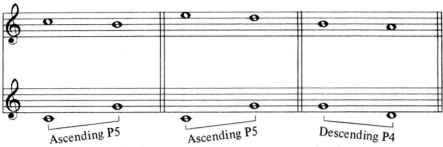

Weak Interior Cadence Points

Very weak interior cadence points will be observed from time to time. These take on a variety of resolutions, but most often resolve to a 3rd or 5th. Generally a hocket (rest) is present to interrupt the final interval.

Lassus: Qui vult venier post me

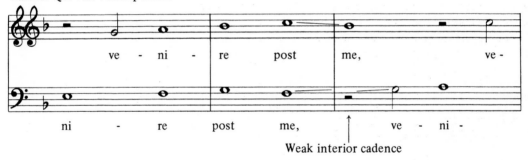

FORM

One of the most popular forms used in the sixteenth-century choral style is the *motet* of which an example, *Beatus Homo* is printed in its entirety here. The musical setting of the words follow the general formal design:

A Each line of words is considered a *section* and is set musically so that a cadence or at least a pause will occur at the end of the line.
B Each section of music begins with imitation that may be free or strict and may be abandoned before the end of that section.
C After each interior cadence a new imitation begins and follows as described above.

D   The rhythm is seldom the same in two successive measures, and each voice generally has a different rhythm from its simultaneous counterpart.

E   Melodic sequences are seldom found.

THE HOCKET

Means "rhythm" according to some sources and to others, "hiccough." The device developed in the thirteenth century and referred to single notes alternated between the different parts in such a way that one voice was silent while the other was singing. In the sixteenth century the term refers to the truncation or interrupting of the melody at interior cadences. Instead of both voices singing the final tone of the cadence, one voice is silent (rest), then takes up the beginning of the next phrase.

Hocket and overlapping phrases: (Measures 23 and 24)

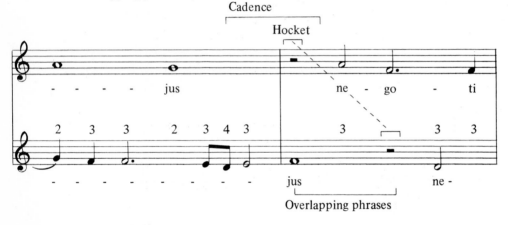

Overlapping phrases

PARALLEL MOTION

Parallel P5ths, P8ths, and P1s were not a part of the sixteenth-century motet style.

Parallel P5ths
avoided in this style

However, M3rds, m3rds, M6ths, and m6ths were common, though these did not exceed four (rarely 5) in succession.

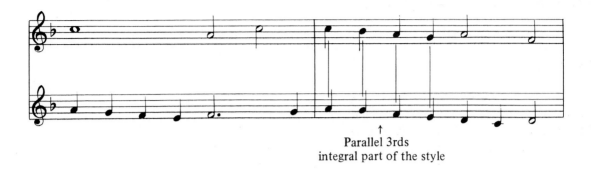

Parallel 3rds
integral part of the style

TEXT SETTING

Although the setting of texts for sixteenth-century polyphony is sometimes extremely complicated, a few general observations may be made.

A   Syllables are assigned only to half-note (or larger) values. A quarter note may carry a syllable only when it is preceded by a dotted half note and followed by a white note.

B   After a run of quarter notes the syllable is not changed until at least the second white note value that follows.

Palestrina: Motet, Alleluja Tulerunt

Syllable changes on 2nd white note

C   Text settings in general try to emphasize the rhythm or accents of the words themselves. Since dynamic accents are foreign to the style, accented syllables often are given *agogic* (durational) stress.

Al Le Lu Ja

Palestrina: Motet, Alleluja Tulerunt

Accented syllable is given longer duration
(Agogic accent)

TEXT PAINTING (WORD PAINTING)

Use of obvious musical patterns to illustrate particular words or phrases of a text.

A   The use of an ascending pitch pattern to accompany words or phrases indicating motion upward. In the example below, the words *Ye Go Heavenward* are sung to a melodic figure that climbs an entire octave.

Arcadelt: Voi ve n'andat' al cielo

    *Voi   ve   n'an - dat'   al   cie - lo

*Translation: Ye go heavenward

B   Use of a descending pitch pattern to accompany words or phrases indicating downward motion. In the example below the word *descend* is sung to a melodic figure that descends a M6th.

Palestrina: Dies Sanctificatus

    *Des -   - cen - dit

*Translation: Descend

C   In the following illustration the words *In the name of* are set to a motive suggesting a trumpet call, which traditionally precedes an important pronouncement.

Lassus: Missa pro Defunctis: Benedictus

    *In   no - mi - ne   Do - mi - ni   in   no - mi - ne

*Translation: In the name of God

D   Many other such instances of text or word painting can be found in this period. The word *crucifixus* meaning *cross* has been attended by a musical figure in which two of the parts (as for instance the soprano and alto voices) cross each other.

E   On other occasions, words depicting sorrow and sadness are given a setting of minor triads in which words of anguish or suffering are accompanied by augmented triads, diminished triads, or in some instances especially strident suspensions.

14

Analysis: Beatus Homo, A Sixteenth-Century, Two-Voice Motet

ABOUT THE COMPOSER

Orlando Di Lasso was born in Mons, Belgium in approximately 1532. He began his musical career as a choir boy, and was said to have had such a beautiful voice that he was kidnapped three times for his services as a singer. He was subjected at a very early age to the influence of the Italian style of composition.

At age 23 his first works were published and were sung in both Antwerp and Venice. This launched a career as a composer that was to encompass a broad spectrum of sixteenth-century forms ranging from masses and motets to magnificats, passions, psalms, Italian madrigals, French chansons, German choral lieder, and chorale-motets. His style includes every resource of sixteenth-century choral technique. Of the nearly sixty volumes of his music about twenty-two have so far been published. He died in 1594 at the age of 62.

ABOUT THE MOTET

The term first appeared in the early thirteenth century through the addition of words to the upper part of a two-part clausula. The motet then became an independent composition and underwent many changes on its way to the sixteenth century where it enjoyed its greatest popularity.

In the sixteenth century, a motet was considered to be the setting of a sacred text in the current style of the period, for solo voices and/or choir, with or without instrumental accompaniment.

Beatus Homo, printed here in its entirety, is from a group of two-voice motets. Two-voiced motets are comparatively rare in the sixteenth century. This one was selected because it displays a wide variety of techniques found in more complex compositions, yet it is simple in design and reveals the true genius of interrelating voices more simply than the larger, multivoiced compositions.

The text for this motet is taken from the Bible: Proverbs 3: 13, 14.

Motet: Beatus Homo

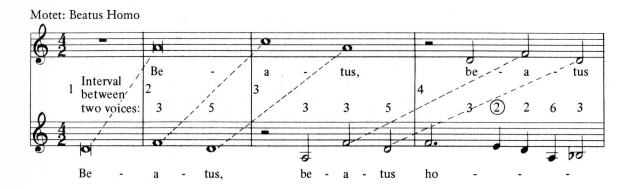

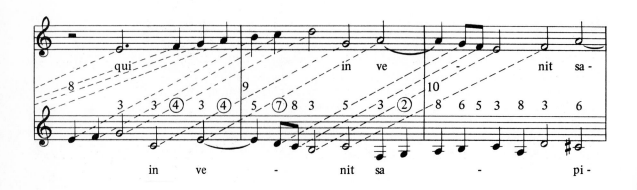

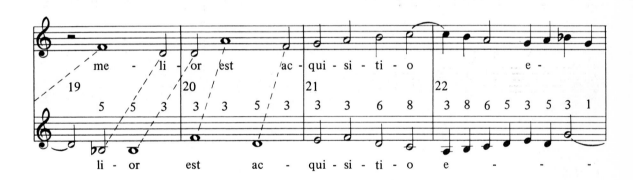

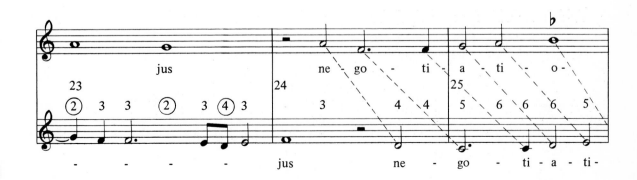

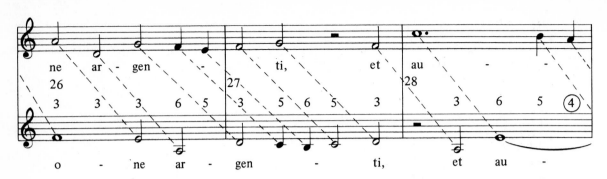

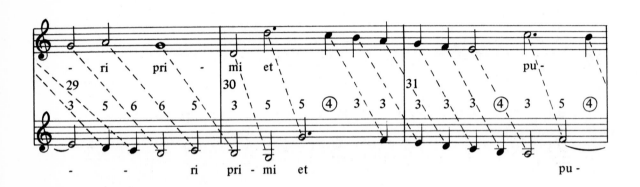

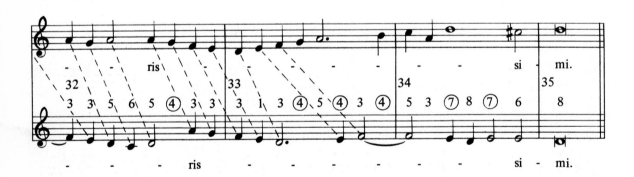

MODE

The composition is in the Dorian mode. The reasons for this choice are:

A   Of the five cadences, four end on *D*.

B   The pitches selected for this composition are primarily those without accidentals. Two accidentals appear—*C sharp* three times, and *B flat* six times. These tones are examples of musica ficta, with the *B flat* used to avoid the melodic tritone, and the *C sharp* employed to provide the leading tone for the cadences.

C   Since *D* is obviously the central tone in this composition and most of the pitches conform to this scale, the Dorian mode is vigorously manifested.

Dorian mode with musica ficta tones:

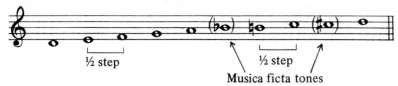

½ step

½ step

Musica ficta tones

MELODY

A   The melody line is preponderantly stepwise.
B   Triads are outlined on occasion.

Measure 7:

Outlined triad

C   Step progressions are plentiful.

Step progression

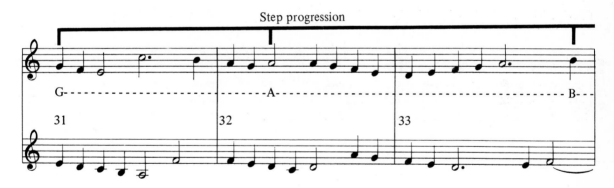

G - A - B - - -

31   32   33

- - C - - - - - - - - - - - - - - - - - C♯ - - - - D

34   35

D   There are no melodic sequences.
E   There are no repeated (in the same voice) melodic motives.
F   The composition is essentially through composed.
G   There are five phrases (in both voices), each ending in a cadence. The phrases of the music coincide with the lines of the verse.

Phrases

PHRASE	MEASURES
1	1 through 5½
2	5½ through 12
3	12 ¾ through 17
4	17¼ through 24
5	24½ through 35

VERTICAL INTERVALS

Consonance

The vertical intervals include primarily the consonances: Perfect unison, fifth, and octave, and major and minor thirds and sixths. Consonances predominate in this composition as in most others of the period.

Dissonance

In the analysis the dissonances (4ths, 2nds, 7ths, and all diminished and augmented intervals) have been circled. There is one instance of a lower, neighboring tone eighth note, and a single accented passing tone occurs in measure 34. However, by far the largest number of dissonances are passing tones, suspensions, and portamentos. The unaccented passing tone is the most popular single dissonance in the composition. Suspensions generally decorate the precadence beats.

CADENCES

The cadences in this composition are as follows:

Cadences

MEASURE	ON	TYPE	REMARKS
5	D	Plagal	Somewhat weaker and less convincing than the clausula vera cadence.
12	D	Clausula vera	With hocket.
16–17	D	Plagal	With hocket. Again somewhat weaker than the clausula vera.
23–24	F	Clausula vera	With hocket.
34–35	D	Clausula vera	7–6 suspension on precadence beats lends strength to this final cadence.

All three clausula vera cadences are preceded by suspensions, and one contains a portamento figure in addition.

Here are the cadences extracted from the composition:

First cadence: Plagal (Meas. 5)   **Second cadence: Clausula vera with hocket:**

Third cadence: Plagal with hocket:

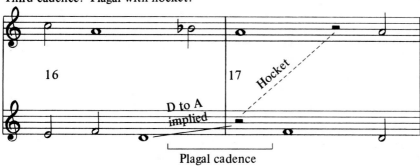

Fouth cadence: Clausula vera with hocket: **Fifth cadence: Clausula vera:**

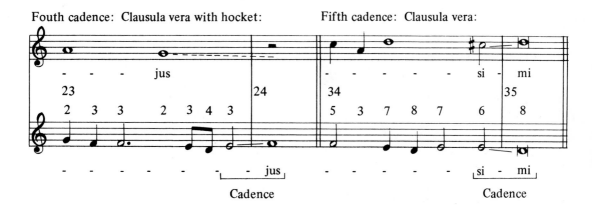

IMITATION

Imitation is the heart of sixteenth-century polyphony. Much of the imitation is strict, but at certain points the interval of imitation changes.

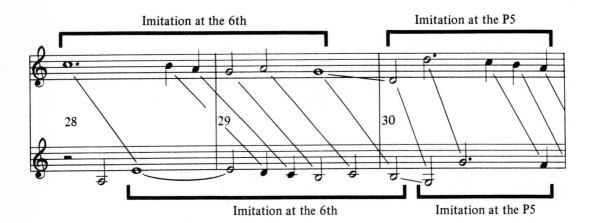

Imitation

MEASURES	TIME LAPSE BETWEEN LEADER AND FOLLOWER	IMITATION AT PITCH INTERVAL	LENGTH OF IMITATION
1–4	1 measure	P5 changing to P8	4 measures
5–10	1 measure	P5 changing to P4	6 measures
12–15	1 measure	P8	3 measures
17–20	½ measure	3rd (M & m)	3¾ measures
24–33	½ measure	P4 changing to 6th, changing to P5	10 measures
			26¾ total measures

Out of the 35 total measures 26¾ contain imitation. Customarily imitation ceases near the cadence to allow for greater flexibility in directing the lines to a suitable final tone.

In this composition note values are most often retained when the second voice (follower or COMES) takes the imitation. However, here is an instance in which the note values are not maintained.

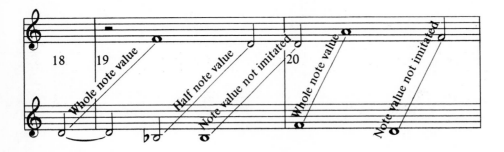

FORM

The five phrases analyzed under "2. Melody" comprise the form of the composition. Here is the text as it relates to the music.

Text

BEATUS HOMO Happy is the man	First section ending in measure 5 with plagal cadence
QUI IN VENIT SAPIENTIAM Who finds wisdom	Second section ending in measure 12 with a clausula vera cadence
ET QUI AFFLUIT PRUDENTIA MELIOR EST ACQUISITIO EJUS And who is rich in understanding. The acquiring of it	Third and fourth section ending in measure 24 with a clausula vera cadence
NEGOTIATIONE ARGENTI ET AURI PRIMI ET PURISSIMI Is better than the purchase of silver and the finest and purest gold.	Fifth section ending in measure 35 with a clausula vera cadence

TEXT SETTING

A   *Melismatic technique.* This motet shows a preference for the melismatic (one syllable of the words to more than one note, usually several, of music). Measures 31, 32, and 33 are good examples of this approach:

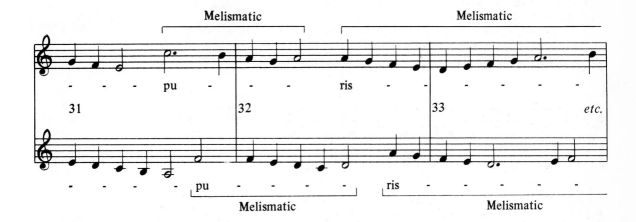

In the preceding illustration the syllable "ris" is set to ten successive
tones of the melody in the upper voice

B   *Syllabic treatment.* Although melismatic style is emphasized in this composition, syllabic (one syllable of the words to each note of the melody)
treatment is in evidence in the first 4¼ measures of the composition:

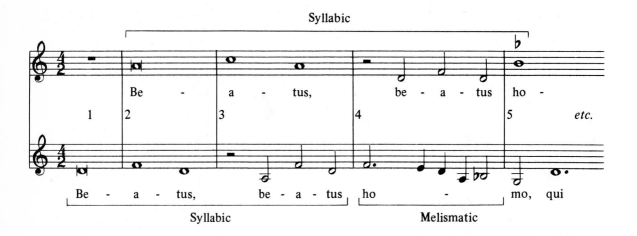

ASSIGNMENT 1   Analyze the following two-voice, sixteenth-century motet in the manner followed
in this chapter. Use a separate sheet of paper for your analysis.

Di Lasso: Serve Bono

Matthew 25: 23—Well done, good and faithful servant; because thou hast been
faithful over a few things I will place thee over many things:
enter thou into the joy of thy Lord.

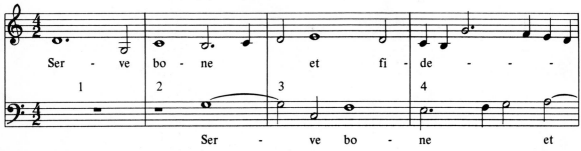

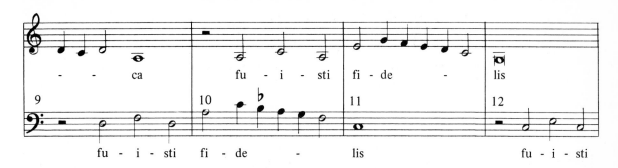

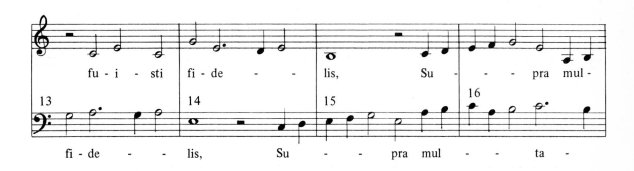

Assignment 1 (continued)

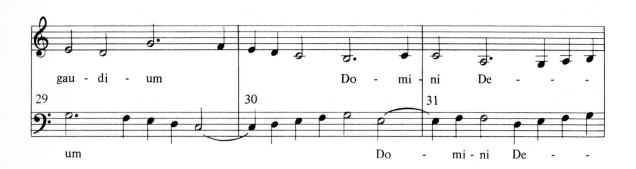

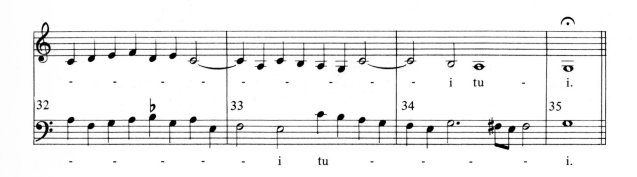

ASSIGNMENT 2   In each exercise that follows there is at least one error in style. Circle the note or notes that create the error and pencil in a correction.

1.

2.

3.   **4.**

5.   **6.**

ASSIGNMENT 3   1   Complete the measure with a clausula vera cadence. Include a suspension.

2   Complete the measure with a Clausula Vera Cadence. Include a suspension decorated with a portamento figure.

3   Complete the measure with a Clausula Vera Cadence. Include a suspension.

4   Complete the measure with a Clausula Vera Cadence. Include a suspension decorated with a portamento figure.

5   Complete the measure with a Clausula Vera Cadence. Include a suspension.

6   Complete the measure with a Clausula Vera Cadence. Include a suspension.

ASSIGNMENT 4   Write one phrase of music (about six measures).

1   Sixteenth-century Palestrina style counterpoint.
2   Two parts only.
3   Dorian mode.
4   Clausula vera cadence on *D.*
5   Use the words:
        Latin: Benedictus qui venit
     Translation: Blessed is he that cometh
6   Maintain imitation at the P5th for at least three measures.

ASSIGNMENT 5   Add a second phrase of music to Assignment 4 above.

1   Sixteenth-century Palestrina style counterpoint.
2   Two parts only.
3   Dorian mode.
5   Use the words:
4   Clausula vera cadence on *D.*
        Latin: In nomine domini
     Translation: In the name of the lord
6   Maintain imitation at the P8 for at least three measures.

15

Two-Voice, Eighteenth-Century Counterpoint

Micro-Rhythm	*Nonharmonic Intervals*	*Augmentation*
Macro-Rhythm	*Harmonic Rhythm*	*Fragmentation*
Portamento	*Motive*	*Embellished Melody*
Nota Cambiata	*Countermotive*	*Extension of Melody*
Implied Harmony	*Retrograde*	*Diminution*
Harmonic Intervals	*Contrary Motion*	*Sectional Form*

COMPARISON OF SIXTEENTH- AND EIGHTEENTH-CENTURY STYLES OF COUNTERPOINT

Before embarking on a study of eighteenth-century counterpoint, some comparisons with sixteenth-century polyphony should be made. The following chart enumerates some of the major similarities and differences.

SIXTEENTH-CENTURY COUNTERPOINT	EIGHTEENTH-CENTURY COUNTERPOINT
SIMILARITIES	
1. Successive parallel 5th, octaves, and unisons avoided.	1. Same as in sixteenth-century counterpoint
2. Consonances consist of: P8, P5, P1, M & m 3rds and 6ths.	2. Same consonances as in sixteenth century
3. Dissonances are: 2nds, 4ths, and 7ths as well as all diminished and augmented intervals.	3. Same dissonances as in sixteenth century

SIXTEENTH-CENTURY COUNTERPOINT	EIGHTEENTH-CENTURY COUNTERPOINT
	DIFFERENCES

1. Modal (church modes)
2. Much use of micro-rhythm

3. Vertical sonority based on intervals above the lowest sounding voice. Not constituted as functional harmony.

4. Dissonance regulated metrically according to beats and portions thereof.

5. Dissonant tones restricted to passing tone, suspension, portamento, nota cambiata, and an occasional neighboring tone.

6. Melodic sequences infrequent to nonexistent

7. Rhythmic figures seldom repeated immediately in the same voice

8. No bar lines in original manuscripts

---

1. Tonal (key-oriented)
2. Micro-rhythm not an essential part of the style

3. Based on functional harmony

4. Dissonance still regulated but not so strictly organized metrically.

5. Nonharmonic devices extend to passing tone, neighboring tone, suspension, anticipation, appoggiatura, escape tone, changing tone, and pedal tone.

6. Melodic sequences an intrinsic part of the style.

7. Rhythms frequently repeated in same voice.

8. Bar lines are used in original manuscripts.

While vocal and instrumental counterpoint existed side by side in both centuries, counterpoint of the sixteenth century was prejudiced by vocal demands as eighteenth-century counterpoint was greatly influenced by the instrumental idiom.

However, the major changes that took place in music between the two periods had little to do with either vocal or instrumental dictates but by the gradual shift from the modal to the tonal system and the advent of functional harmony that developed and matured during the seventeenth century.

EIGHTEENTH-CENTURY COUNTERPOINT

The writing of two-voice, eighteenth-century counterpoint is similar in most respects to the harmonization and composition of four-voice chorales. The two outer voices (soprano and bass) of a chorale incorporate the same principles expressed in the two-voice counterpoint of two-part inventions.

IMPLIED HARMONY

In the four-voice chorale all harmony is directly stated—all three factors of triads are present, and generally all four factors of 7th chords are included. On the other hand, in two-voice counterpoint the harmonic intervals can supply only two factors, and consequently must *imply* those not stated.

Harmonic Intervals

P unisons   — Seldom found in two-voice writing except at cadences or to indicate tonic or dominant harmony.

M & m 3rds — Depending upon the position in the scale and the surrounding harmony, 3rds may imply root position or first inversion triads.

P 5ths   — Indicate root position triads.

M & m 6ths — Most often indicate 1st inversion triads, but when composed of factors of the tonic triad may indicate second inversion.

P octaves   — Seldom found in two-voice writing (do not provide sufficient sonority) except at cadence points or to indicate tonic or dominant harmony.

Nonharmonic Intervals

M & m 2nds — Nonharmonic intervals. Exception is the 2nd which indicates 3rd inversion of a seventh chord.

P 4ths   — Nonharmonic intervals. Generally treated as a passing tone, neighboring tone, or suspension. Sometimes in harmonic elaboration the 4th is found as one of the arpeggiating tones and is thus considered a consonant tone. *In arpeggiating figures the lowest sounding tone of the figure is considered the tone from which the position of the chord is determined.*

M & m 7ths — Nonharmonic intervals. Exception is the tones of the V^7 chord and less often the tones of other 7th chords.

All diminished and augmented intervals—Nonharmonic intervals. Exceptions occur when outlining diminished triads or diminished 7th chords.

The excerpt below from a Bach Two-Part Invention illustrates the use of arpeggiated figures:

The 4th and 2nd used in arpeggiating figures:

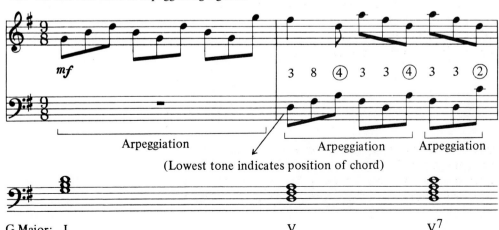

G Major: I   V V^7
                                                                   Mm

Harmonic Rhythm

Just as in 3- and 4-voiced compositions, two-voice counterpoint is governed by harmonic rhythm, implied though it may be. A single triad may be extended through arpeggiation or through repetition of its factors. The two-part invention on page 298 has a harmonic rhythm of one chord per measure while others vary from irregular to regular and from one beat to two measures.

VOICE LEADING IN TWO-PART EIGHTEENTH-CENTURY COUNTERPOINT

A *Generally partwriting procedures are the same as described previously for four-part, eighteenth-century chorales.*

B *Successive parallel P8ths, P5ths, and P1s are avoided in the style.*

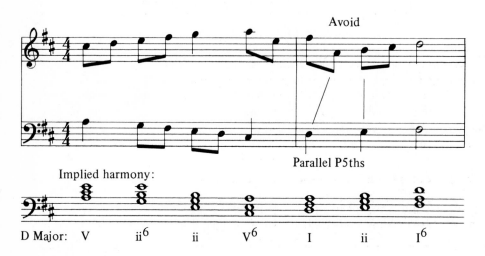

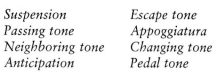

C *Nonharmonic tones should be limited to the following types:*

Suspension	*Escape tone*
Passing tone	*Appoggiatura*
Neighboring tone	*Changing tone*
Anticipation	*Pedal tone*

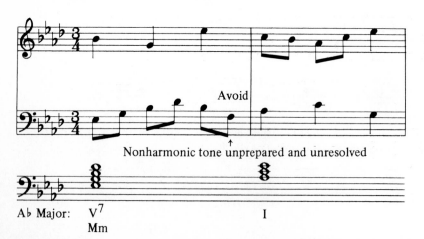

D $^6_4$ *chords should be one of the following types:*

    1. *Cadential*   3. *Arpeggiated*
    2. *Passing*   4. *Neighboring tone*

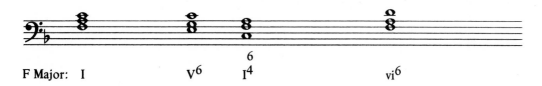

$^6_4$ chord approached and left by leap

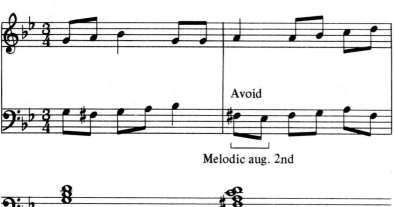

F Major: I   V^6 I$^6_4$ vi^6

E   *Avoid augmented and diminished intervals in the melodic line except
when a chord that contains such an interval is arpeggiated.*

Melodic aug. 2nd

G minor: i   V$^6_5$
                                   Mm

F   *Successive harmonic dissonances tend to confuse the implied harmony.*
     Seldom are two such dissonances found successively.

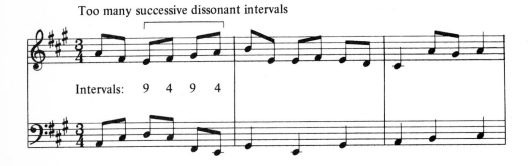

Intervals: 9   4   9   4

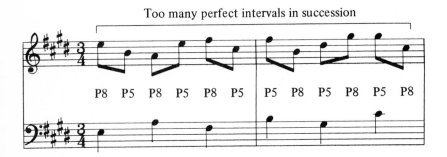

A Major: vi^6 IV   IV^6 V^6 I

G   *Although composers such as Bach used perfect intervals (P8, P5, or P1,*
     especially) at cadence points, to imply triads, such use is by no means
     a common practice. 3rds and 6ths provide more sonority and are used
     regularly in the body of two-part compositions.

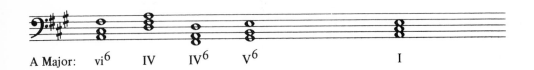

P8   P5   P8   P5   P8   P5 | P5   P8   P5   P8   P5   P8

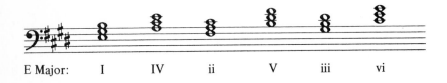

E Major: I   IV   ii   V   iii   vi

H *Dissonant intervals intended as suspensions should be resolved down one step (either half or whole).*

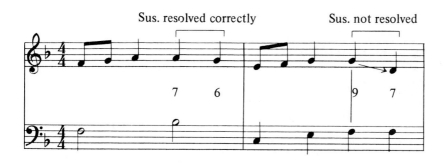

I *Although nonharmonic tones are common within a particular implied harmony, leaps to and from a nonchord tone tend to confuse and weaken the orderly progression of harmony.*

Confusing implied harmony

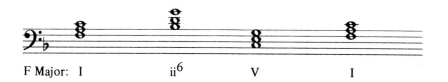

J   *Successive P8ths, P5ths, or P unisons occurring at accented points (even though they may be separated by other consonant intervals) give the effect of parallel movement and are avoided by composers in this style.*

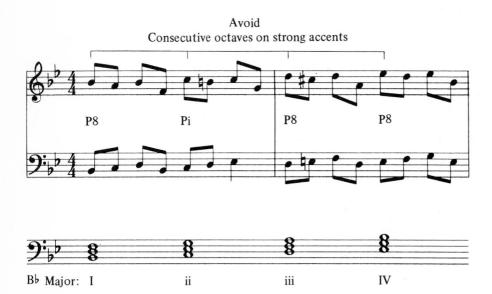

K   *Chord factors that form dissonant intervals (such as the tritone from 3rd to 7th and the 7th from root to 7th in the Mm7th chord) may be used somewhat freely and treated as consonances during the period of a single implied harmony, but under other circumstances should be treated as any other dissonance.*

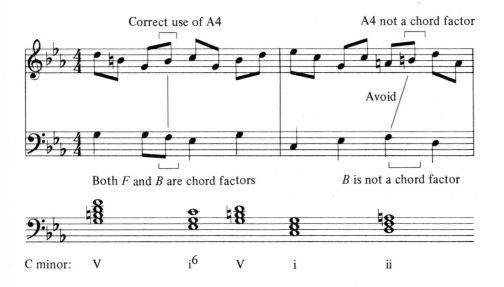

DEVELOPMENT OF THE MOTIVE

The following are some ways in which a motive may be elaborated, modified, or developed in the two-part invention. Bach utilized some but not all in his two-part inventions.

TWO-PART INVENTION

A two-voice composition in which a musical idea (motive) is stated, then developed immediately.

A   A two-part invention may be based on a rhythmic, harmonic, or melodic idea (sometimes termed *motive* or *subject*). It could contain any sectional or nonsectional form, and it might be in any style from eighteenth-century to the most contemporary.

B   Surely the best known two-part inventions are those composed by Bach. Bach wrote fifteen two-part inventions, and these have become the model for many successive compositions of this type.

Characteristics of Bach Two-Part Inventions

A   Contrapuntal texture.

B   Based on one melodic motive (and accompanying counterpoint).

C   The melodic motive is immediately developed.

D   The composition is in *sectional form* (each section is set off by a strong cadence).
Two main sections: Inventions No. 8 and No. 10.
Three main sections: Inventions No. 1, No. 4, and No. 7.

Detailed Analysis of Invention No. 4

SECTION 1

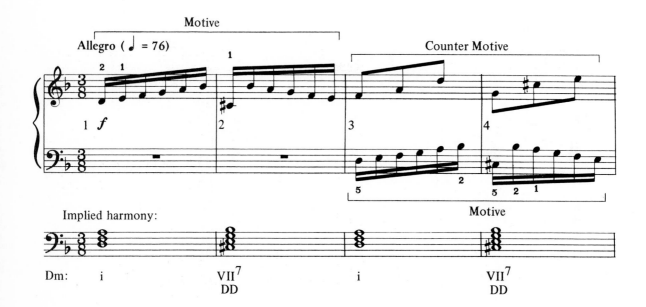

Motive (Meas. 1 & 2)	—	The subject of the entire two-part invention.
Countermotive (Sop. Meas. 3 & 4)	—	*A counterpoint accompanying the motive.* Some inventions utilize the countermotive material in ensuing developments while others do not. This particular invention utilizes the countermotive extensively.
Sequence A (Meas. 7–10)	—	Diatonic sequence in both voices utilizing the motive material (upper voice) and countermotive material (lower voice).
Sequence B (Meas. 11–16)	—	Diatonic sequence in both voices utilizing the first three tones of the motive (in the soprano) and slightly altered motive material (in the lower voice).
Cadence (Meas. 17–18)	—	A strong authentic cadence in *F* major (relative major of the original key, *D* minor).

SECTION 2

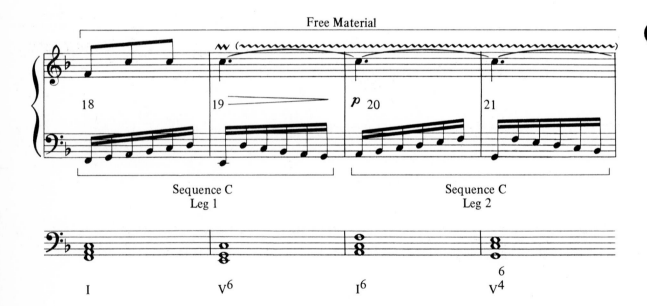

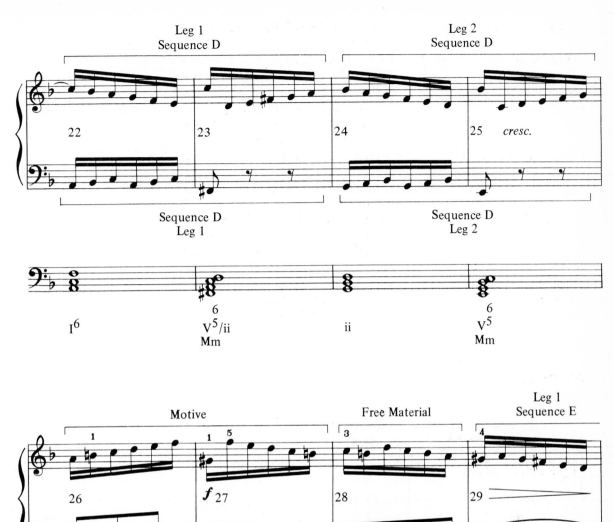

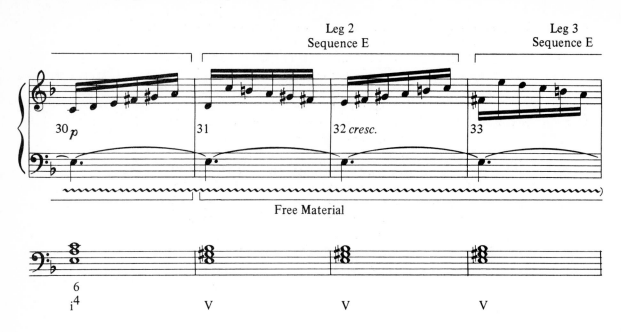

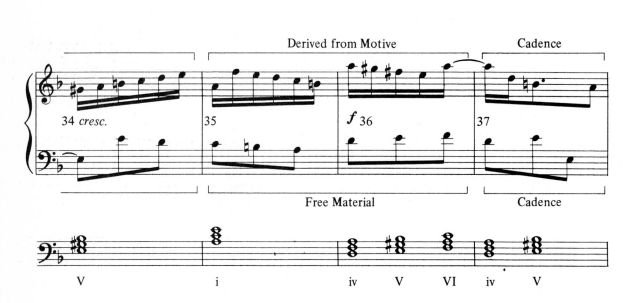

Sequence C (Meas. 18–21)	— Sequence in lower voice only with material from the motive.
Sequence D (Meas. 22–25)	— Sequence in upper voice is an *inversion* of the motive material. Lower voice utilizes first three tones of the motive in *A* minor. 2 legs.
Motive (Meas. 26 & 27)	— Motive accompanied by free treatment of countermotive.
Sequence E (Meas. 29–34)	— Scale material in inversion derived from the motive. Sequence in upper voice only. 3 legs.
Motive derived (Meas. 35 & 36)	— Contains lead-in material to prepare for the cadence. Derived from the motive (upper voice).
Cadence (Meas. 37–38)	— A strong authentic cadence in *A* minor (dominant minor of the original key).

SECTION 3

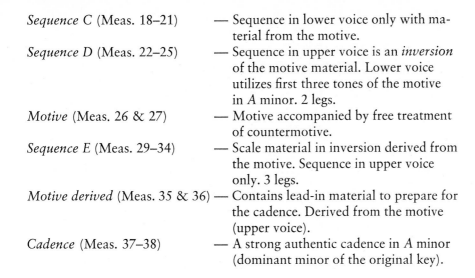

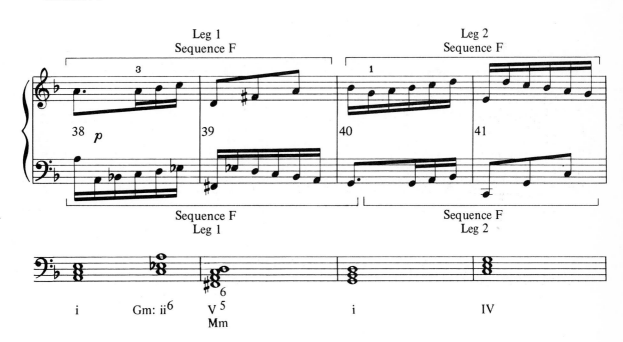

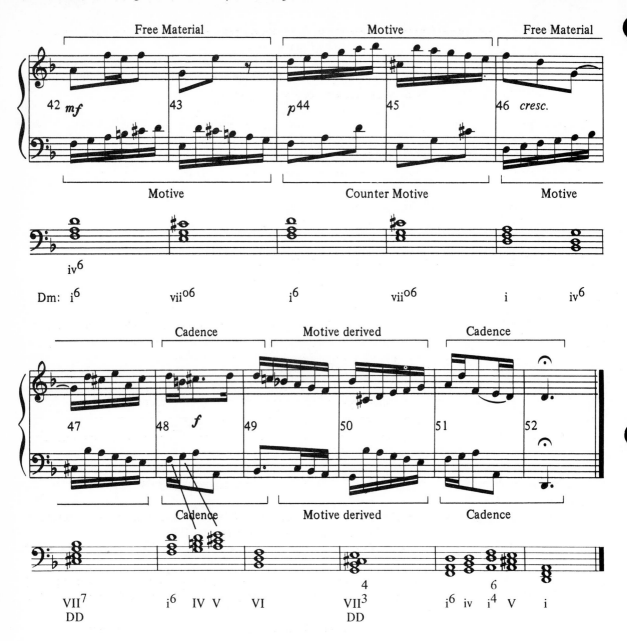

Sequence F (Meas. 38–41)   — A sequence in which the melodies switch voices in the second leg.

Motive (Meas. 42–43)   — Motive in the lower voice with free material in the upper voice.

Motive (Meas. 44–47)   — Return of the motive in the original key (D minor)

Cadence (Meas. 48–49)   — Typical instance of Bach's use of the deceptive cadence very close to the final cadence.

Motive derived (Meas. 49–50) — Motive derived material (inverted) that leads to the final cadence in D minor.

Cadence (Meas. 51–52)   — Strong authentic cadence in D minor.

ASSIGNMENT 1

Following is a two-part invention composed by a student. Omissions have been made so that only one voice at a time is present.

1   The motive and countermotive:

Motive:

Countermotive:

2   Analyze the invention with its present omissions first:

  a   Identify the various entrances of the motive and countermotive. Compare them with the entrances in the Bach *D* minor invention.

  b   Determine the extent of each of the three sections.

  c   Observe the new key of the second section.

  d   Analyze carefully the harmonic rhythm that is the key to successful harmonic counterpoint.

3   Then, reconstruct the two voices of the invention.

  a   Use the motive or countermotive or material derived from them whenever possible. (See the Bach *D* minor invention.)

  b   Free material should be used sparsely.

  c   Fill in all blank measures—do not use more than one quarter rest in any given measure.

  d   Avoid parallel P5ths, octaves, and unisons, and observe partwriting recommendations found early in this chapter.

  e   Plot the implied harmony as you write. Place the chords on the blank staff beneath the score.

4   When you have completed the two voices of the invention, make a complete analysis (melodic and harmonic) along the same lines as that provided in this chapter.

5   Arrange the invention for two instruments and perform it in class.

Assignment 1 (continued)

ASSIGNMENT 2   1   Write a two-part invention.
                    2   Use one of the motives provided or make up your own.

Motive No. 1

Motive No. 2

Motive No. 3

Motive No. 4

3   Use the following general form:

No. of Measures	Content
	First Section:
2	Motive alone in upper voice.
2	Motive in lower voice with countermotive above.
2–3	Sequence (derived from motive or countermotive) of two or three legs that does not modulate.
2–3	Sequence (derived from motive or countermotive) that modulates to the dominant or relative major (if in a minor key).
1	Cadence ending on the dominant of the new key.

No. of Measures	Content
	Second Section:
2	Motive alone in lower voice and in the new key.
2	Motive in upper voice accompanied by countermotive in the lower voice (new key).
2–3	Sequence (derived from motive or countermotive) of two or three legs leading to a third key (closely related).
2	Motive in third key accompanied by countermotive.
2–3	Sequence (derived from motive or countermotive) of two or three legs leading back to original key.
1	Cadence ending on dominant of the original key.
	Third Section:
2	Motive accompanied by countermotive in original key.
2–4	Material derived from either motive or countermotive ending in a deceptive cadence in the original key.
2–4	Material derived from either motive or countermotive ending in an authentic cadence in the original key.

26–34 Total Measures

    4 Arrange the invention for two instruments and perform it in class.

    5 Have the students determine the following through listening only:

        a The relationship of new keys to the original.

        b The cadence points.

        c The sequences.

        d Motive and countermotive derived material.

16
The Fugue

Exposition (of a Fugue)   *Episode (of a Fugue)*
Real Answer   *Recapitulation (of a Fugue)*
Tonal Answer   *Stretto*
Countersubject   *Augmentation*
Bridge (in a Fugue)   *Diminution*
Codetta (in a Fugue)   *Inversion at the Octave*
Melodic Link   *Inversion at the 10th*
Lead Passage   *Contrary Motion (Melodic Inversion)*
Development (of a Fugue)   *Retrograde*

DEFINITION

A contrapuntal composition in two or more parts, built on a subject (theme) that is introduced at the beginning in imitation and recurs frequently in the course of the composition. In addition to the broad general contrapuntal design, the fugue is highly structured and its form is well-established.

EXPOSITION

The first (of three) sections is the exposition, which includes the entrance of all voices. The exposition ends when all voices have completed either the subject or answer. Most often the conclusion of the exposition is signaled by a cadence.

311

Fugue Answer

The fugue subject is heard first alone (unaccompanied) after which the subject is imitated usually at the interval of a P5th higher (P4th lower). This imitation is called the answer.

REAL ANSWER
An interval by interval transposition.

TONAL ANSWER
Transposition of the subject is modified. Tonal answers exist for a variety of reasons, but two very basic ones are:

A   A strong tonic-dominant relationship in the subject is often transposed as a dominant-tonic relationship.

Bach: Fugue No. 8 in E-flat Minor, Well-Tempered Clavier, Vol. 1

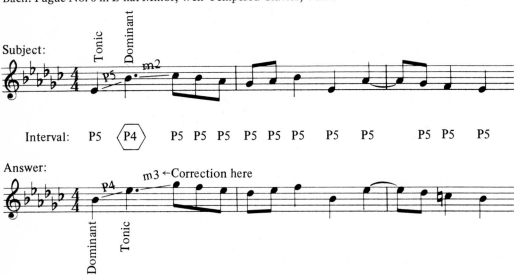

B   A subject that modulates usually takes a tonal answer to prevent the key system from spiraling off out of the closely related key range.

Bach: Fugue No. 7 in E-flat Major, Well-Tempered Clavier, Vol. 1

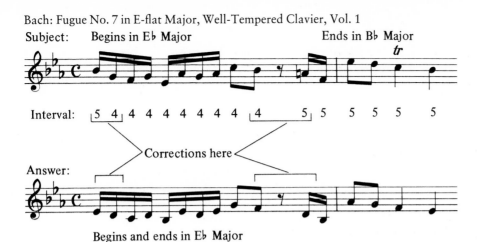

Subject: Begins in E♭ Major   Ends in B♭ Major

Interval: 5 4   4   4   4   4   4   4   4   4   5   5   5   5   5   5

Corrections here

Answer:

Begins and ends in E♭ Major

In this illustration the answer is *below* the subject. If it were above as in the preceding illustration all intervals would be reversed, that is, 5ths would become 4ths and vice versa.

Here is the real answer to the fugue subject that preceded. As can be seen it leads immediately to a key that is outside the orbit of closely related keys.

Real Answer

Begins in B♭ Major   Ends in F Major
                                          (not a closely related key to E♭)

Bach avoided this real answer and used the tonal answer

Countersubject

The continuation of counterpoint in the voice that has just completed the subject. This continuation is only termed a countersubject when it is used again in the fugue.

Bridge

A short passage in the exposition of a fugue between entrances of the subject or answer. The bridge is often employed by composers as a modulatory passage for the next entrance of either the subject or answer.

Codetta

A short series of tones at the end of the subject that provides a smooth passage to the countersubject. Many subjects have no codetta and approach the countersubject directly and smoothly, but others end on tones that afford no equitable and easy connection with the countersubject. Consequently, in such instances, a short passage (often scalewise) of faster notes is added to link the subject with the countersubject. Other terms used in place of *codetta* are: *lead passage,* and *melodic link.*

Exposition Design

Although the design of the exposition differs from fugue to fugue, here is one fairly common pattern that is often found in the literature of music.

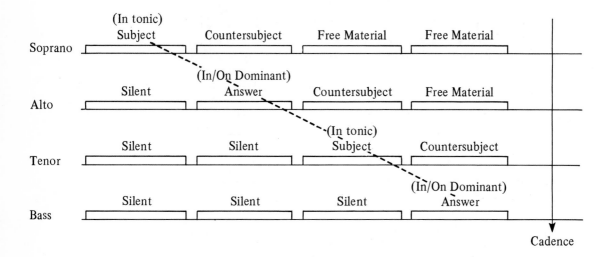

Exposition Alternatives

Common alternatives to the above pattern are:
A   The order of entrances may be: subject, answer, answer, subject.
B   Any voice (soprano, alto, tenor, or bass) may have the first statement of the subject.
C   The countersubject may not always appear three times as above.
D   Between entrances of the subject or answer there may be short excerpts interposed. These are sometimes called bridges.

DEVELOPMENT

After the exposition has been completed the subject or answer is stated in various keys (closely related keys in the Baroque).

Episode

In the development the entrances of the subject or answers are often set apart by episodes. *An episode is a short section that does not contain the subject or answer, often embraces sequences, is rather free in nature, and sometimes functions as a modulatory passage.*

RECAPITULATION

The 3rd and final part of the fugue containing the return of the subject and/or answer in the tonic key of the composition. Not all fugues have recapitulations, and in some the recapitulation is quite abbreviated.

DEVICES AND TYPES OF IMITATION

Stretto

Overlapping of subjects (or answers) in different voices. Usually occurs in the development section of a fugue.

Stretto

Theme Statement 1

Overlap

Theme Statement 2
(Overlaps Statement 1)

Augmentation

A device in counterpoint in which the note values of a given melody, subject, theme, etc. are lengthened (usually doubled).

Example of Augmentation

Theme (above) in augmentation

Diminution

A device in counterpoint in which the note values of a given melody, subject, theme are shortened.

Diminution

Above theme in diminution

Inversion

A device in counterpoint in which the vertical order of the two voices is reversed. Known also as invertible counterpoint.

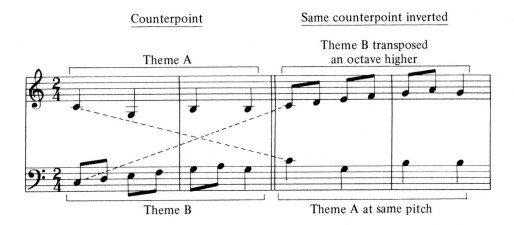

In the Baroque style where dissonance (2nds, 7ths, 4ths, and all diminished and augmented intervals) must be resolved properly, counterpoint that can be inverted is an essential technique of composition. As an example *it is wise to plan a countersubject that can be placed below the answer as well as above it since it may occur later in such a context.*

Here is a chart that indicates inversions and intervals that must be handled with special care when composing invertible counterpoint. For instance, the P5th (a consonance) inverts into a P4th (a dissonance), so the P5th must be treated as if it were a dissonance so that it will be handled properly when it becomes a P4th (in inversion).

Inversion at the Octave

INTERVAL:	1	2	3	4	5	6	7	8
	Both Consonant	Both Dissonant	Both Consonant	Dissonant Interval Inverts into Consonance	Consonant Interval Inverts into Dissonance	Both Consonant	Both Dissonant	Both Consonant
WHEN INVERTED BECOMES:	8	7	6	5	4	3	2	1

Counterpoint in two voices may be inverted at any interval. The above example, inverted at the octave (octave axis), is the most popular, but here is an illustration in which the inversion is at the 10th (octave and a 3rd).

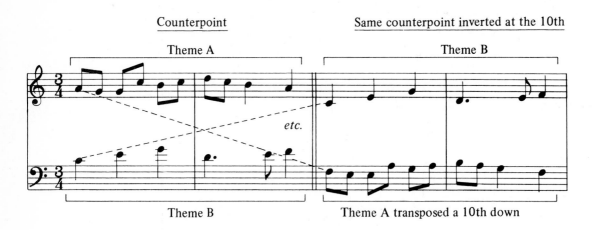

Here is a table showing each interval and the interval that will be created by inversion:

TABLE FOR INVERSION AT THE 10TH

INTERVAL:	1	2	3	4	5	6	7	8	9	10
	Both consonant avoid parallels however	Both dissonant	Both consonant avoid parallels however	Both dissonant	Both consonant avoid parallels however	Both consonant avoid parallels however	Both dissonant	Both consonant avoid parallels however	Both dissonant	Both consonant avoid parallels however
WHEN INVERTED BECOMES:	10	9	8	7	6	5	4	3	2	1

Contrary Motion (Melodic Inversion)

A device in counterpoint in which the direction of a melody, subject, theme, etc. is reversed. Sometimes called the inversion of a melody, but the term "contrary motion" is preferred because it eliminates confusion with the word "inversion" as it applies to invertible counterpoint.

Contrary motion

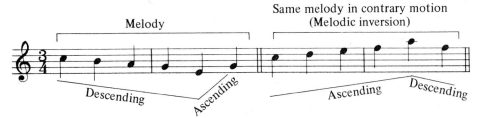

Retrograde

The tones of a melody, theme, subject, etc. in reverse order (back-wards).

Retrograde

This melody is the retrograde (reverse order) of the soprano melody

---

ASSIGNMENT 1   The subject for Fugue No. 2, Well-Tempered Clavier, Volume Two, by J. S. Bach is printed below.

Beneath the subject are eleven transformations (of the subject) plus the countersubject.

Place the name of the relationship in the blank provided. Listed are:

Retrograde	Embellished subject
Contrary motion	Subject extended
Countersubject	Change of interval (direction maintained)
Augmentation	Diminution
Change of Mode	Tonal answer
Motivic use	Real answer

320   The Fugue

Assignment 1 (continued)

Subject:

1.

2.

3.

4.

5.

6.

7.

8.

9.

10.

11.

12.

17
Analysis: Fugue No. 2 in C Minor by Bach

Unquestionably the most famous of Bach's works for the clavier is the set of preludes and fugues entitled *The Well-Tempered Clavier*. "Clavier" is a broad term meaning keyboard, so these compositions were written to be played on any keyboard instrument with strings. At the time of Bach such instruments included the clavichord, the harpsichord, and the pianoforte (piano). Nowadays *The Well-Tempered Clavier* is most often performed on the piano.

The complete work is divided into two sections, Part 1 and Part 2. Each part contains a prelude and fugue in each of the twelve possible major and minor keys—thus, a total of twenty-four preludes and fugues in each part.

Bach's primary purpose in preparing the work was to demonstrate the flexibility of the equal-tempered system of tuning, which at that time was considered experimental. Sometime after 1500 meantone temperament was generally adopted for keyboard instruments, and this method prevailed until the time of Bach. Meantone temperament was cumbersome and did not permit the free use of all keys (especially those with a number of sharps or flats in the signature). With the use in composition of the cycle of twelve major and twelve minor keys as manifested by Bach in *The Well-Tempered Clavier* the system of equal temperament began to gain in popularity. Gradually it earned acceptance over the more limited meantone system, but it should be mentioned that universal use did not take place until the nineteenth century.

The Fugue No. 2 in C minor Part 1 is selected for inclusion here since it exhibits a wide variety of imitative devices but at the same time displays fairly conventional fugal practice and form.

Subject

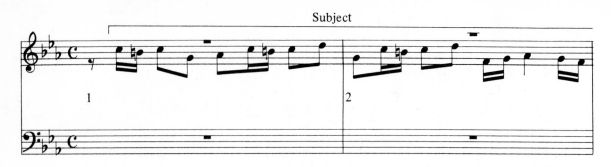

Answer

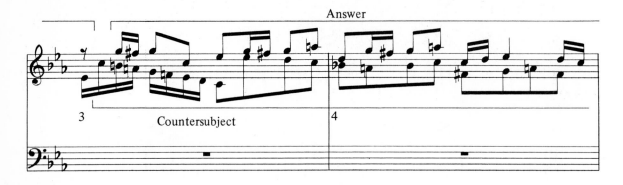

Countersubject

Bridge between answer and next entrance of the subject

Sequence, Leg 1   Sequence, Leg 2   Sequence, Leg 3

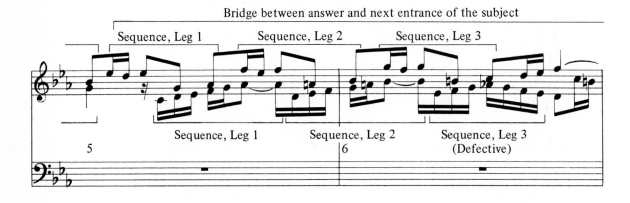

Sequence, Leg 1   Sequence, Leg 2   Sequence, Leg 3
(Defective)

Countersubject

Free Material

Subject

End of | Beginning of
exposition | development

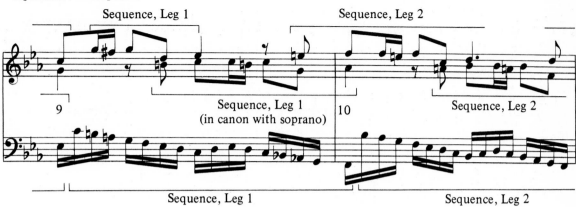

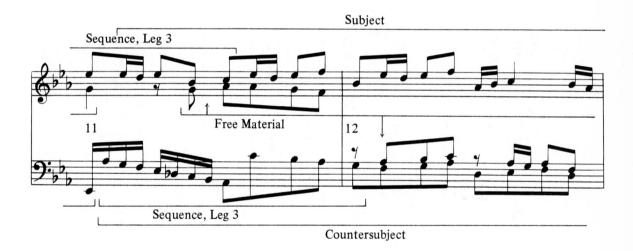

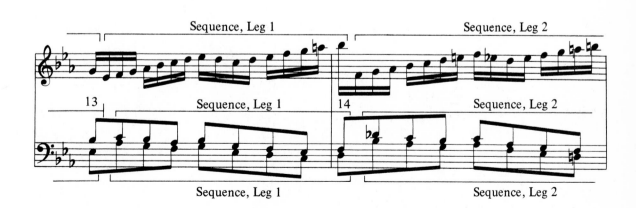

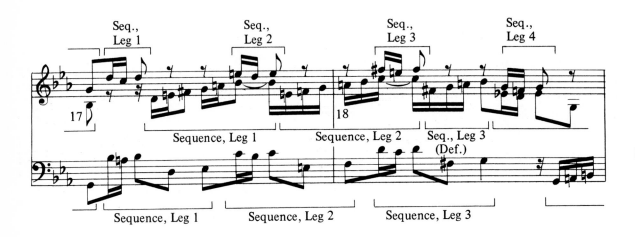

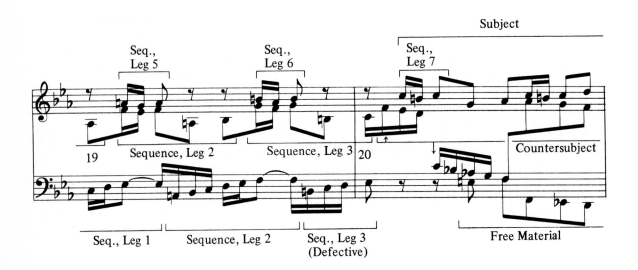

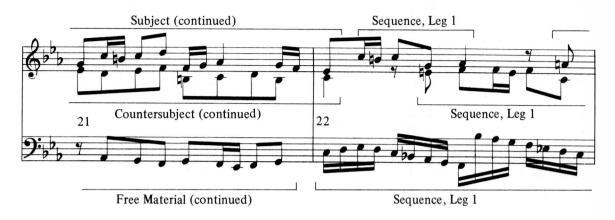

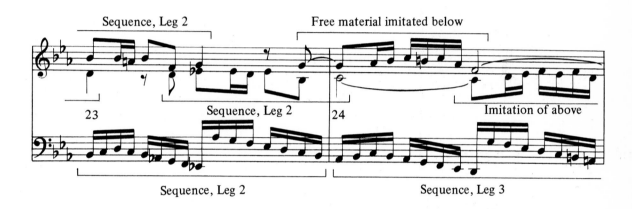

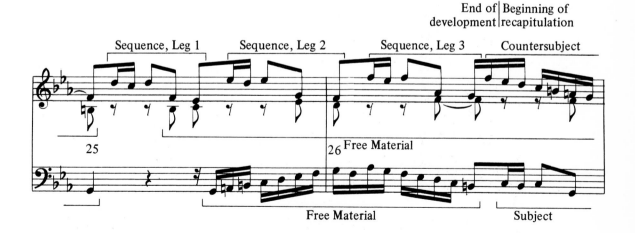

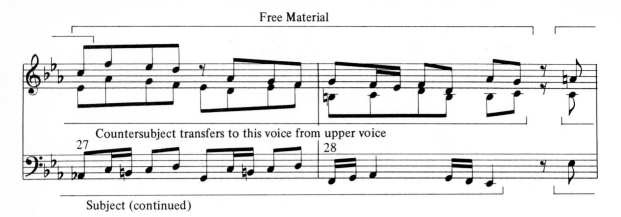

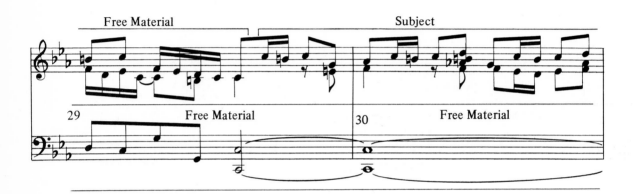

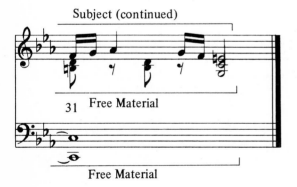

FORM

Exposition

This three-voice fugue follows convention in that the order of entrances is subject-answer-subject. The subject appears alone at first, but both the answer and the second entrance of the subject is accompanied by the countersubject. A short bridge separates the answer from the second entrance of the subject. The bridge serves the function of modulating from G minor back to C minor for the second entrance of the subject.

Development

As is customary in fugues the development consists of a series of episodes between entrances of either the subject or answer. Consistent with convention this fugue displays a variety of different keys in the development all of which are "closely related" to the original key.

Recapitulation

Although not all fugues have substantial recapitulations this particular one does. Beginning in measure 26 the subject is heard twice in the tonic key, the last statement appearing in the final two measures over a tonic pedal tone.

Chart with Analysis of Form

EXPOSITION:

Upper Voice:	1	2	3	4	5	6	7	8	9
				answer in Gm		bridge		countersubject	
Middle Voice:	1	2	3	4	5	6	7	8	9
		subject in Cm		countersubject		bridge		free material	
Lower Voice:	1	2	3	4	5	6	7	8	9
								subject in Cm	

DEVELOPMENT:

Upper Voice:	9	10	11	12	13	14	15	16	17
		episode		subject in E-flat		episode		countersubject	
Middle Voice:	9	10	11	12	13	14	15	16	17
		episode		free material		episode		answer in Gm	
Lower Voice:	9	10	11	12	13	14	15	16	17
		episode		countersubject		episode		free material	

Upper Voice:	18	19	20	21	22	23	24	25	26
		episode		subject in Cm			episode		
Middle Voice:	18	19	20	21	22	23	24	25	26
		episode		countersubject			episode		
Lower Voice:	18	19	20	21	22	23	24	25	26
		episode		free material			episode		

RECAPITULATION:

Upper Voice:	26	27	28	29	30	31	
		countersubject		free mat		subject in Cm	
Middle Voice:	26	27	28	29	30	31	End
		free material		free mat		free material	
Lower Voice:	26	27	28	29	30	31	
		subject in Cm		free mat		free material	

THE SUBJECT

The subject, stated in the first two measures, is the basis of the entire composition.

Subject:

The subject, stated in its entirety, is heard six times in the composition:

Table of Subject Entrances

MEASURE	KEY	ACCOMPANIED BY COUNTERSUBJECT
1	C minor	No
7	C minor	Yes
11	E-*flat* major	Yes
20	C minor	Yes
26	C minor	Yes
29	C minor	No

THE ANSWER

The answer, derived of course from the subject, is tonal rather than real.

Subject and answer placed together to show the slight alteration in the answer

The answer in its entirety is heard twice in the fugue:

Table of Answer Entrances

MEASURE	KEY	ACCOMPANIED BY COUNTERSUBJECT?
3	C minor to G minor	Yes
15	C minor to G minor	Yes

THE COUNTERSUBJECT

The countersubject plays a principle role in this fugue accompanying both the subject and answer throughout except in two entrances of the subject, one of which is at the beginning where the subject is traditionally stated alone. Furthermore, Bach makes good use of countersubject-derived material in the episodes of the development section.

Countersubject:

EPISODES

There are five episodes, four of which occur in the development, and one (consisting of less than a measure and inserted simply for the purpose of cadence construction) in the recapitulation.

All of the episodes except the last are based on fragments or motives from the subject or countersubject and are composed primarily of sequences.

Here is an illustration showing the derivation of episodic material:

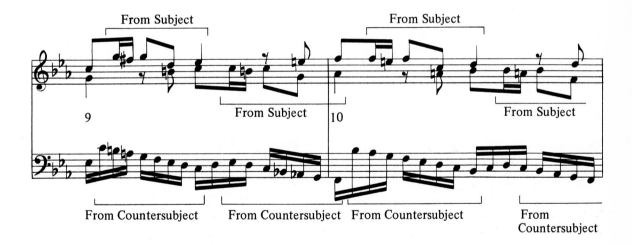

Even the lines marked "free material" often allude to the subject or countersubject.

Table of Episodes

	MEASURES
Episode 1	9–11
Episode 2	13–15
Episode 3	17–20
Episode 4	22–26
Episode 5	28–29

KEY RELATIONSHIPS

As with most compositions of the Baroque period, modulations are usually to closely related keys (subdominant, dominant, and the relative minor [or major] of the original, subdominant, and dominant).

Here are the key relationships in C minor.

ORIGINAL (3 flats)	*SUBDOMINANT* (4 flats)	*DOMINANT* (2 flats)
C minor	F minor	G minor
RELATIVE MAJOR (3 flats)	**RELATIVE MAJOR* (4 flats)	*RELATIVE MAJOR* (2 flats)
E-flat major	A-flat major	B-flat major

* This is the only key not found in the fugue.

Here is a table showing the various keys found in the fugue. As indicated in the table some of the key changes that are of very short duration are indicated as appearing only in a leg of a sequence. An alternate analysis of these would be to recognize each such change only as an instance of secondary dominant use.

Table of Keys

MEASURES	KEY	CIRCUMSTANCES
1–3	C minor	
3–6	G minor	
6–10	C minor	
11–13	E-*flat* major	
13–14	B-*flat* major	Modulating sequence, leg 1 only
14–15	F minor to C minor	Modulating sequence, leg 2 only
15–18	G minor	
18–19	C minor	Modulating sequence, leg 1 only
19	B-*flat* major	Modulating sequence, leg 2 only
19–20	C minor	Modulating sequence, leg 3 only
20–22	C minor	Modulating sequence, leg 1 only
22	F minor	Modulating sequence, leg 2 only
22–23	E-*flat* major	
24–31	C minor	

MISCELLANEOUS IMITATION

In addition to the form and contrapuntal relationships already mentioned, there are instances throughout the composition of additional imitation.

One example is in measures 9 and 10 where imitation is carried on between two voices that is in the nature of overlapping sequential material and is alternately heard in each of the voices.

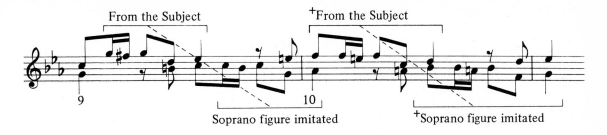

A similar example is that of measures 22 and 23 in which the same type of imitation occurs.

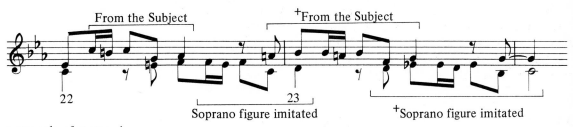

+ example of stretto also

The melody in the lower voice in measures 9 and 10 (derived from the countersubject) appears again in measures 13 and 14 in contrary motion (melodic inversion) in the upper voice.

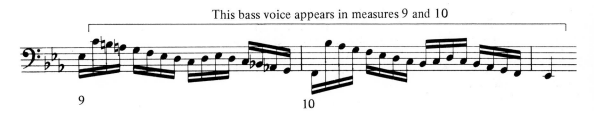

ASSIGNMENT 1   10 fugue subjects follow.

1._____

2._____

3._____

4._____

5._____

6._____

7.

8.

9.

10.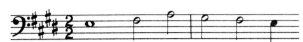

1 Determine whether each should have a real or tonal answer and write the type of answer in the blank provided above the music. Remember:

   a Tonal answers are usually given to subjects which:
     (1) Begin on the dominant tone.
     (2) Begin on the tonic and move to the dominant immediately.
     (3) Modulate.

2 Select one of the subjects that takes a real answer and write a countersubject. Remember that the countersubject accompanies the answer *not* the subject.

3 With this same subject write a fugue exposition. Use the Bach fugue analyzed in this chapter as a general guide. Remember, however, that different subjects require different treatment, so do not expect to handle your exposition *exactly* as Bach did.

4 When the exposition is completed, write a fugue development to follow the exposition.

5 Complete the fugue with a recapitulation.

6 Perform the fugue in class. Ask the class members to identify the subject and countersubject, the type of answer, the three sections of the fugue, and other compositional devices that might be present.

ASSIGNMENT 2

This is the first fugue in the first volume of the Well-Tempered Clavier by J. S. Bach. In the frame of its bare twenty-seven measures there are twenty-six entrances of the fugue subject!

1   Make a complete analysis of this fugue following the outline found in this chapter.

2   Arrange the fugue for three instruments and perform it in class.

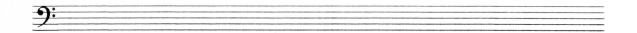

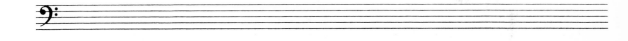

Assignment 2 (continued)

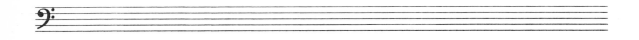

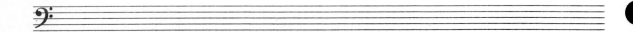

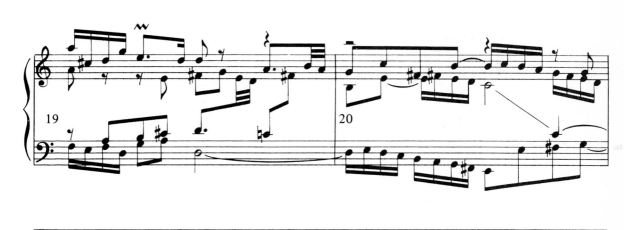

Assignment 2 (continued)

18
Devices of the Late Nineteenth and Early Twentieth Century

Whole-Tone Scale
Gregorian Modes
Pentatonic Scale
Melodic Doubling in Parallel
Added Tone Chords
Chords of Omission
Consonant Quartal Chords

Dissonant Quartal Chords
3rd Relationship
Parallel Chords (Planing)
Linear Cadence
3rd Relationship Cadence
Altered Dominant Cadence
Altered Tonic Cadence

WHOLE-TONE SCALE

The scale in which each degree is a whole step from the next.
A   The whole-tone scale has only six tones—a *hexatonic* scale.
B   Only two different whole-tone scales are possible:
   1   A whole-tone scale utilizing the following tones:

Any pitch may be spelled enharmonically:

1   2   3   4   5   6

2   The other possibility selects the remaining tones of the chromatic scale. An *aggregate* of the chromatic scale is formed by the two scales illustrated.

Any pitch may be spelled enharmonically:

C   There are no P5ths or P4ths between any two degrees of the whole-tone scale.

D   The whole tone scale is not diatonic—it contains no key or tonal center and may begin on any of the six tones.

E   An illustration from the Preludes of Debussy demonstrate the scale in context:

Debussy: Voiles (Sails). Copyright 1910, Durand et Cie. Used by permission of the publisher Elkan-Vogel, Inc. sole representative, United States.

GREGORIAN MODES

Composers of this style period often utilized modal resources to create new and unusual melodic effects. A knowledge of modal practices of previous periods is interesting and helpful, but is by no means essential to the understanding of modal treatment at the turn of the present century. More recent composers did not limit themselves to the same idiomatic use of the modes as in earlier (up to the 17th century) periods. The *Chanty* from the group of piano compositions *Poems of the Sea* (1924) by Ernest Bloch illustrates the use of the Dorian mode.

Dorian mode beginning on *A*

"Chanty" from POEMS OF THE SEA by Ernest Bloch. Copyright © 1923 G.
Schirmer, Inc. Used by permission.

From the Italian composer, Ottorino Respighi, the excerpt below illustrates the use of the Phrygian mode beginning on *A*. The composition is *Trittico Botticelliano* (1927), a suite for small orchestra.

Phrygian mode beginning on *A*

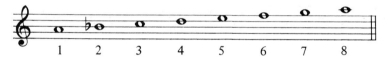

Respighi: Trittico Botticelliano

PENTATONIC SCALE

The pentatonic (five-tone) scale found frequent use in compositions of this style period. Since it is a *gapped* scale (contains intervals larger than a whole step between adjacent tones) there are several possible arrangements of intervals available. Some of the more popular pentatonic scales are:

Some of the more frequently found pentatonic scale formations:

The following excerpt from the *Preludes*, Volume 1, by Debussy demonstrates the use of the pentatonic scale. The composition was written in 1910.

Pentatonic Scale

Debussy: Voiles (Sails). Copyright 1910, Durand et Cie. Used by permission of the publisher Elkan-Vogel, Inc. sole representative, United States.

MELODIC DOUBLING IN PARALLEL

Doubling of melodic lines to create parallel movement. The doubling may be simply the addition of a single harmonic tone:

Melody

Same melody with melodic doubling

While treated in a unique way in this period, melodic doubling is by no means the invention of twentieth-century composers. Such doubling has been in existence for many centuries and can be found in *Fauxbordon* and *English Discant* of the fifteenth century:

Fauxbordon

Dufay: Mass (circa 1465)

Melodic doubling may be contrived to coincide with conventional harmonic progressions, a practice not often found in music of the late nineteenth and early twentieth centuries:

America with melodic doubling at the 6th

More appropriate to Impressionism is the following excerpt illustrating the use of melodic doubling at the interval of the 2nd.

Debussy: Ce qu'a vu le vent de l'Ouest (What the West Wind Saw). Copyright 1910 Durand et Cie. Used by permission of the publisher. Elkan-Vogel, Inc. sole representative, United States.

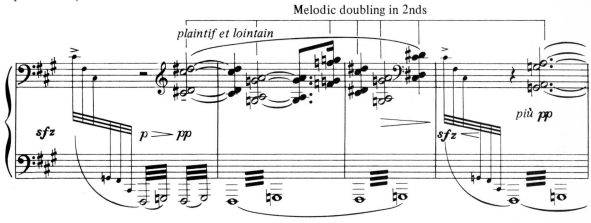

Similarities exist between the terms *melodic doubling* and *parallelism (planing)*. Both terms refer to parallel motion. Melodic doubling implies a clearly defined melody that has been thickened with additional tones but supported by a harmonic context that is not related to the doubling. Parallelism (planing) is a term more suited to the description of an entire vertical sonority that is moved about in equidistant blocks. Despite the explanations, there are instances in music that could be expressed by either term.

7TH, 9TH, 11TH, AND 13TH CHORDS

These chords are employed in considerably more frequency during the late Romantic and Impressionistic period, and the incidence of resolution of the dissonant factors is greatly diminished.

The following excerpt from Ravel's *Sonatine* (1903) illustrates the use of 7th and 9th chords in succession. Note the circle of descending 5ths (ascending 4ths) progression, a vestige of the Baroque, Classical, and Romantic periods.

Ravel: Sonatine (2nd movement)

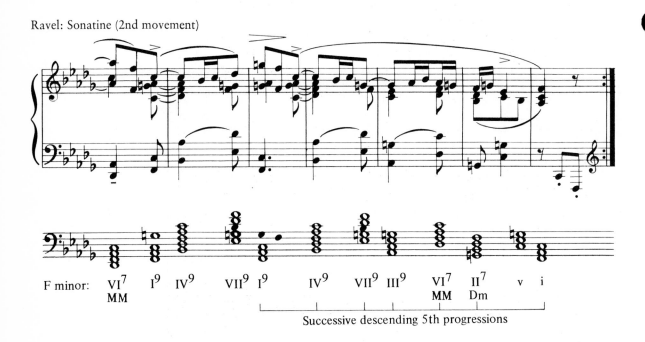

CHORDS OF OMISSION AND ADDITION

Chords with added or deleted tones. In order to thicken the sound of some sonorities composers of the period often added a 6th, a 4th, or a 2nd to the traditional triad. Using the same procedure, tones were on occasion deleted from chords, thus thinning the sound. Some examples that are found frequently are:

Added 6th   Added 4th   Added 2nd   Omitted 3rd Omitted 3rd

Added Tone Chords

Chords with added tones are often very similar in construction to 9th, 11th, and 13th chords. Here are two suggestions that may assist in avoiding confusion:

A   If a chord is made up of a triad *only* with an added factor (6th, 4th, 2nd) the chord is definitely an added tone chord. The chords shown immediately above are good examples.

B   7th chords may sometimes contain added tones, but 9th, 11th, and 13th chords already contain a number of dissonant factors, and added tones would only be confusing and ineffective.

C   Distinguishing between 7th chords with an added tone and 9th, 11th, or 13th chords depends entirely upon the arrangement of the chord. In 9th, 11th, and 13th chords the highest factor is usually in the upper voice, and, when in this position, the characteristic nature of such chords is clearly emphasized.

D   However, when the highest factor (9th, 11th, or 13th) is in a lower voice the tendency is to hear it as a tone added to a 7th chord.

E   When a chord is given an added tone, one of its factors is often deleted.

Both chords contain the same tones   Both chords contain the same tones

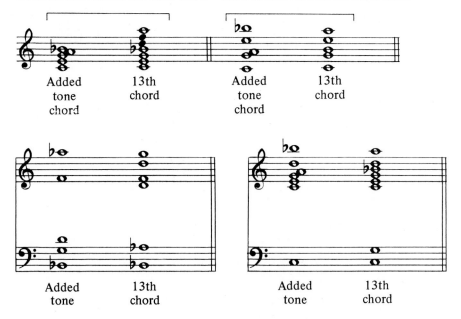

Added   13th   Added   13th
tone   chord   tone   chord
chord   chord

Added   13th   Added   13th
tone   chord   tone   chord

The added sixth chord is especially prominent in the following excerpt:

Ravel: Sonatine (1st movement)

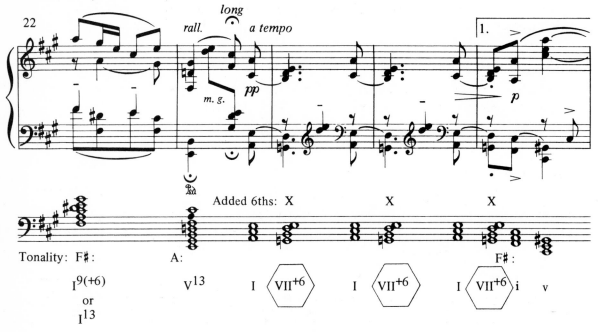

The above examples of added tones are diatonic, but chromatic added tones are also found. Such chromatic tones usually produce a split root, 3rd, 5th, or 7th. The example below contains five chromatic added tones.

Ravel: Valses Nobles et Sentimentales. Copyright 1911, Editions Durand et Cie. Used by permission of the publisher. Elkan-Vogel, Inc., sole representative, United States.

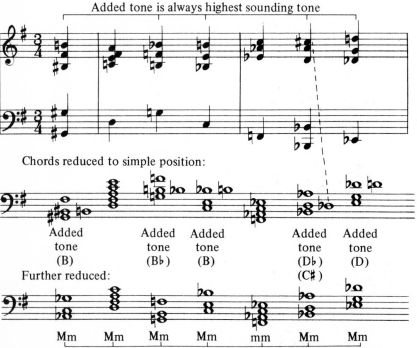

Chords of Omission

While the term is obviously vague the late nineteenth- and early twentieth-century composers sometimes included chords in which vital factors have been deleted.

TRIADS

The 3rd is the only factor of a triad that may be deleted to form a chord of omission. Omitting the root destroys the identity of the chord, while the removal of the 5th does not eliminate enough sonority to provide a noticeable thinning out.

Debussy: Soirée dans Grenade

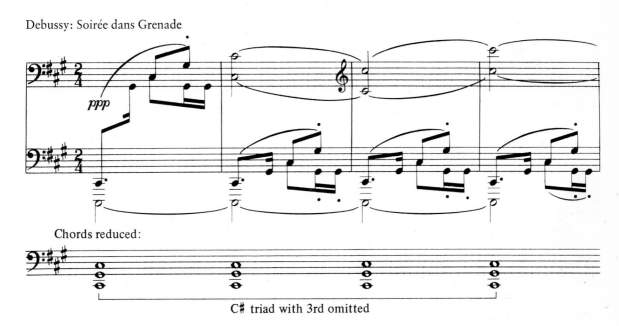

C♯ triad with 3rd omitted

Debussy: Soirée dans Grenade

A Major: I   V⁷   I   V⁷
          (3rd omitted) Mm (same)   Mm
                    (Added 4th)   (same)

7TH CHORDS

As with triads omitting the 3rd gives the 7th chord a definitely thinner sound, but the cancellation of any other factor either destroys the identity of the chord or does not create a sufficiently different sound.

9TH, 11TH, AND 13TH CHORDS

Since 9th, 11th, and 13th chords are already considerably thickened in comparison with triads and 7th chords, the omission of any single interval does not provide sufficient thinning to yield a characteristically different sound.

CHORDS OF ADDITION WITH DELETIONS

Frequently chords of addition also contain deleted tones. The deletions are made to heighten the effect of the additions. Any chord that contains an added tone is called a chord of addition whether it contains deletions or not.

QUARTAL CHORDS

Chords built in 4ths. Although by no means a common occurrence, chords built in 4ths can be found in this style period.

Consonant Quartal Chords

Three, four, or five factors built in P4ths.

Dissonant Quartal Chords

A Quartal chords that contain one or more A4ths.
B Quartal chords that contain more than 5 factors.

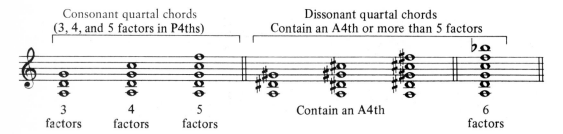

Consonant quartal chords (3, 4, and 5 factors in P4ths) — 3 factors, 4 factors, 5 factors

Dissonant quartal chords — Contain an A4th or more than 5 factors — Contain an A4th — 6 factors

Quartal Chords in Impressionism

Quartal chords in Impressionism are not an intrinsic part of the style. They sometimes appear as parallel chords in nonfunctional harmony. This excerpt from a Debussy Prelude for piano illustrates such use.

Debussy: La Cathédrale engloutie (Engulfed Cathedral). Copyright 1910, Durand et Cie. Used by permission of the publisher. Elkan-Vogel, Inc., sole representative, United States.

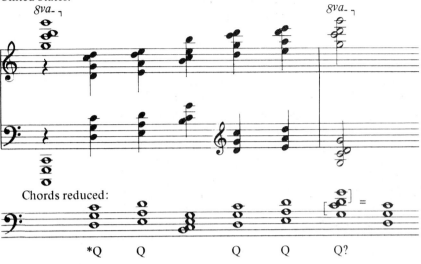

Chords reduced:

*Quartal chords

Quartal Chords in Contemporary Music

More common in the Contemporary period, quartal chords are a part of the harmonic vocabulary of several composers. The illustration below is a somewhat rare example of pure quartal chords employed almost exclusively throughout the composition:

Ives: The Cage (No. 64 of 114 Songs) Copyright 1955 by Peer International Corporation. Used by permission.

Chords reduced to simple position:

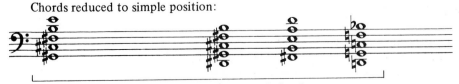

All are 5 factor consonant quartal chords

Frequently quartal chords are not pure—that is, other intervals are interspersed in the chord thus creating a mixture of quartal and tertian harmony. The following excerpt from Alban Berg's first opera (in 1921) illustrates the intermixing of 3rds and 4ths. The parallel 4ths in contrary motion (treble against bass) create a counterpoint that adds to the interest of the composition.

Berg: Wozzeck (Marie's Lullaby). Used by permission of Universal Editions, Ltd.

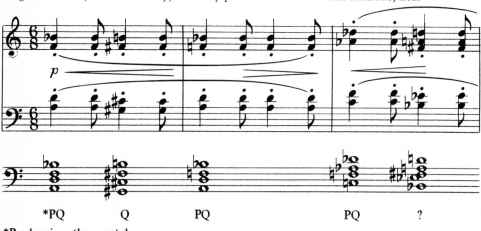

*Predominantly quartal

This excerpt below from a composition written in 1958 by Paul Pisk also illustrates the mixing of quartal with tertian (triadic) harmony. Note also that the melody contains a motif made up of two intervals, the m2nd and the tritone. In its last two appearances in this excerpt the m2nd is maintained, but the tritone gives way first to a P5th and then a M3rd.

Pisk: "Nocturnal Interlude" from New Music for the Piano. Copyright 1963 Lawson-Gould Music Publishers, Inc. Used by permission.

*Quartal chords
**Tertian (Triadic)

Both quartal and tertian harmony often contain the same tones, each distinguished only by the arrangement of the chord factors.

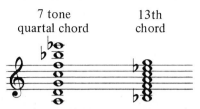

Both contain the same pitches

3RD RELATIONSHIP

Root movement in 3rds. Chord progressions where the roots lie a P4th or P5th apart are considered the strongest type and tend to reinforce tonality especially when the tonic and dominant chords are involved. When prominent progressions employ root relationships such as the M or m3rd in concentration or in succession, particularly ascending, the tonality becomes less emphasized. This pattern is one of the distinguishing features of the late nineteenth- and early twentieth-century style and is common in the music of this period. The second of Debussy's *Nocturnes, Fetes* (1899) contains an excellent illustration:

Debussy: Fêtes (Festivals). Copyright 1923, Editions Jean Jobert. Used by permission of the publisher. Theodore Presser Company, sole representative, United States, Canada and Mexico.

Chords reduced to simple position:

Root relation: 3rd   3rd   3rd   3rd   3rd

From the second movement of Debussy's *Pour le Piano* (For the Piano) suite written in 1901 3rd relationships are prevalent:

Debussy: Sarabande

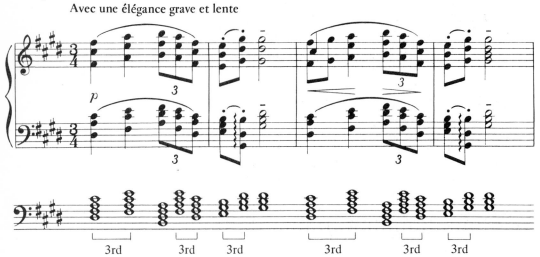

PARALLEL CHORDS (PLANING)

Chords in which all factors or voices move in parallel motion. Generally planing reduces or negates the effect of harmonic progression, but occasionally chords such as the tonic and dominant may produce the feeling of harmonic progression.

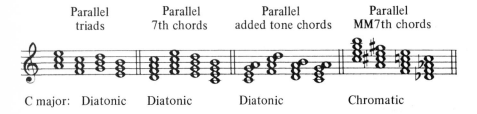

The following example of planing contains only Mm7th chords.

Debussy: Sarabande

Parallel Major-minor 7th chords

This illustration contains mixed major and minor triads in first inversion:

Debussy: Soirée dans Grenade

poco cresc. - - - - - - - - - -

Chords reduced:

Planed 1st inversion M and m triads

CADENCES

A wide variety of cadences are found in this style period ranging from the traditional authentic cadence of the eighteenth and nineteenth century to the 3rd relationship cadence, a type peculiar to the late nineteenth and early twentieth century.

Traditional Authentic Cadence

The traditional authentic cadence of earlier periods is frequently adorned with 7th, 9th, 11th, or 13th chords:

Debussy: *Pelleas et Melisande* (opera) (1902)

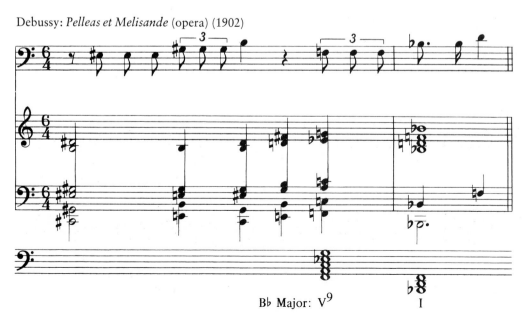

Bb Major: V⁹   I

Linear Cadence

Melodic lines that converge or diverge to form cadence points. The usual concept that a cadence is made up of harmonic progressions is not valid in the linear (sometimes called line) cadence. Diverging, converging, or oblique motion create line cadences:

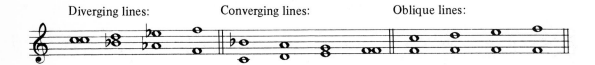

From the first volume of *Preludes* by Debussy the final cadence results from oblique motion:

Debussy: Le vent dans la plaine (The Wind on the Plains). Copyright 1910, Durand et Cie. Used by permission of the publisher. Elkan-Vogel, Inc., sole representative, United States.

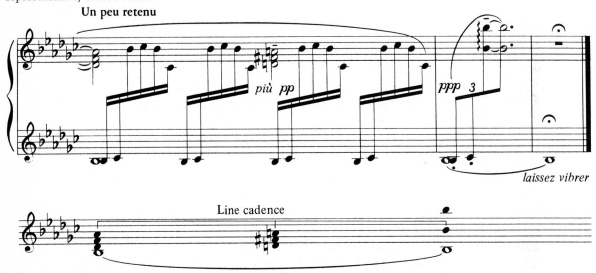

3rd Relationship Cadences

Very common is the cadence that results from the harmonic progression in which the roots lie a 3rd apart. This highly decorated cadence by Ravel is of the 3rd relationship type.

Ravel: Sonatine (2nd movement) (1903)

From the *Suite Bergamasque,* third movement, *Clair de lune* (circa 1903), by Debussy, the following illustration contains a 3rd relationship cadence.

Debussy: "Clair de lune" (Moonlight)

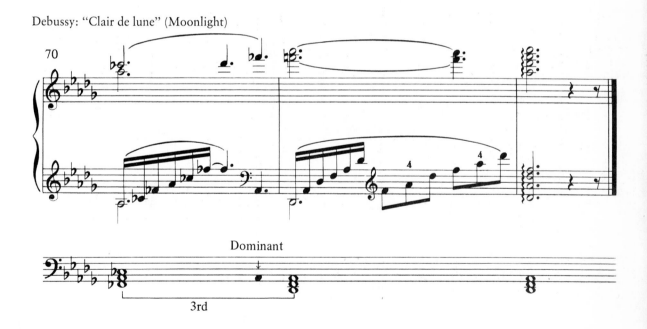

A final example of a 3rd relationship cadence by Ravel:

Ravel: Sonatine (1st movement) (1903)

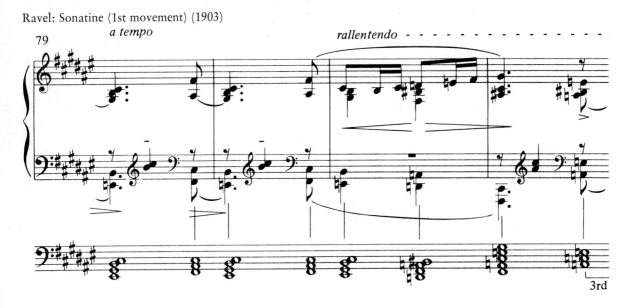

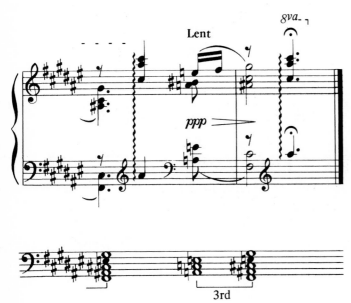

Cadences Containing Altered Dominants or Tonics

Although the authentic cadence of the eighteenth and nineteenth centuries is sometimes found in its unaltered state in this style period, the dominant-tonic function is often camouflaged by chords to which additional factors have been added or deleted.

Cadences with modified tonics or dominants:

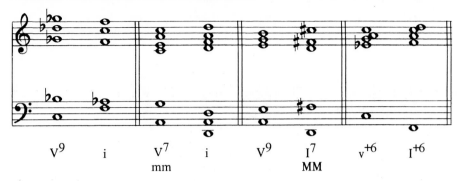

$$V^9 \quad\quad i \quad\quad V^7 \quad\quad i \quad\quad V^9 \quad\quad I^7 \quad\quad v^{+6} \quad\quad I^{+6}$$

mm   MM

The following final cadence from the second movement of *Suite Bergamasque* contains a dominant 7th chord with an added 4th. In some respects this chord contains elements of both dominant and tonic harmony.

Debussy: Menuet (from Suite Bergamasque) (1906) Copyright 1925, Editions Jean Jobert. Used by permission of the publisher. Theodore Presser Company, sole representative, United States, Canada and Mexico.

Cadence with altered dominant

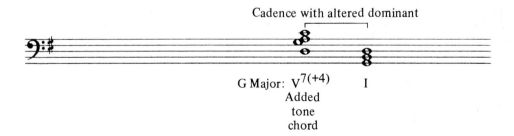

G Major: $V^{7(+4)}$ I
Added
tone
chord

The *Polka* from the ballet *L'Age d'or* written in 1930 by Shostakovitch illustrates the use of a dominant 9th and 13th chord with lowered 5th.

Shostakovitch: Polka from L'Age d'or (The Golden Age)

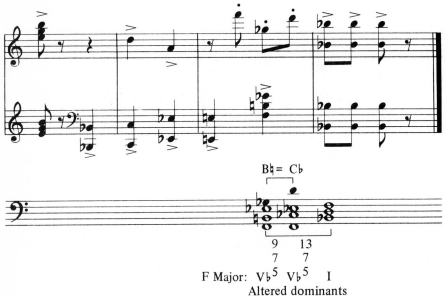

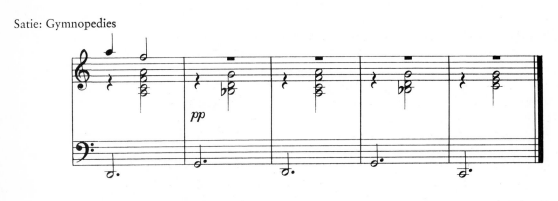

Other Cadences

A variety of other cadences are also a part of the late nineteenth- and early twentieth-century style. Most are simply derivations of more established cadences from previous periods. The short piano composition *Gymnopedie* (Greek ceremonial dance) by Eric Satie, written in 1888, ends with a dominant-tonic cadence in the mixolydian mode:

Satie: Gymnopedies

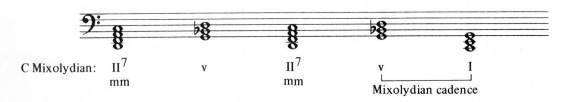

19

Analysis: La Cathédrale Engloutie by Debussy (1862-1918)

ABOUT THE COMPOSER

Debussy (1862–1918), as most other French composers, was trained in the Central European classical tradition. He spent eleven years at the French Conservatoire where he was trained in the principles and techniques that were in themselves not characteristic of French musical creativity. Despite his background and training Debussy's language and intent are entirely different from those of his predecessors and contemporaries. His music, like Impressionist paintings and symbolist poetry of the time, reflect through perceptive allusions and stylistic inflections the sights and sounds of nature.

Though his music is tonal it contains many departures from the accepted techniques of earlier styles. He developed a new harmonic vocabulary, adapted Gregorian modes, utilized other scales such as the whole tone, and employed such devices as harmonic parallelism.

Melody, rhythm, and harmony in the hands of Debussy become simply different aspects of one basic idea. Sounds and sound patterns relate to each other by rather arbitrary and sensual aural criteria rather than by the old necessities of harmonic resolution as governed by dictates of the past. The elaborate and graceful tonal imagination of Debussy is given a much wider and more profound field of action and expression than its apparently limited character might seem to suggest at first. Traditional techniques such as sequence act as extending or delaying devices and produce a pleasing ambiguity that reinforces the over-all motion. Indeed, Debussy is a master of subtlety, veiled clarity, and hinted suggestion.

Debussy's style functions as a transition from the eighteenth and nineteenth century concept of tonality to the twentieth century ideas of tonal organization. Since he stands at the dividing line between the old and the new his music richly deserves our careful attention.

SCALES AND MODES

The wide variety of scale and modal patterns found in this composition
contribute heavily to the unique style represented here. The following chart
indicates the various scales and modes for the smaller units of the work,
and, although few if any can be distinguished separately in performance,
the presence of each is important to the homogeneous sound of the
composition as a whole.

MEASURES	KEY OR MODE	CHORD ROOT	SCALE USED	TONES MISSING
1–2	C major		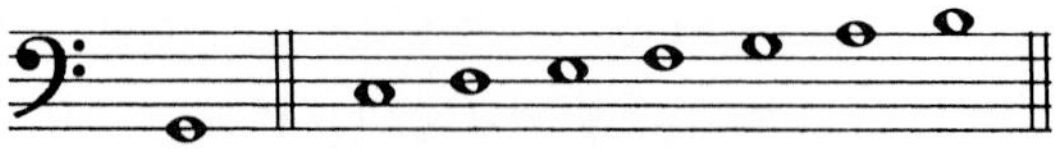	None
3–4	C major		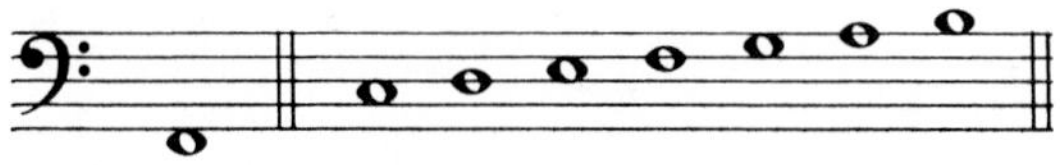	None
5–6	C major		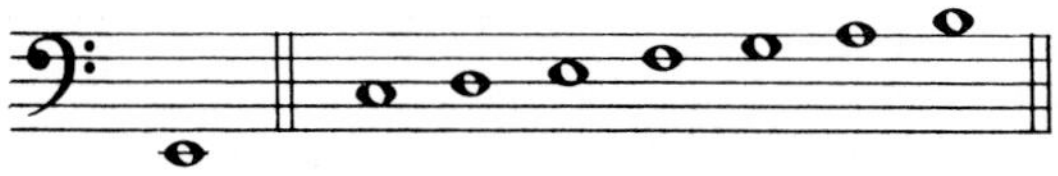	None
7–13	E Lydian mode (or C♯ Dorian mode)			F♯
14–15	C major		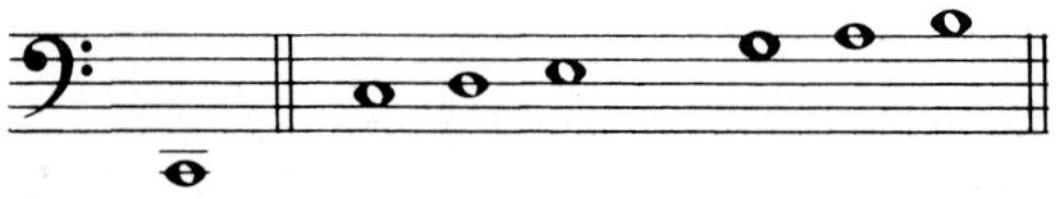	F
16–18	B pentatonic		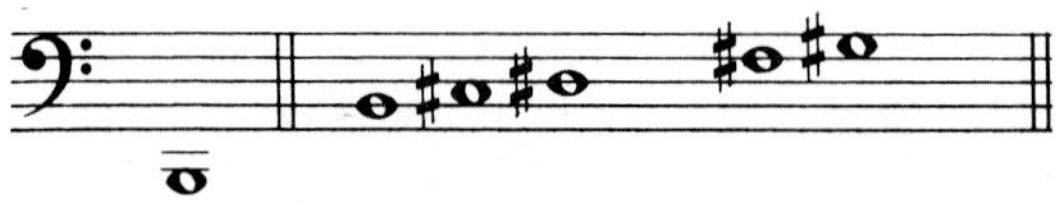	None
19–21	E-*flat* major		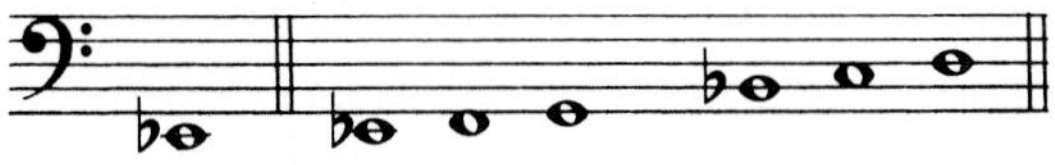	A-*flat*
22–27	C pentatonic			None (B & E used only as non-harmonic tones
28–32	C major		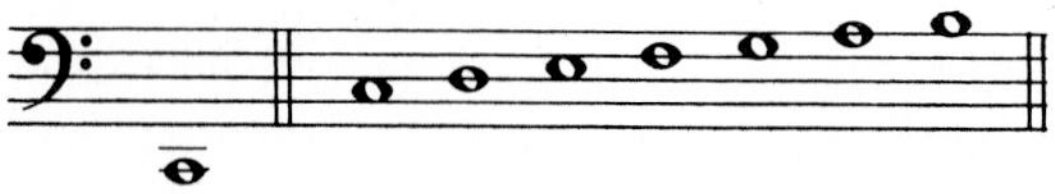	None

MEASURES	KEY OR MODE	CHORD ROOT	SCALE USED	TONES MISSING
33–41	C Mixolydian mode			None
42–43	Transition			
44–46	Transition			
47–54	C# Dorian mode			F#
55–62	C# Aeolian mode			E
63–71	Transition			
72–76	C major			None
77–83	C Mixolydian mode			None
84–89	C major			None

TONALITY

The tonality of this composition is vague compared to that of works from the Baroque, Classical, and Romantic periods. Contributing to this indecisiveness is the slow harmonic rhythm of the composition. In one instance (measures 47–71) a single root spans a total of twenty-four measures. It may be further noted that many of the chord roots are simply extended pedal tones that abound in this work.

The following illustration presents the roots found in the entire composition—an extremely small number for a composition of eighty-nine measures.

Chord roots with measures indicated:

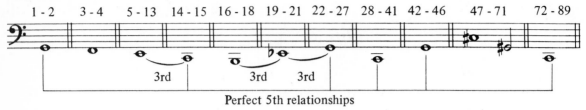

Perfect 5th Relationships

The illustration above demonstrates the strong P5th relationship between *G* and *C* thus strengthening the dominance of *C* as a tonal center. Since a slightly ambiguous interplay of Dorian, Mixolydian, and Aeolian modes may be found, it would not be accurate to indicate the *key* of *C* for this composition. Rather the more inclusive term *tonality* should be selected since this term embraces any scale formation so long as the tonal center is not disturbed.

The chart on pages 362 and 363 shows *C* as the tonal center through 46 of the 89 measures of the composition.

Sections Utilizing *C* as the Tonal Center

MEASURES	TOTAL MEASURES	TYPE OF SCALE OR MODE
1–6	6	C major
14–15	2	C major
22–27	6	C pentatonic
28–32	5	C major
33–41	9	C Mixolydian
72–76	5	C major
77–83	7	C Mixolydian
84–89	6	C major

MELODY

As is typical of Debussy and many other composers of this style period the delicate fusion of harmony, rhythm, and melody makes it difficult to speak of one without considering the others.

Melody emerges to prominence at four different points of the composition. Its appearance seems to evolve unobtrusively out of the general context, it declaims its brief existence, and just as quietly dissolves into the blend of color so adroitly conceived by the composer.

The sections of the composition in which melody emerges to predominate are:

Theme A

Measures: 7   8   9   10   11   12   13

Theme A is of seven measures length only and is ambiguous in that it favors both the tonality of *E* and *C♯*. Since the harmonic constituents that accompany it tend to support *E* (long *E* pedal tone persists throughout) the tonality of *E* prevails.

Theme B

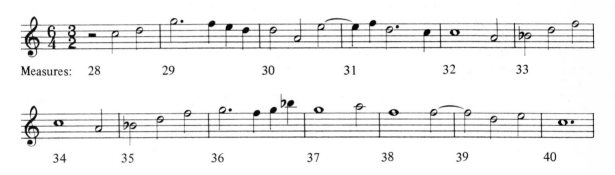

Measures: 28   29   30   31   32   33

34   35   36   37   38   39   40

Theme B is of thirteen measures length and clearly defines the tonality of *C*. Bars 33 through 36 utilize the Mixolydian mode (note the *B-flat*), but the tonality remains *C*. The harmonic fabric strongly reinforces the tonality through the use of a *C* pedal tone.

Theme A′

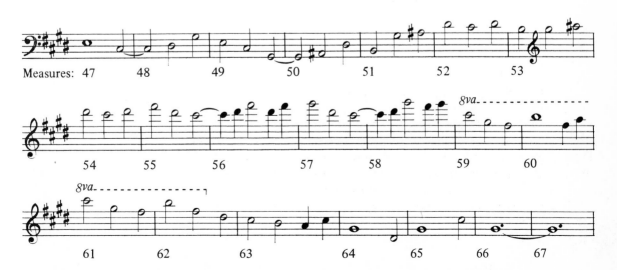

Measures: 47   48   49   50   51   52   53

54   55   56   57   58   59   60

61   62   63   64   65   66   67

Theme A′ appears in measure 47 this time extended considerably. Also, instead of emphasizing *E* tonality the strong *G♯* and *C♯* relationships of the harmony fortify the latent *C♯* tendencies.

Theme B

Measures: 72   73   74   75   76   77

78   79   80   81   82   83

Theme B reappears again in measure 72 exactly as before except for the final three tones. The tonality of *C* is obvious.

FORM

The form of the entire composition is determined for the most part by the appearance of the melodies above (A, B, A′, B). The form may be summarized thus:

MEASURES	SECTIONS
1–27	A
28–46	B
47–71	A′
72–89	B

HARMONY

Harmonic Vocabulary

The following reduction illustrates the harmonic vocabulary used by Debussy in this composition. *Parallelism* (chords in parallel motion) is one of the most important elements of the work, but since the device negates basic harmonic progression such instances have been eliminated from the analysis and will be discussed later in the chapter.

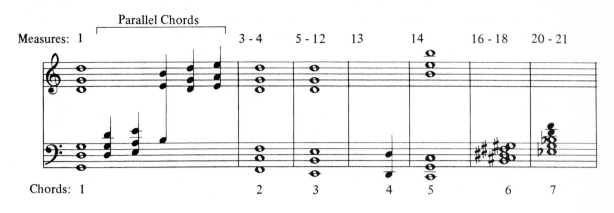

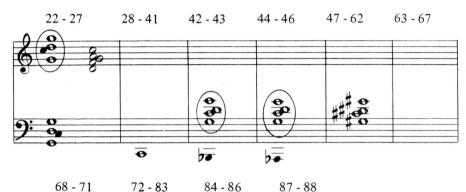

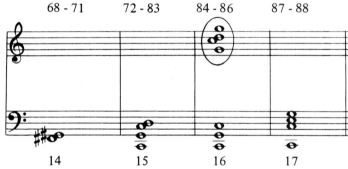

Chord 1 (measures 1 & 2):   Chord of omission—*G* and *D* (missing the third factor)

Chord 2 (measures 3 & 4):   May be analyzed in any of the following ways:

1.   Chord of omission *F C F* with upper pedal *D G D*.
2.   Chord of omission *D G D* similar to measure 1 with *F C F* as passing tones to *E* in measure 5.
3.   A single *quintal* (chord built in P5ths) chord *F C G D*.

Chord 3 (measures 5–12):   May be considered in one of the following ways:

1.   Chord of omission *E B E* with upper pedal *D G D*.
2.   Chord of omission *D G D* similar to measure 1 with *E B E* as passing tones toward *C* in measure 14.
3.   A single 7th chord *E G B D*.

Chord   4   (measure 13):   Passing tone to C in measure 14.

Chord   5   (measure 14):   Similar in nature to chords 2 and 3, but because of its strength both formally and tonally will probably sound as a MM7th chord on C (C E G B).

Chord 6 (measures 16–18):   Major triad with added 2nd and 6th. Traditionally it is a leading tone (C tonality) chord, but through its function as part of a 3rd relationship it cannot be analyzed in the normal functional way. It contains all the tones of the B pentatonic scale.

Chord 7 (measures 20–21):   E-*flat* major triad that acquires both a 7th and a 9th at times. Part of a 3rd relationship, so its harmonic strength has been somewhat reduced.

Chord   8   (measures 22–27):   This chord composed of two superimposed P4ths (G to C and D to G) is a harmonic and melodic figure that appears regularly throughout the composition. The chord represented by the un-stemmed half notes is a II^7 with added 4th.

mm

Chord   9   (measures 21–41):   Pedal tone with parallel chords that do not generate harmonic progression.

Chord 10 (measures 42–43):   The same harmonic figure as in chord 8. The B-*flat* is a passing tone to the A-*flat* (G♯).

Chord 11 (measures 44–46):   The same harmonic figure as in chord 8. The A-*flat* in the bass becomes a pedal tone and changes to G♯.

Chord 12 (measures 47–62):   The same harmonic figure as in chord 8 but transposed up one-half step.

Chord 13 (measures 63–67):   Parallel chords that do not for the most part generate progressions. Measures 64 & 65 contain the V^7 and V^7 of IV in C♯ minor, which, even in parallel motion, are of sufficient strength to define harmonic movement.

Chord 14 (measures 68–71):   Pedal tone composed of F♯ and G♯.

Chord 15 (measures 72–83):   A version of the harmonic figure from chords 8, 10, 11, and 12 (above). At this point the effect is that of a *quintal* chord.

Chord 16 (measures 84–86):   Pedal tone C with the harmonic figure from chords 8, 10, 11, 12, and 15 above it.

Chord 17 (measures 87 & 88):   C major triad—tonic triad. Appears in measures 86–89.

Further Observations of Harmonic Vocabulary

Although most of the chords are basically *triadic* (built in 3rds from the root) there are examples that bear resemblance to *quintal* (built up in P5ths) chords or *quartal* (built up in P4ths) chords.

The chords below sometimes relate to familiar triadic structures although their arrangements often suggest quartal or quintal tendencies:

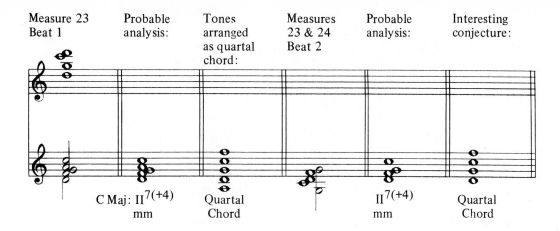

| Measure 23 Beat 1 | Probable analysis: | Tones arranged as quartal chord: | Measures 23 & 24 Beat 2 | Probable analysis: | Interesting conjecture: |

C Maj: II⁷(+4) mm — Quartal Chord — II⁷(+4) mm — Quartal Chord

The chords found in measures 85 and 86 also give considerable suggestions of quartal or quintal construction:

Measure 85:   Measure 86:

Chords reduced:

Quintal   Quartal?

Chord Progressions

The effect of regularly recurring harmonic progressions is minimized in this composition. The reasons are:

A   The actual progressions occur at widely spaced intervals of at least two measures and in one instance at a distance of thirteen measures. The harmonic rhythm is extremely slow.

B   Some of the harmonic progressions (such as from meas. 18 to 19 and 21 to 22) contain chords whose roots lie in 3rd relationship to each other. When the thirds are ascending the harmonic strength is weakened considerably.

Cadences

Traditional harmonic cadences are suggested (as at measures 86–89) but seldom stated clearly as in earlier styles. Even the authentic cadence at measures 27–28 is veiled with added tone chords and a running figure in the lower voice.

The cadence points are as follows:

MEASURES	CADENCE TYPE	TONALITY	CHORDS
27–28	Authentic	C	V_2^4 (implied) to I
39–40	Linear (parallel motion)	C	I (pedal)
65–66	Half	C♯	V^7/V to V^7
			Mm
86–89	Authentic (modified dominant)	C	V (or quartal) to I
			I

Pervading the composition as a whole is the *C G D* figure that invades both the melody and the harmony. This figure contains the P5th of both the tonic and dominant triads (in C tonality), and at the final cadence (86–89) suggests an authentic cadence.

Measure 86:

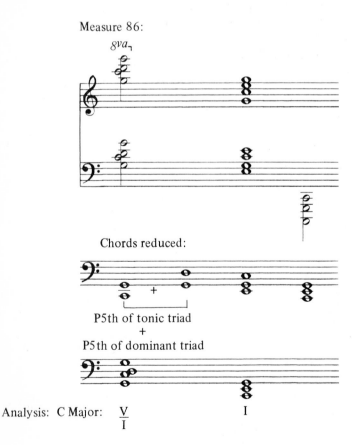

Chords reduced:

P5th of tonic triad
+
P5th of dominant triad

Analysis: C Major: $\dfrac{V}{I}$ I

RHYTHM AND METER

Meter

$\frac{6-3}{4-2}$ meter, indicated at the beginning of this composition is normally interpreted to mean that the quarter note value remained fixed and that in some measures they would be grouped in duples and in others as triplets. However, in his own performance of this work, Debussy plays in a fashion that would indicate:

♩ IN $\frac{6}{4}$ METER = ♩ IN $\frac{3}{2}$ METER

Rhythm

Since the meter vacillates somewhat irregularly from groupings of two to groupings of three the rhythm, although interesting and diverse, is not stressed. The underlying desire of Debussy to fuse the rhythm, melody, and harmony into a single amorphous mass is demonstrated in this composition very well. Note how the gentle rhythmic figures appear and disappear without creating undue attention. Using its most literal meaning rhythm is an insignificant factor in this work, but considering the rhythm as a part of the total "color" it plays a very important role.

TEXTURE

The texture of this composition is nearly an antithesis of polyphony. With the numerous pedal tones and the parallel movement of chords, conflict of opposing melodies is almost totally absent. The motion is predominantly parallel or oblique as shown in this typical measure:

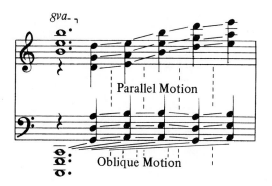

SUMMARY OF LATE NINETEENTH- AND EARLY TWENTIETH-CENTURY DEVICES

DEVICE	MEASURES
Planing (parallelism)	62–67, 72–83, 84–85
Gregorian modes (*E* Lydian or *C♯* Dorian)	7–13, 47–54
Quintal chords and planing	14–15
Added 6th chord	16–18
Pentatonic scale	16–18
3rd relationship of chord roots (*B* to *E-flat* to *G*)	16–27
7th and 9th chords	19–21, 62–67
Chord with added 4th (*D F A C* with added *G*)	23, 26
Planing of triads in 2nd inversion	28–40
Quartal or quintal chords	42–45, 83–86
Chord with added 2nd (*B D♯ F♯* with added *C♯*)	60

Debussy: La Cathédrale engloutie. Copyright 1910, Durand et Cie. Used by permission of the publisher. Elkan-Vogel, Inc., sole representative, United States.

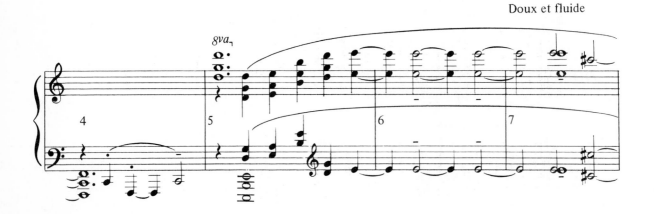

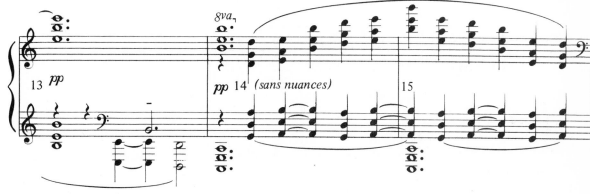

Peu à sortant de la brume

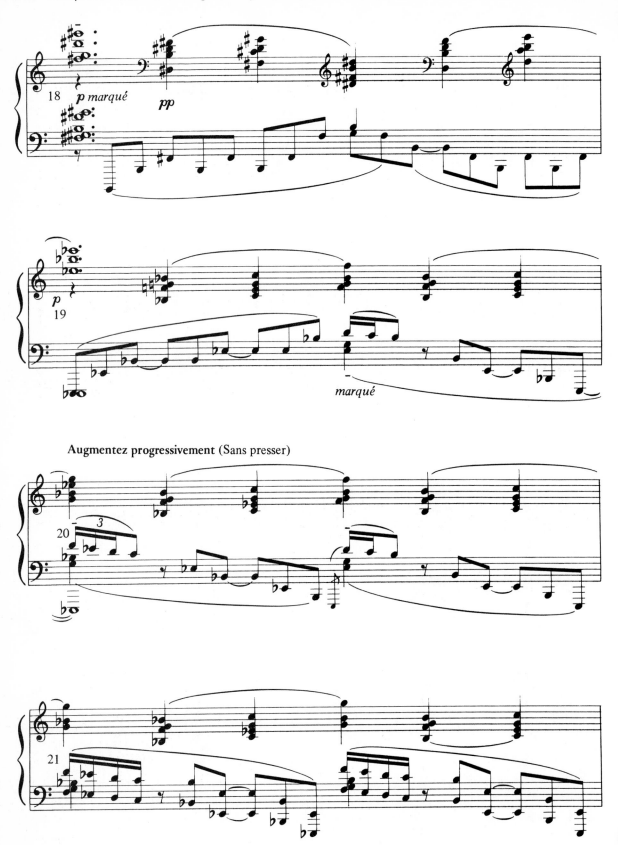

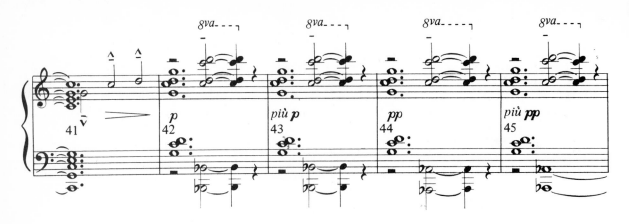

Un peu moins lent (Dans une expression allant grandissant)

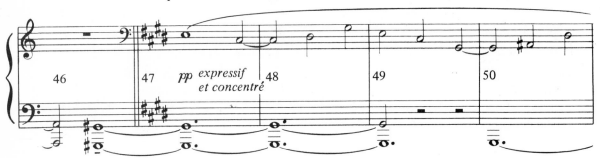

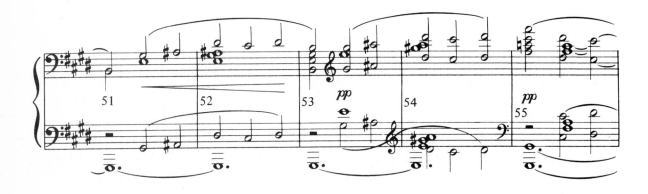

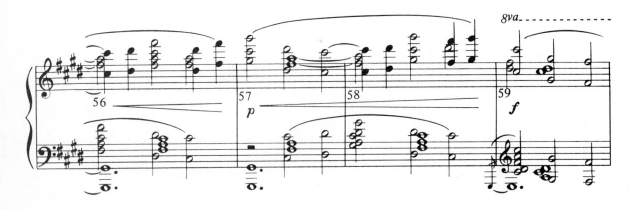

ASSIGNMENT 1   On a separate sheet of paper make a complete analysis of the following composition using the same approach as is used for ''La Cathédrale Engloutie.'' Before preparing the analysis have a student perform the composition two or three times in class or listen to a recording until the work is thoroughly familiar.

Claude Debussy: Sarabande from "Pour le Piano"
Avec une élégance grave et lente

Assignment 1 (continued)

Assignment 1 (continued)

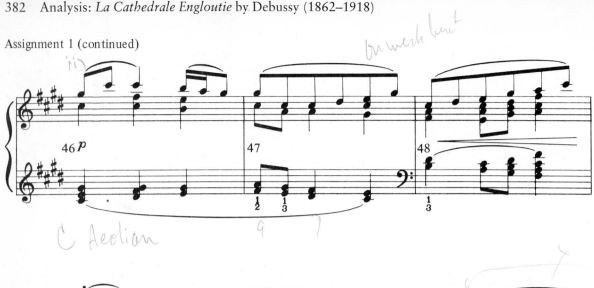

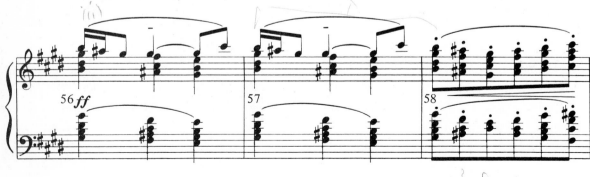

ASSIGNMENT 2

1   Using some of the devices listed below, write a short composition (16 to 30 measures) in the style of "La Cathedrale Engloutie."

Third relationship	Melodic doubling
Parallel chords	Altered dominants or tonics
Modal melody	Changing meters
Pedal tone	
7th, 9th, 11th, & 13th chords	
Chords of addition and omission	

2   Write for any combination of instruments played by class members.

3   Perform the compositions in class.

4   After each student composition is performed, members of the class should enumerate (from listening only) the various devices employed in the work.

20

Analysis: Prelude No. 3 Op. 74 by Alexander Scriabin (1872-1915)

Synthetic Scale   *Octatonic Scale*   *Tetrachord*

ABOUT THE COMPOSER

A Russian pianist and composer, Scriabin was the son of a lawyer father and a concert pianist mother. He enjoyed considerable success during his lifetime as a concert pianist, and toured the United States in 1907 playing in New York, Chicago, Washington, and Detroit. He taught piano for a while at the Moscow Conservatory, but proved constitutionally unsuited to teaching and moved to Switzerland, where, thanks to an annuity provided him by a wealthy student, he was able to concentrate on his compositions.

From early childhood he was a mystic and deeply involved in religion. During a brief stay in Brussels he attended meetings of a Theosophy Circle, an experience that influenced him considerably and had a profound effect on the style of his compositions.

His compositions can be arranged into definite periods according to the style of writing. His earliest works are obviously patterned after those of Chopin; then, during the Opus 30's a gradual maturing took place. At this point he divorced himself from the traditional tonal system of his youth, and experimented with scales he contrived from chords that were built in combinations of perfect, diminished, and augmented 4ths. One of these is known as the "mystic chord," but he also developed other synthetic scales as well. After Opus 58 key signatures were eliminated.

A work by Scriabin is included in this text because it represents a unique departure from the traditional style of composition prevalent in the Romantic period. Although Scriabin does not rank in stature with some of his contemporaries [Debussy, (1862–1918), R. Strauss (1864–1949), Sibelius (1865–1957), Ravel (1875–1937)], his works are typical of composers who sought release and freedom from the tyranny of the Romantic system of keys and functional harmony. Among the more innovative contemporaries of Scriabin are Charles Ives (1874–1954), Arnold Schoenberg (1874–1951), and Eric Satie (1866–1925) while those who continued to build on the traditions of Romanticism are Gustav Mahler (1860–1911), Giacomo Puccini (1858–1924), and Serge Rachmaninoff (1873–1943).

ABOUT THE COMPOSITION

Scale

A   This composition is based entirely on one SYNTHETIC (developed by the composer) scale:

This is called an OCTATONIC (8-tone) scale, a departure from the seven-tone major and minor scale. A unique feature of the scale is the division into two *tetrachords* (four-tone arrangements) that are symmetrical (same arrangement of half and whole steps).

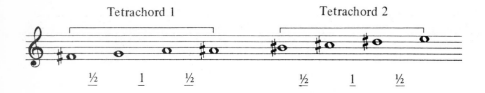

The interval from any given tone to the 5th scale degree above or below is a tritone.

Also, using either the odd or even scale degrees a diminished 7th chord sound will result (superposition of minor thirds):

Diminished 7th chord sound

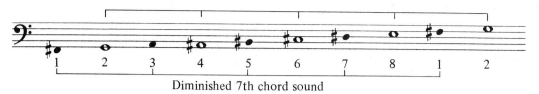

Diminished 7th chord sound

Tonality

A   The tonality of this composition is considerably shrouded because of the large number of melodic and harmonic tritones. Tritones tend to confuse tonality and weaken stronger relationships such as the P5th, P4th, and M3rd.

B   Most of the chords contain at least five factors that further aids in weakening the tonality.

C   A survey of bass tones and chord roots favors *F♯* as the tonal center. Here are the bass tones (whole notes) and chord roots (unstemmed quarter notes) found in this composition:

Bass tones = o   Chord roots = ●

F♯ appears most often both as a bass tone and chord root.

Melody

MELODIC PATTERNS

A   The composition is based on a motive that appears in ten of the twenty-six measures.

The same motive is used in 10 different measures:

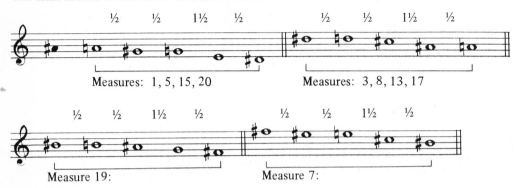

B   A second motive appears in 6 measures:

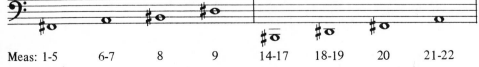

C   In addition to the melody in the upper voice the accompaniment also presents some interesting relationships. Here is an illustration of a figure that appears often in the composition. Although spelled in various ways the sound is always that of a diminished seventh chord:

The diminished 7th chord pattern in various melodic applications:

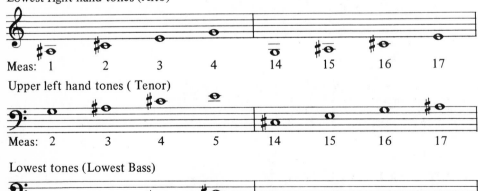

Form

A   The melodies in measure 1–11 and 13–23 (upper voice) are identical
except that the second melody is transposed down a tritone. Here is an
illustration showing the first four measures of each:

B   The melodic form is:

MEASURES	SECTION	
1–8	A	The following motive (and its transpositions) appear five times in this section:

| 9–12 | B | This is a pseudo-transposition back to the motive material in section A. This motive (and transposition) appears three times: |

13–20	A′	This is section *A* material transposed down a tritone.
21–24	B′	Except for measure 24 this is *B* material transposed down a tritone.
25–26	CAD	This is a two measure extension of B′ added to provide a cadence.

Harmony

CHORDS

A   Most of the chords have at least five factors. Illustration:

Chord in Measure 3

Factors

B   Most chords contain at least two tritones thus providing a high level of harmonic tension throughout the composition.

C   Because of the number of factors and the high tension level the roots of the chords are of only minor concern since the ear finds it difficult to hear them clearly.

D   Here is an illustration showing the chords in the first five measures of the composition. Play each chord on the piano and note the difficulty in identifying a pronounced root:

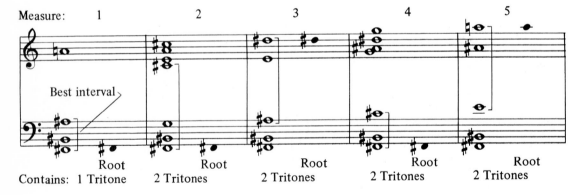

The roots are determined by the root of the best interval in the chord:

BEST INTERVAL IN DIMINISHING ORDER	ROOT OF THE INTERVAL
Perfect 5th	Lower tone
Perfect 4th	Upper tone
Major 3rd	Lower tone
Minor 6th	Upper tone
Minor 3rd	Lower tone
Major 6th	Upper tone
Major 2nd	Upper tone
Minor 7th	Lower tone
Minor 2nd	Upper tone
Major 7th	Lower tone
Tritone	No root

E   Note (in the example above) that the roots of the chords do not form strong intervals with each other.

F   None of the chords in this composition are triadic (based on a super-position of thirds).

G   Two chords (heard in the right hand only) have the sound of first inversion triads, but they are combined with harmony in the left hand, which negates the effect of the clear sound:

Meas: 2 & 16   4 & 14

1st inv. triad   1st inv. triad

H   Obviously the chords are selected from the synthetic scale, and since Scriabin chooses to emphasize the tritone relationships, chords and chord relationships bear little resemblance to those of the nineteenth century.

I   Chords are selected to highlight the tritone effect and the particular sound of the superimposed minor 3rds (diminished 7th chord), which has already been pointed out. The diminished 7th chord sound is found melodically in the lower voices often, and the diminished triad can be extracted as a component of most of the harmonic sonorities:

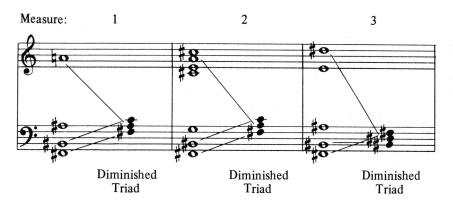

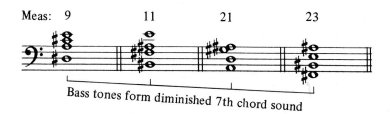

CADENCES

A   Harmonic cadences are virtually nonexistent in this composition.
B   At the point marking large section changes (meas. 12–13) and at the
    end of the composition (meas. 25–26) all eight tones of the synthetic
    scale are found (either melodically or harmonically).

HARMONIC RHYTHM

A   Since the difference in chord makeup is generally minimal (most chords
    contain at least two tritones and 5 or 6 factors) the effect of harmonic
    rhythm is considerably reduced.
B   Chords are sounded in the following frequency:

SECTION	FREQUENCY
A	1 per measure
B	1 per four measures
A′	1 per measure
B′	1 per two measures
CAD	1

Rhythm and Meter

METER

The meter is 9/8 with no changes throughout.

RHYTHM

A   The following rhythmic figure predominates in the melody (upper
    voice):

B   Two rhythmic figures are prominent in the lowest voice:

Rhythmic figure <u>A</u>   Rhythmic figure <u>B</u>

C   Here is an illustration showing the use of these two figures throughout
the composition:

Measure:	1	2	3	4	5	6	7	8	9	10	11	12	13	14
Rhythm used:	A	B	A	B	A	B	A	A	..Held Chord..			A	B	

Measure:	15	16	17	18	19	20	21	22	23	24	25	26
Rhythm used:	A	B	A	B	A	A	.......Held Chord.......					

Scriabin: Prelude No. 3 from Five Preludes, Op. 74

Allegro drammatico

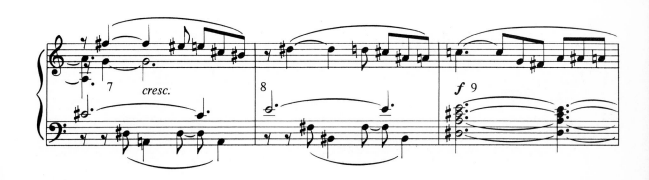

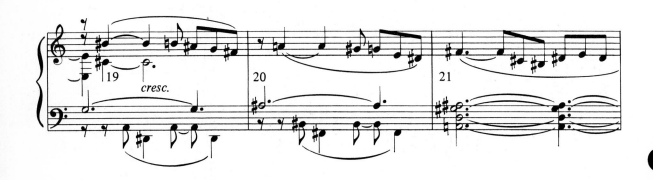

ASSIGNMENT 1
On a separate sheet of paper make a complete analysis of the following composition using the same approach as is used for Prelude No. 3, Op. 74 by Scriabin (above).

Before preparing the analysis have a student perform the composition two or three times in class or listen to a recording until the work is thoroughly familiar.

Alexander Scriabin: Poëme, Op. 69, No. 1

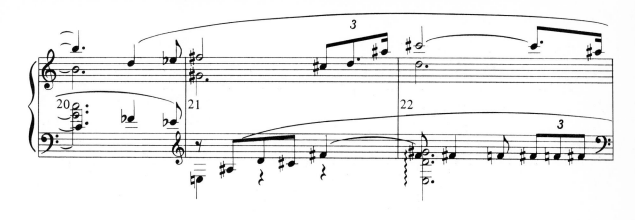

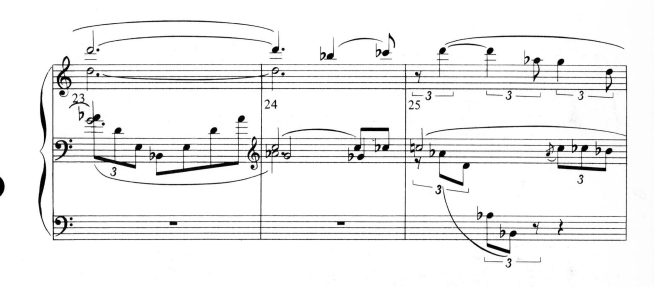

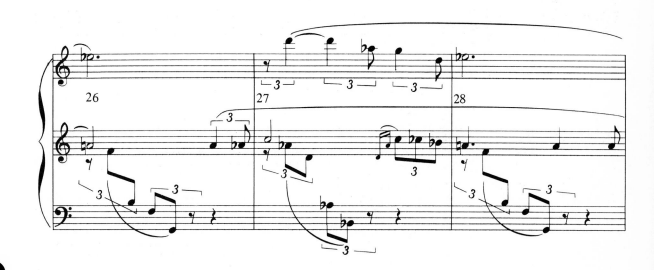

Assingment 2 (continued)

ASSIGNMENT 2

1 Using the synthetic scale from either Prelude, Op. 74, No. 3, or Poeme, Op. 69, No. 1, or a synthetic scale of your own invention, write a short composition of sixteen to thirty measures in the approximate style of either of the Scriabin compositions.

2 Write for any combination of instruments played by class members.

3 Perform the compositions in class.

4 After each student composition is performed, members of the class should try to determine the scale upon which the work is based.

21
The Contemporary Period (1910-Present)

Neoclassicism
Expressionism
Primitivism
Duodecuple Scale
Polytonality

Polychords
Free Tonality
Shifted Tonality
Dual Modality
Pandiatonicism

Chord Clusters
Changing Meters
Asymmetric Meters
Nonaccentual Rhythms

Concurrent with the surge of Post-Romantic and Impressionistic music, several newer and quite different styles were beginning to surface. As the works of such composers as Debussy (1862–1918), Delius (1862–1934), Wolf (1860–1903), Faure (1845–1924), and Richard Strauss (1864–1949) were being premiered, other voices new to the scene were writing music in considerably different idioms: Alexander Scriabin (1872–1915), Arnold Schoenberg (1874–1951), Charles Ives (1874–1954), Béla Bartók (1881–1945), and Igor Stravinsky (1882–1971). Some maintained tertian harmony but abandoned functional harmony while others experimented with chords constructed in 4ths, 5ths, or combinations of several intervals. Some preserved tonality while others discarded it in favor of atonality. Experimentation ranged even to tampering with the pitch of conventional chromatic scale tones, which led to the development of microtonal (less than a half-step interval) scales.

A few (but by no means all) important attitudes and influences during this period in which a wide spectrum of styles developed will be discussed.

NEOCLASSICISM

A reaction to the extreme individualism of the Romantic period. A return to discipline and order as essential ingredients in music. With the unbridled freedom allowed in Romantic music, many composers lacked restraint in their compositions and thus produced a kind of effusive disorganization. The Neoclassic composers (Stravinsky, Hindemith, and Bartók among others) sought to expunge from their music the pictorial, the onomatopoetic, the visionary, the literary, and other meanings and extra-musical intent that had been attached to music throughout the Romantic period.

EXPRESSIONISM

Related to Neoclassicism. A reaction to Impressionism. Actually the term has no intrinsic meaning, but its proponents hoped to create music that would be an expression of their inner world and would probe such new mysterious areas as the subconscious and psychoanalysis. The Impressionists had intended their music to represent their own impressions of the external world. Typical composers exemplifying this movement were Schoenberg and Berg.

PRIMITIVISM

A reaction to the extremely refined and fragile music of such composers as Debussy and Ravel. Its followers sought simple and clearly defined melodies of a folk nature that operated within a narrow range. Sharp percussive effects with thickly textured chords and much parallel movement typified this style of writing. Bartók's *Allegro Barbaro* (1911) and Honegger's *Pacific 231* represent examples of this movement.

In addition to the compositional devices described earlier in chapter 18, Devices of the Late Nineteenth and Early Twentieth Century, composers of the Contemporary period developed a variety of other practices some of which are:

DEVICES OF THE CONTEMPORARY PERIOD

Duodecuple Scale

The twelve tones of the octave each with equal status. Since these tones are not considered to have preconceived tendencies, spelling is not a critical factor. In contrast, the older term, "chromatic" scale, implies altered or secondary tones within a key system.

Schoenberg: No. 5 of 5 Pieces for Piano, Op. 23 © for all Countries by Wilhelm Hansen, Copenhagen. Used by permission.

12 tone set:

Duodecuple Scale:

Polytonality

Simultaneous use of two tonalities.

Polytonality

Ziebart: Overture

Polychords

Two or more triads, 7th chords, or other chords sounded simultaneously and spaced far enough apart to make each recognizable as separate structures. Two triads containing common tones and spaced a distance apart may not be perceived as separate structures if the combination of the two form a chord very familiar to us. But, if the triads contain no common tones and are of sufficiently contrasting nature, fusion will not result and each triad will maintain its own identity.

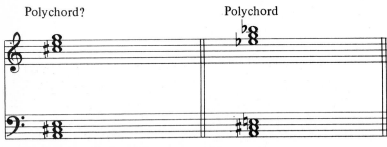

Chords contain 2 common tones   No common tones
Tones fuse into Mm7th chord   Each chord retains separate sound
Little polychordal effect   Polychordal effect is emphasized

The following excerpt illustrates the wide spacing and diverse nature of the simultaneous chords making up *polychords*.

W. Schuman: Three Score Set from THREE SCORE SET by William Schuman.
Copyright © 1943 G. Schirmer, Inc. Used by permission.

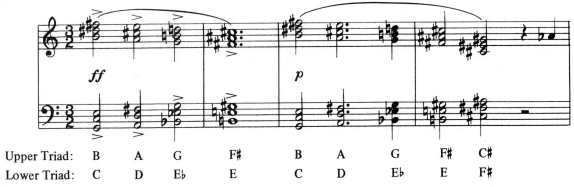

| Upper Triad: | B | A | G | F♯ | B | A | G | F♯ | C♯ |
| Lower Triad: | C | D | E♭ | E | C | D | E♭ | E | F♯ |

Free Tonality

Tonality without key. Includes the following conditions:

A A clear tonal center.
B Any combination of the twelve tones of the octave may be used.
C The traditional functioning of the diatonic tones of a key based on that same tonal center is minimized or avoided entirely.

D   The dominant-tonic axis of key-centered tonality is absent.
E   In the following excerpt by Hindemith:
   1   All twelve tones of the octave are present.
   2   The tonality of *F* is achieved without a single dominant-tonic
      progression.
   3   Enharmonic equivalents such as *C-sharp* and *D-flat* appear in the
      same chord (measure 3).
   4   The Phrygian mode is hinted.

Free Tonality

Chords reduced: (● = root)

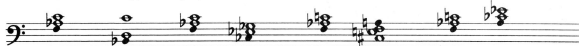

F   The Bartok excerpt below also illustrates free tonality.
   1   Lacks key-related harmonic function.
   2   Although the upper voice by itself reflects the "A" natural minor
       scale ("F" natural missing) the bass voices share only the "A" and
       "E" while introducing all other tones of the chromatic scale.

UPPER VOICE TONES: A   B   C   D   E   G

BASS CLEF TONES: A   A#   C#   D#   E   E# F#   G#

Bartok: No. 150 in Mikrokosmos, Vol. VI. Copyright 1940 by Hawkes & Sons
(London) Ltd., Renewed 1967. Reprinted by permission of Boosey and Hawkes
Inc. and Boosey and Hawkes (Canada) Ltd.

Chords reduced: (● = root)

Roots extracted:

Shifted Tonality

Sudden tonality change without preparation.

Shifted Tonality

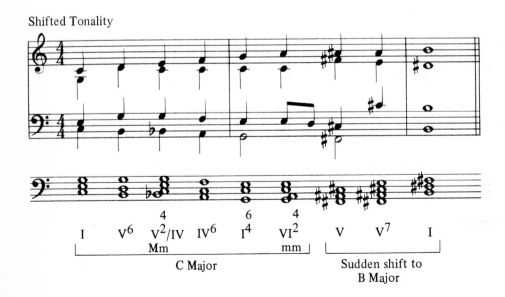

Dual Modality

Simultaneous use of major and minor mode or combinations of Gregorian modes. Usually the two have the same tonic.

Dual Modality
Bartok: No. 59, Mikrokosmos, Vol. 2. Copyright 1940 by Hawkes & Sons (London) Ltd. Renewed 1967. Reprinted by permission of Boosey & Hawkes, Inc. and Boosey and Hawkes (Canada) Ltd.

Treble clef notes: Minor

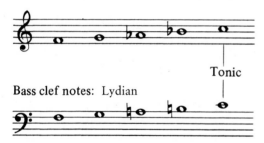

Pandiatonicism

The use of the tones of a diatonic scale in such a way that each tone is stripped of its usual function. The traditional characteristics and functions of the individual tones (such as dominant, subdominant, mediant, etc.) of the diatonic scale are negated.

The following excerpt by Stravinsky demonstrates the use of pandiatonicism.

A   Absence of functional harmony.
B   Use of all seven tones of the *D* major scale.
C   Thick harmonies (most are 5 factor chords).
D   No nondiatonic tones.

Pandiatonicism

Stravinsky: Sonata for Two Pianos. Reprinted by permission of Belwin Mills Publishing Corp., Melville, New York. United States distributor for B. Schott's Soehne, Mainz, Germany. All rights reserved.

Chord Clusters

Chords with three or more factors of which each is no more than a whole step from its adjacent factor.

Cluster Chords

Changing Meters

Meter changes within a composition to show rhythmic patterns more clearly than with a single constant meter. Instead of making the rhythm fit into the rigid system of a single meter, the signature is changed as often as necessary to clarify rhythms that would be at odds with any single metric signature.

Changing meters

Strickler: Overture for Band

Asymmetric Meters

Meters in which the beats are not grouped into symmetric units.

Asymmetric meters

Gillion: Suite No. 1

Nonaccentual Rhythms

Absence of dynamic accents. Such absence focuses increased attention on agogic (accents by virtue of duration) accents.

Nonaccentual rhythm

Lucerne: Dirge

22

Analysis: Marche du Soldat from L'Histoire du Soldat by Igor Stravinsky (1882-1971)

ABOUT THE COMPOSER

Stravinsky's professional activity as a composer lasted nearly sixty years and evolved through nearly every style found in the twentieth century. Born in St. Petersburg, Russia in 1882 he began studying with Rimsky-Korsakov in 1907 and by 1911 had achieved success in Paris with two ballets, *The Firebird,* and *Petrouchka.* Just before World War I he left Russia and took up residence in Switzerland where he remained until 1920. After a long residency in France (1920–1939) he moved to America and became an American citizen in 1945.

With twenty-one works for the theater and nineteen orchestral compositions his professional accomplishments are indeed impressive; moreover, he wrote for a variety of other media including chamber music, concertos, sacred choral-orchestral works, solo songs, and piano music.

Stravinsky is considered by many to be the most important musical figure of the twentieth century since he achieved considerable success and acclaim during his lifetime, was a significant influence on other composers of the period, and remained a vital and ever-unfolding master of composition and orchestration throughout his lifetime.

Since his music represents the style gamut from Post-Romantic to serial technique, a serious study of Stravinsky's works provides an insight into a wide panorama of twentieth-century trends and techniques.

The following chart provides an undetailed overview of the various phases of Stravinsky's professional life.

APPROXIMATE YEARS	PERIOD	REPRESENTATIVE COMPOSITIONS	BRIEF DESCRIPTION OF TECHNIQUES
1904–1912	Post-Romantic Nationalistic	The Firebird Petrouchka	Extreme modulations, rich harmonic schemes, full orchestral sounds, changing and asymmetrical meters
1913–1923	Transition to Neoclassic	L'Histoire du Soldat Les Noces	Chromaticism, polytonality, more dissonant harmony, polyrhythms, thinner textures
1923–1951	Neoclassic	Symphony of Psalms Symphony in Three Movements	Somewhat less chromaticism, pandiatonicism, thin textures, use of song and sonata-like forms
1952–1971	Serial technique	In Memoriam Dylan Thomas Movements Orchestra variations	Tone rows of 5 to 7 tones, fully developed serial technique suggested by a study of Webern's music

While the composition selected for analysis in this chapter represents only the second period of Stravinsky's writing, a study of at least one composition from each of the above periods would represent an ideal semester project for an honors student.

Stravinsky: *Marche du Soldat* from *L'Histoire du Soldat*. By permission of J&W Chester Edition Wilhelm Hansen, London Limited.

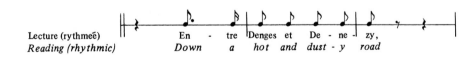

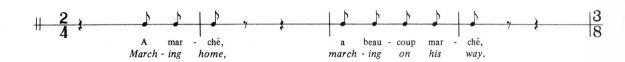

A   mar - ché,   a   beau - coup   mar - ché,
March - ing   home,   march - ing   on   his   way.

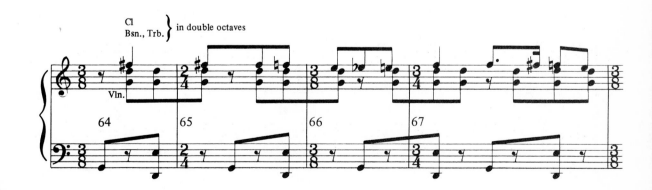

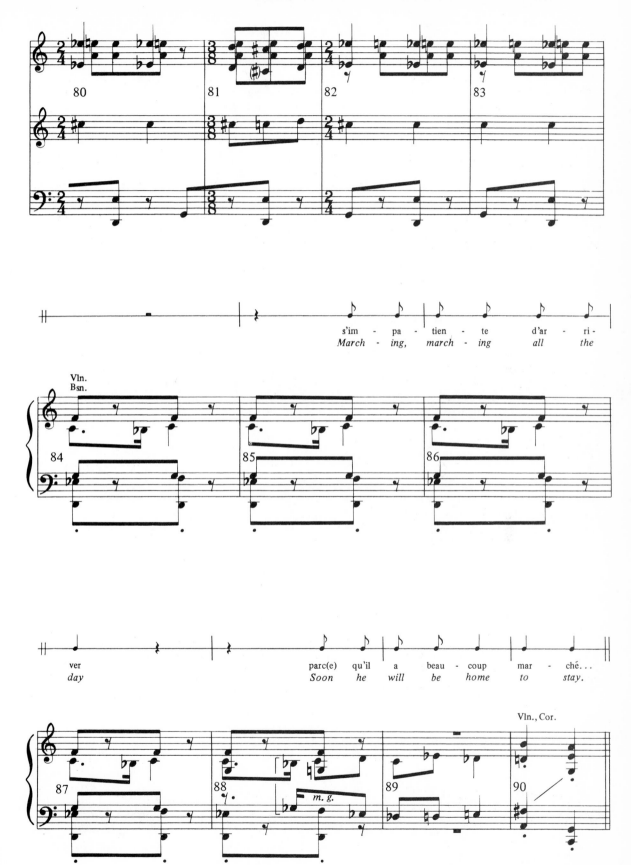

s'im - pa - tien - te   d'ar - ri -
March - ing,   march - ing   all   the

Vln.
Bsn.

ver
day

parc(e)   qu'il   a   beau - coup   mar - ché...
Soon   he   will   be   home   to   stay.

Vln., Cor.

m. g.

ABOUT THE COMPOSITION

Scales

Although Stravinsky alludes at times to the modes in this composition the melodic line is based primarily on the *D* and *A* major scales. Bitonality is present throughout. Shown here are the scale formations found in the melodic line (and often throughout the entire fabric) of this work:

MEASURES	SCALE USED IN THE MELODIC LINE
1–2	F major
3–4	Whole tone
6–20	A major
21–29	A major with chromatic tones
30–45	D major
46–47	E Lydian mode
48–59	A major
60–90	D major with chromatic tones

Bitonality

Bitonality predominates in the composition.

A   Because of the strong dominant-tonic (*D-G*) relationship that pervades the lower voice the tonality of *G* is overriding.

B   Stravinsky employs very clear major melodies in the upper voices that clash head on with the well-established tonality of *G* in the lower voice. Shown here are the bitonal relationships in the composition:

Upper voice tonality:	F M	W T			A major						A major			
Measures:	1 2	3 4	5	6 7 8	9	10	11	12	13	14	15
Lower voice tonality:	A♭M				G tonality						

				A major									
16	17	18	19	20	21	22	23	24	25	26	27	28
	G tonality						G tonality				

				D major								
29	30	31	32	33	34	35	36	37	38	39	40	41
G. ton.				D major						

	D major			E Lydian		A major						
42	43	44	45	46	47	48	49	50	51	52	53	54
					G tonality					

	A major					D major						
55	56	57	58	59	60	61	62	63	64	65	66	67
					G tonality					

				D major								
68	69	70	71	72	73	74	75	76	77	78	79	80
				G tonality						

	D M		F major							
81	82 83	84	85	86	87	88	89	90
	G T		D tonality					C M

The following two examples demonstrate how tonality is established in the upper voice:

Measures 11 through 18

A Major Triad

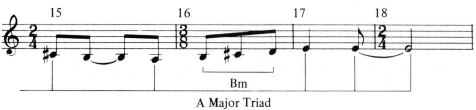

Bm

A Major Triad

In the above excerpt the tonic triad, *A* major, is clearly outlined and emphasized by the fact that such triad tones are provided metric accents and longer durational values.

Measures 45 - 47

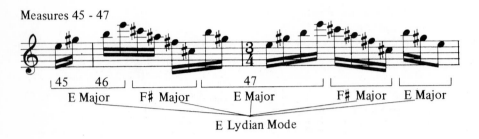

In the above brief excerpt two major triads, outlined as they are, direct attention strongly to the tonality of *E*—and in this case the *E* Lydian mode.

Melody

MELODIC CHARACTERISTICS

A   A clear and ascendant melody in the upper voice often with contrapuntal associates.

B   Homophonic texture applies throughout most of the composition.

C   The melody is based essentially on major scales.

MOTIVES

The melody utilizes three motives.

Motive A

Motive A is simply a descending scalewise passage that then turns in the opposite direction and ascends. Here are several examples of the use of this motive:

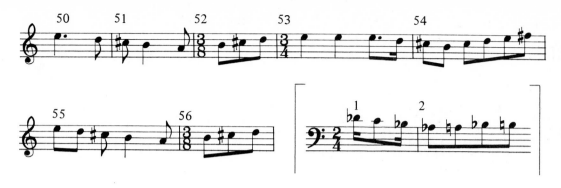

Motive B

Motive B by contrast consists of outlined triads. Examples of the second motive are:

Motive C

Motive C is very similar in direction to motive A, but differs in that it is made up entirely of half steps.

Motive C is used exclusively beginning in measure 64 and continuing on through measure 83. A close look at measures 64–79 reveals the technique of phrase extension as employed by Stravinsky.

The following illustration compares measures 64–70 with measures 71–79. Whole notes are used to represent all tones so that a comparison is more visible.

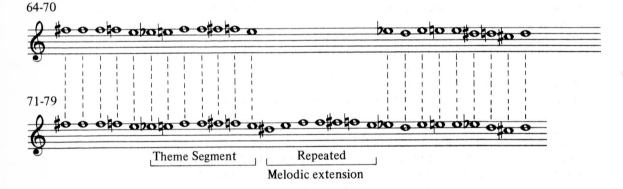

From this illustration it can be seen that phrase 64–70 and phrase 71–79 are identical except for the phrase extension (melodic extension), which is a repetition of the previous seven tones.

Form

A   Through the generous use of the three motives an overall sectional form is not apparent.

B   Since one of the overriding factors is the ostinato figure in the lower voice, its presence or absence exerts an important influence on the organization of the composition and might well have the following form:

MEASURES	LOWER VOICE	SECTION
1–30	G, D, G, D ostinato figure	A
31–41	Pedal tone D	B
42–83	G, D, G, D ostinato figure (return)	A
84–90	Pedal tone D (return)	B

C   From the standpoint of motive order the form appears to be somewhat quixotic.

MEASURES	MOTIVE	LENGTH	MEASURES	MOTIVE	LENGTH
1–18	A	18 meas.	39–43	B	5 meas.
20–21	B	2 meas.	44–46	A	3 meas.
22–26	C	5 meas.	46–47	B	3 meas.
26–30	B	5 meas.	47–57	A	11 meas.
31–32	A′	2 meas.	57–59	B	3 meas.
33–34	B	2 meas.	64–83	C	19 meas.
34–35	A′ Inv.	2 meas.	84–90	Ostinato	7 meas.
37–38	A′ Inv.	2 meas.			

Harmony

BASS LINE

The bass line consists entirely of short ostinato figure G and D with an occasional D pedal tone.

MELODIC LINE ABOVE THE OSTINATO

The melodic lines above this ostinato deny rather than reinforce the tonality of G as implied in the strong tonic-dominant relationship (G-D).

BITONAL MIX

Although to an extent a combination harmony results from the bitonal mix, the effect is not of a single force or direction. The ear hears two separate functions and two harmonic directions. As an example:

MELODIC CADENCES

Melodic cadences, such as the one below, occur frequently in the upper voices, but they are not often supported by the lower voice because of the strict ostinato figure.

PHRASE OVERLAPPING AT CADENCES

Overlapping phrases are fairly common. A melodic cadence is completed in one voice, but at the same time a new phrase begins in another voice.

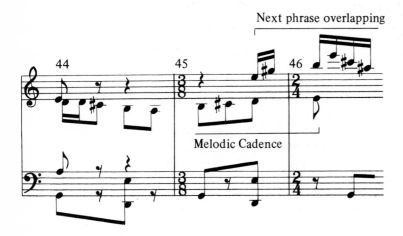

Rhythm and Meter

A   Contains frequent meter changes, but in most instances the steady ostinato figure disregards these and plods on as if the 2/4 meter had not been altered. Here is an example showing Stravinsky's actual notation along with another version illustrating how it might have been written keeping the steady 2/4 meter intact:

The passage as written:

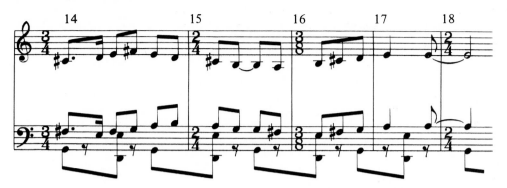

The same passage in strict 2/4 meter:

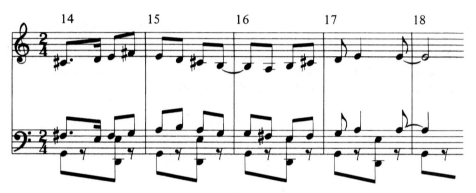

B   The basic value found in this composition is the eighth note with the sixteenth note and quarter note action also in evidence.

C   Aside from the ostinato figure utilizing a simple metric pattern, there are no significant rhythmic ideas that recur often enough to warrant attention.

D   Of the three motives used throughout, none have an unusual rhythmic import. The second motive is somewhat distinctive in that it is essentially of sixteenth-note movement, but its rhythmic pattern is not of a distinguished or unique nature.

Texture

A thin and principally homophonic texture persists throughout. The upper voices on occasion (as in measures 11–18) engage now and then in mild contrapuntal display.

ASSIGNMENT 1

Make a complete analysis of an excerpt from one of the following. Select a small section that can be treated thoroughly rather than a large section superficially.

Le Sacre du Printemps (either full score or a two-piano arrangement)
Petrouchka (either full score or excerpts arranged for two pianos by Victor Babin)
Circus Polka (either full score or arranged for piano solo, violin & piano, two pianos)
L'Oiseau de Feu (Firebird) Suite

ASSIGNMENT 2

1 Using the same techniques found in *Marche du Soldat,* write a short composition (16 to 30 measures).
2 Write for any combination of instruments played by class members.
3 Perform the compositions in class.
4 The class should discuss each composition, its strengths and weaknesses, its proximity to the style of the *Marche du Soldat,* and its general musical qualities.

23

Analysis: No. 148, Six Dances in Bulgarian Rhythm, No. 1, from the Mikrokosmos by Béla Bartók (1881-1945)

Arch Form   *Wedge Form*   *Polytonality*
Polymodality   *Free Tonality*

ABOUT THE COMPOSER

A composer of considerable stature in the twentieth century, Bartok was born in a farming region of Hungary and migrated to the United States in 1940. He was beset most of his life with financial difficulties, and eventually died almost penniless in a New York hospital of leukemia in 1945. Bartok's creative life can be divided into the following three periods:

1881–1908

Youthful work influenced by composers he admired such as Liszt, Brahms, and Strauss. This period consisted mainly of small chamber works, piano compositions, and songs. A piano sonata (in manuscript) (1897), and Twenty Hungarian Folksongs (1906) are among the works composed during this period.

1908–1928

Much experimentation and the development of a dissonant harmonic vocabulary of almost expressionistic fervor. Three string quartets, two violin sonatas, most of the works written for piano, and *Dance Suite* for orchestra are among the compositions written during this period.

1928–1945

Techniques developed during the middle period became an integral part of Bartok's musical expression, and most of the works that are well-known today come from this last period. Among them are *Music for Strings, Percussion, and Celesta (1936). Concerto for Orchestra (1943),* and the 4th and 5th string quartets (1928 and 1934 respectively).

Folk Music

Throughout his entire life span Bartok was interested in folk music. Almost all of his music is in some way influenced by or is based on folk music material. Of Magyar, Slovak, Transylvanian, and Rumanian tunes he has collected in excess of 6,000!

Influences

Of all composers of the twentieth century, Bartok was least influenced by contemporaries. He remained within his own inimitable style, working and experimenting as he went along, but he was extremely impervious to outside influences. He did not embrace the twelve-tone technique, he did not imitate the major composers of his own era such as Stravinsky, nor did he show any more than passing interest in the native styles of his adopted land, America.

Musical Style

Some of the more salient features of his musical style are:

A   *Melodies influenced by or actually taken from folk song sources.*
B   *Considerable use of church modes*—developed from his study of folk music.
C   *Use of striking and unique rhythms* developed out of accentual patterns in the Hungarian language and the rhythmically free folk songs of his native land.
D   *Preference for polyphony in later and more mature works.*
E   *Adopted standard forms such as sonata-allegro, rondo, fugue, etc.* but utilizes each in his own way.
F   *Developed some less-used forms such as the* arch *and the* wedge.

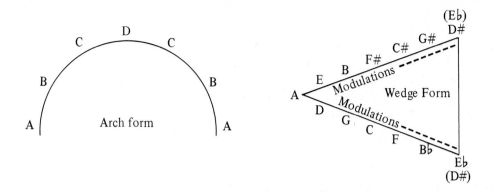

The *arch* form is found in *Music for Stringed Instruments, Percussion, and Celesta (1936)*—third movement. The letters above refer to themes and sections. The *wedge* is found in the same composition, first movement. The letters denote simultaneous modulations (the key schemes used in various voices of the fugue.

Arch form simply means the thematic scheme: A B C D C B A

Wedge form is in reality not a form but a scheme of keys to be followed. In the above illustration the composition starts in the key of A, but the upper voice modulates to *E* while the lower voice modulates to *D* and so forth. Note that the modulations in the upper voice progress in P5ths *up* while the modulations in the lower voice progress in P5ths *down*. Both meet on *E-flat* after six modulations.

G *Harmony is taken from the scales used*—frequently modal.
H *Favors dissonant harmony (harmony containing 2nds and 7ths),* and as can be seen from the ensuing analysis, he favors (45%) chords without tritones.
I *Polytonality and polymodality are a part of his style.*
J *Cadences are often weak* with authentic cadences either highly decorated or avoided altogether.

Mikrokosmos

The series of compositions known as the *Mikrokosmos* is a group of 153 piano compositions, graded from easy to difficult. They are often assigned as "teaching pieces" and illustrate in miniature form the compositional techniques Bartok used in his larger works. He was in the process of composing this set for eleven years (1926–1937) thus forming a kind of bridge between his middle and late period of composition.

ABOUT THE COMPOSITION

Scales

The composition is fairly typical of Bartok's use of various modes.

A   At certain points, especially in transition sections (measures 20–21) and (51–52) the stricter modal treatment is abandoned and considerable chromaticism takes over.

B   The simultaneous use of modal or scale patterns is dominant. As an example, measures 4 through 13 demonstrate the use of the *E* major scale in the bass clef against the *E* Phrygian mode in the treble clef. The following table presents the modes found in the composition:

TREBLE:	E PHRYGIAN MODE		C AEOLIAN MODE
MEASURES:	1 2 3 4 5 6 7 8 9 10 11 12 13	14 15 16 17	
BASS:	E PHRYG. E MAJOR SCALE	C LYDIAN MODE	

TREBLE:	TRANSITION	A AEOLIAN MODE
	18 19 20 21 22 23 24 25 26 27 28 29 30 31 32 33	
BASS:	A LYDIAN TRANSITION B MAJOR SCALE CHROMATIC	

TREBLE:	A AEOLIAN MODE	A DORIAN	B AEOLIAN MODE
	34 35 36 37 38 39 40 41 42 43 44 45 46 47 48 49		
BASS:	CHROMATIC	A AEOLIAN A MEL. MI.	

TREBLE:	TRANSITION	E PHRYGIAN MODE
	50 51 52 53 54 55 56 57 58 59 60	
BASS:	TRANSITION	E PHRYGIAN MODE

C   The scales and modes illustrated:

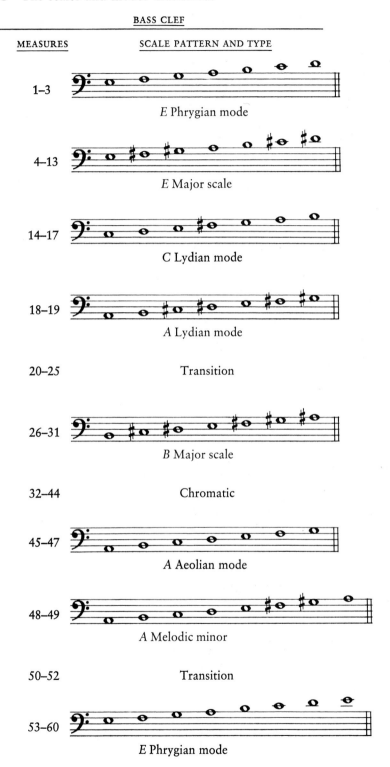

MEASURES	SCALE PATTERN AND TYPE
1–3	*E* Phrygian mode
4–13	*E* Major scale
14–17	*C* Lydian mode
18–19	*A* Lydian mode
20–25	Transition
26–31	*B* Major scale
32–44	Chromatic
45–47	*A* Aeolian mode
48–49	*A* Melodic minor
50–52	Transition
53–60	*E* Phrygian mode

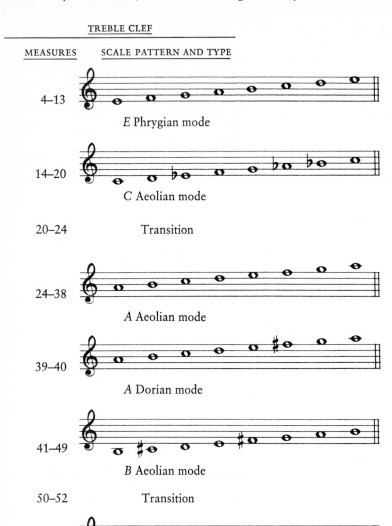

TREBLE CLEF

MEASURES	SCALE PATTERN AND TYPE
4–13	E Phrygian mode
14–20	C Aeolian mode
20–24	Transition
24–38	A Aeolian mode
39–40	A Dorian mode
41–49	B Aeolian mode
50–52	Transition
53–60	E Phrygian mode

Tonality

The movement of chord roots favors E tonality—the work begins and ends in E tonality. The tonalities represented in the composition according to root movements:

MEASURES	TONALITY
1–13	E
14–17	C
17–27	A
28–30	B
31–33	Ambiguous A#?
34–36	Ambiguous F#?
37–39	D
40–44	E
45–49	A
50–52	Ambiguous F?
53–60	E

Note that the tonalities if placed in a scale represent most of the tones of the *E* Phrygian mode:

E (F) (G) A B C D   (only *F* and *G* tonalities are missing)

The composition also (as with root movements) begins and ends with melodies that have an *E* tonal center.

Melody

A   A clear and sustained melody throughout—except for transitions.

B   Homophonic texture predominates.

C   Entire melody, except for transitions, is modally oriented.

D   Phrases are uneven in length:

PHRASE	MEASURES	LENGTH OF PHRASE	PHRASE	MEASURES	LENGTH OF PHRASE
1	1–3	3	7	32–36	4
2	4–8	5	8	36–38	3
3	9–13	5	9	37–44	8
4	14–17	4	10	45–49⅔	4⅔
5	18–21	4	11	50–52	3⅓
6	22–31	10	12	53–60	8

E   The melodic elements in the first phrase (measures 4–8) are utilized
    often in succeeding phrases:

Measures 4 - 8

Measures 9 - 11

Measures 32 - 34

Measures 37 - 39

Form

The form is roughly binary although the "B" section in many instances resembles the "A" in melodic contour and rhythm. The overall form is:

MEASURES	SECTION
1–19	A
20–31	Transition
32–49½	B
50–52	Transition
53–60	Coda (*E* pedal)

Harmony

Included in the following table is the list of chord types in this composition. See appendix A for the meaning of symbols under columns "Chord Category" and "Includes."

CHORD CATEGORY	INCLUDES		CHORDS MUST NOT CONTAIN	FREQUENCY OF USE
I	I_1 &	I_2	Tritones, 2nds or 7ths	26%
II	II_{A1},	II_{A2}	Minor 2nds or major 7ths	10%
	II_{B1},	II_{B2}		
	II_{B3}			
III	III_1 &	III_2	Tritones	45%
IV	IV_1 &	IV_2	None—no intervals excluded	19%
V				One chord only

SOME OBSERVATIONS

A   Bartok's favorite chord (type III) contains no tritone but includes at least one interval of a 7th or 2nd.

B   Major and minor triads (type I) follows next in frequency. These chords also lack the tritone but in addition have no 2nds or 7ths.

C   Occurring often in the transition sections is the type IV chord. Such chords are of very great tension containing not only tritones but also either m2nd or M7th intervals.

D   Type II chords that contain the tritone and mild dissonances (M2nds and/or m7ths) represent only ten percent of the total chords.

E   The entire composition indicating the distribution of chords throughout:

Extracted Melody:

E Phrygian Mode

Extracted Chords:

I_1 III_2 I_1 III_2 I_1 III_2 I_1 III_2

Extracted Roots: E Tonality

E Phrygian Mode

I_1 III_2 III_1 III_2 I_1 III_2

E Tonality

E Phrygian Mode

I_1 III_2 I_1 III_2 I_1 III_2

E Tonality

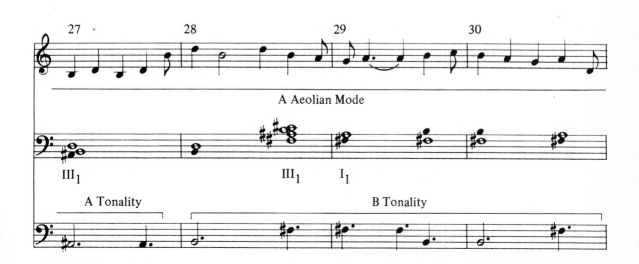

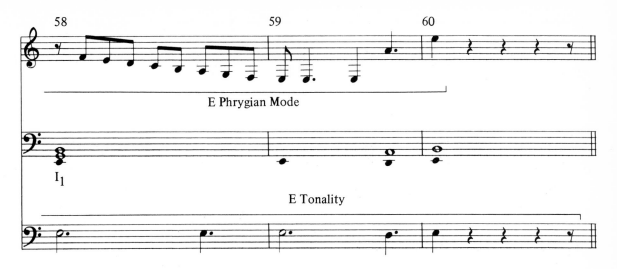

CHORD PROGRESSIONS

The chord roots clearly define the various tonalities through strong root relationships. As an example in measures 4–8 the roots *E* and *B* are prominent, thus emphasizing the tonality of *E*:

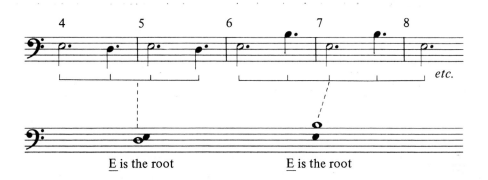

The *E* tonality in the above illustration is proven in the following ways:

A   *E* tonality appears more often than any other tone.
B   *E* falls on the accented beats of the measures.
C   *E* forms intervals with other chord roots and is maintained as the root of the best interval.

The composition represents considerable variety of chord types and fluctuations from one type to another.

HARMONIC RHYTHM

A fairly consistent harmonic rhythm of two chords per measure obtained throughout the composition. Generally the chords change on the 1st and 7th eighth note of the measure:

MEASURE IN EIGHT NOTES: 1 2 3 4 5 6 7 8 9   1 2 3 4 5 6 7 8 9
X = CHORD CHANGE: X   X   X   X

CADENCES

A   Cadence points at phrase endings are determined far more by the
    melodic consideration than the harmonic strength.
B   Harmonic progressions at cadence points are almost indistinguishable
    from those within the phrases.
C   The final cadence consists simply of two open-5th chords a 2nd apart.
D   Pauses of a half note or longer in the melodic line signal the cadence
    points in most instances. This simple slowing-down of the rhythmic ac-
    tivity is a major influence in effecting a cadence in this work.

Rhythm and Meter

METER
The melody is arranged into groups of 4, 2, and 3 eighth notes each.

RHYTHM
Two prominent rhythmic patterns are:

Rhythm 1   Rhythm 2

A   The first rhythmic figure illustrated above is found in eighteen different
    measures throughout the composition.
B   The second rhythmic pattern is found in six different measures.
C   Variations of these two rhythmic figures as well as others are found
    throughout the composition.
D   The division of 4–2–3 eighth notes in the meter are a major influence
    in the many syncopated rhythms that pervade this composition.

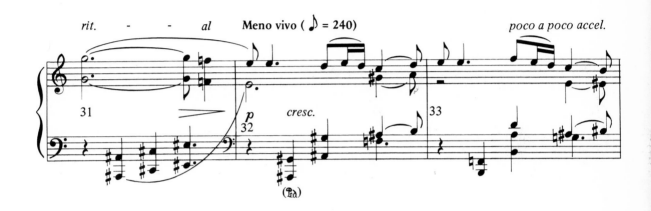

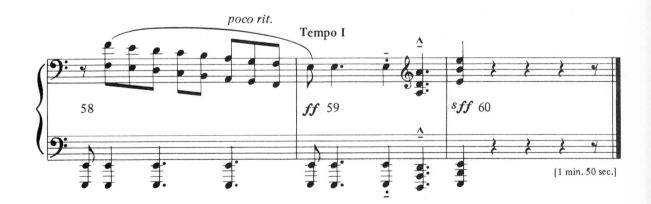

[1 min. 50 sec.]

ASSIGNMENT 1   On a separate sheet of paper make a complete analysis of the following composi-
                      tion using the same approach as is used for No. 1 of Six Dances in Bulgarian
                      Rhythm (No. 148 of Mikrokosmos).

                      Before preparing the analysis have two students perform the composition two or
                      three times in class or listen to a recording until the work is thoroughly familiar.

Bartok: No. 33, Song of the Harvest from Forty-four Violin Duets. Copyright 1933 by
Universal Editions, Ltd. Renewed 1960. Copyright and renewal assigned to
Boosey & Hawkes, Inc. Reprinted by permission.

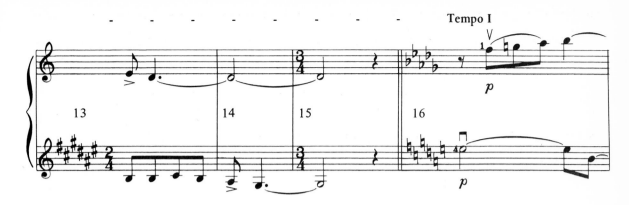

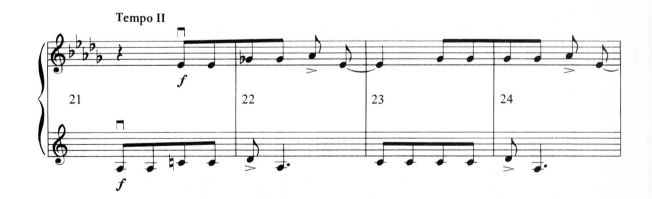

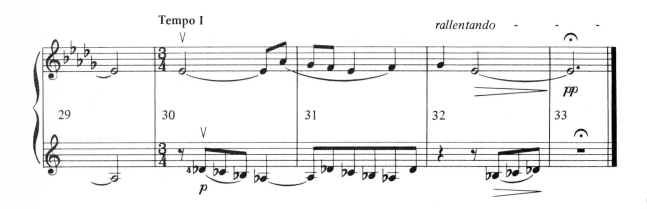

1   Using compositional techniques employed in the Bulgarian Dance analyzed
    in this chapter, write a short composition (16 to 30 measures).
2   Write for any combination of instruments played by class members.
3   Perform the composition in class.
4   After each student composition is performed, members of the class should
    enumerate (from listening) some of the various devices employed in the work.

24

The Viennese Atonalists

ARNOLD SCHOENBERG (1874–1951)

The rich chromatic style of Wagner's *Tristan und Isolde* along with the kind of expression it sought was preserved and extended by such composers as Richard Strauss (1864–1949). Indeed Wagner had many compatriots and imitators who continued after his death in somewhat the same style he had originally developed. However, Arnold Schoenberg (1874–1951), a young composer at the time, became disenchanted with the further piling on of triadic harmony and the excessive use of altered chords and aspired to find a new organizing principle that would eliminate the growing morass of complex harmony. To be sure, he had already demonstrated his ability in the true Wagnerian tradition with his *Verklärte Nacht* (Transfigured Night) and *Gurre-Lieder* and had observed that carrying this style of composition to its very limit obscured tonality and in many instances completely negated it.

Thus, he searched for a new way to organize music so that it would continue in the nontonal (atonal) path, but at the same time relieve it of the excessive and burdensome ties with the harmonic tradition of the now concluding Romantic period.

His contemplation finally netted him a system later known as the "Twelve-Tone Technique" or "Serial" composition. Using this plan he would invent a melodic set of tones using all twelve notes of the chromatic scale and would so arrange these that triads and other traditional marks of tonality would be absent. Generally he would avoid such intervals as the P4th and P5th since these had a tendency to remind the listener of the V to I of the authentic cadence. Negation of tonality being one of his prime goals, he would also arrange the tones so none would be heard twice (except for repetitions during an appearance in the series) until all twelve have been sounded once. Then, through such techniques as inversion (I), retrograde (R), retrograde inversion (RI), and transposition (T) he would be able to maintain unity but at the same time introduce variety and freshness in his compositions. Simultaneous sounds (chords) could be produced through the grouping of three or more tones of the "series" (or "row"), and thus the harmony would depart completely from the older tradition of chords built in thirds.

Schoenberg's professional career as a composer can be divided into three clear and distinct periods:

1874–1908—The earliest songs (opera 1, 2, 3, and 6) were influenced by Brahms, while *Verklärte Nacht* (1899) is in the style of Wagner as is the gigantic *Gurre-Lieder* (literally, Songs of Gurre—after a poem by Jacobsen, 1901). Music of this early period related to Schoenberg's ties with traditional style.

1908–1923—This is the period of *Pierrot Lunaire* (using *Sprechstimme*, which literally means "speaking voice" but is more idiomatically translated as "speech-song") Opus 21 (1912) and "Five Pieces for Orchestra," Opus 13 (1908–1909). During this middle period Schoenberg swung toward atonality (but *not* Twelve-Tone Technique), and frequently employed the motivic or "cell" technique in a way that negated tonality. It was a logical step toward the invention of the Twelve-Tone Technique and utilized thematic material consisting of only a few tones that reappeared in melodic and rhythmic variation. Harmony, too, broke with tradition and was no longer based on triadic construction (7th, 9th, 11th, and 13th chords) of the Romantic period.

1923–1951—This period saw the introduction of the Twelve-Tone Technique, beginning with Opus 25, "Suite for Piano." One of the most important works of this period is the "Variations for Orchestra," Opus 31, (1928).

The students and associates of Schoenberg wielded an important influence in the evolution of the new system and are known along with him as the "Viennese Atonalists."

ALBAN BERG (1885–1935)

One of Schoenberg's most intimate friends was also one of his most distinguished students, Alban Berg. Perhaps Berg's most important contribution to the twelve-tone movement was his lessening of the severity of the system. He treated the technique with some relaxing of strict rules and allowed himself to construct the row (also called "series") using thirds (somewhat similar to broken chords). This difference in itself placed him closer to the tradition of the past and made his music somewhat more familiar. Perhaps his greatest work was *Wozzeck* (not a serial composition), an opera first performed in 1924. It is the story of a hapless soldier, Franz Wozzeck, who is betrayed and taunted by both his superior officer and his mistress.

ANTON WEBERN (1883–1945)

Anton Webern was actually the first of Schoenberg's students although he also obtained a Ph.D. degree in musicology at the University of Vienna in 1906. He was accidentally shot and killed by an American military policeman in 1945.

Characteristics of Webern's music include:

1   Economy. He was very economical with his use of notes so that every tone had a purpose and superfluous tones were avoided.
2   Concentration. Most of his compositions are quite short, but the focus of musical activity is so concentrated and the meaning of each tone so important that an extraordinary degree of attention is required by the listener.
3   Use of small ensembles. Most of his works are for a small number of instruments with thick-textured sounds almost completely absent. As an example, his Symphony (Op. 21) is for nine solo instruments—a contrast to the full symphonic scoring of many of his contemporaries.
4   In summary, a penchant for brevity, frugality, attention to the smallest detail, and a style almost devoid of Romanticism characterizes Webern's compositions.

25

Analysis: No. 1 of Six Short Pieces for Piano, Op. 19 by Schoenberg (1874-1951)

Free Atonality   *Dodecaphony*   *Athematic*   *Cell*

FREE ATONALITY

A term designating music without a tonal center where all twelve tones of the octave may be used impartially, but not *in the structured manner of the twelve-tone serial technique.* Free atonality preceded *dodecaphony* (literally means 12 sounds, but more practically refers to 12 tone serial writing), and was a part of Schoenberg's composing style from Opus 10 through 19 (about 1908–1911). Then, after several years during which he published no music, he began experimenting with serial technique. In Opus 23 (1923) he intentionally used the twelve-tone series, but did not make full use of the technique until Opus 25.

Thematic Material in Free Atonality

Thematic material (themes, motives, etc.) in free atonality is not restricted and controlled in the same manner as in the twelve-tone serial technique. As a matter of fact composers of free atonality have employed a variety of ways in which to achieve unity.

A   Sometimes a single motive will be employed for an entire composition, with the motive acting as the major organizational element for the work. This treatment is sometimes similar to the motivic usage of previous centuries, but in the context of atonality different approaches and applications are available.

B   A motive or motives are sometimes utilized in much the same manner as in the twelve-tone serial technique with the possible transformations such as prime, retrograde, inversion, and retrograde-inversion being employed.

C   Some free atonal compositions are said to be *athematic* (no theme or motive in the traditional sense). This type contains patterns (sometimes only an interval) that are then repeated for a few measures while another figure is then taken up and treated in the same way. These microcosmic elements are not handled in the traditional eighteenth- and nineteenth-century manner where motives are extended into a complete composition through modulation, transposition, elongation, and so forth. In free atonality the figure is somewhat of a passing event that appears for the moment, is picked up and repeated in one context or another, and then allowed to trail into the memory as another event looms on the scene for its brief but important function in the composition.

ABOUT THE COMPOSITION

Free Atonality

A   This composition is atonal but contains no twelve-tone patterns found in serial writing.

B   Atonality is achieved through the use of motives that support a variety of tones and emphasizes no particular tonal center.

C   The composition is not based on tertian harmony.

D   The harmony is not of a functional type from the traditional period of music composition.

Cell Technique

A   In this work, small tonal patterns (similar to motives) are interwoven into the fabric of the composition in such a subtle way that the listener may not be consciously aware of their presence.

B   Such patterns are sometimes called *cells* to distinguish them from the more traditional motivic development found in traditional music of the eighteenth and nineteenth centuries.

C   The dominating cell in this composition is made up of two intervals: the 3rd (and its inversion, the 6th) and the 7th (and its inversion, the 2nd). The 3rds and 7ths occur in various different combinations including both M and m3rds and M and m7ths. The following arrangements are common:

Half steps
from first tone: 0   1   4   0   1   5   0   2   5   0   2   6

D   Not only are the above configurations available, but each may be ar-
    ranged in different orders.

Order
of tones: 1   2   3   1   3   2   2   3   1   2   1   3   3   1   2   3   2   1

E   In addition to the basic arrangements and the different orders each may
    be transposed to eleven other pitches within the octave.
F   Of course this short composition does not contain all of the possibilities
    available, but many occur both melodically and harmonically:

Some combinations (like the above) are quite evident by sight while
others are submerged in the context of the harmonic and melodic
texture:

G   Ingeniously, Schoenberg has incorporated other melodic and harmonic patterns in the composition. As an example, measure 2 contains the following bit of imitation that incorporates techniques that lend themselves admirably to this type of writing but would have been difficult to manage in previous styles.

   The melodic figure (A.) illustrated below is found in the upper voice and is immediately imitated in the lower voice (B.) in different durational values.

Melodic figures in measure 2:

Half step intervals: 1   3   3   1   3   3

   Simultaneous with this imitation, Schoenberg has woven the predominating cell of the composition. Measure 2 is excerpted below to show both the imitation and the cells included in the fabric.

Measure 2:
(Numbers simply indicate the pitches in order of their appearance in the measure.)

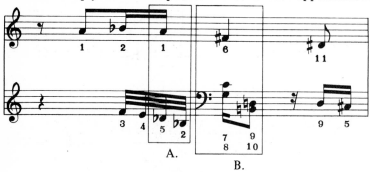

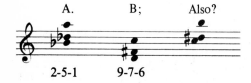

H   Measure 2 has provided an excellent insight into the techniques employed by Schoenberg in this *free atonal* composition. It might be assumed that all compositions written by him during this period (Op. 11 through 19) included the same approach, but such is not the case. Even the remaining five pieces in Op. 19 have varied elements of organization that only serve to demonstrate the restless and inquiring nature of this singularly innovative composer.

ASSIGNMENT 1   Using illustrations on score paper and written explanations continue the analysis of Op. 19, No. 1:

1 Find other micro-imitations as illustrated in measure 2.
2 Find other cells than the one discussed in the chapter.
3 Find other instances of the predominating cell described earlier in this chapter.

Schoenberg: No. 1 of Six Short Piano Pieces, Op. 19. Used by permission of Belmont Music Publishers, Los Angeles, Ca. 90049.

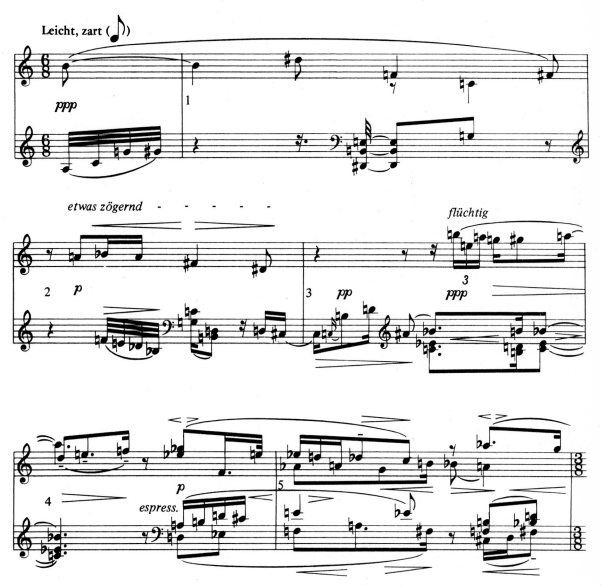

Assignment 1 (continued)

ASSIGNMENT 2   On a separate sheet of paper make a complete analysis of the following composition using the same approach as is used above for No. 1 of Six Short Pieces for Piano, Op. 19.

Before preparing the analysis, have a student perform the composition two or three times in class or listen to a recording until the work is thoroughly familiar.

Schoenberg: No. 5 of Six Short Piano Pieces, Op. 19. Used by permission of Belmont Music Publishers, Los Angeles, California 90049.

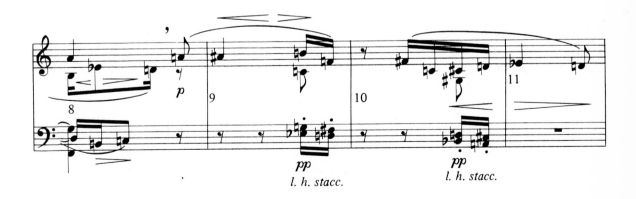

Assignment 2 (continued)

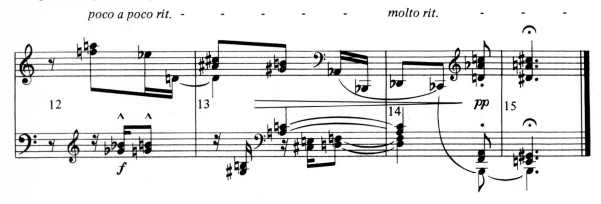

ASSIGNMENT 3

1   Using the same techniques found in the Opus 19 songs by Schoenberg, write a short composition (10 to 15 measures).
2   Write for any combination of instruments played by class members.
3   Perform the compositions in class.
4   After each composition is performed, members of the class should enumerate (from listening only) some of the "cells" employed in the work.

26

Analysis: Wie Bin Ich Froh, No. 1 of Drei Lieder, Op. 25 by Anton Webern (1883-1945)

Twelve-Tone Series	Inversion	Set
Dodecaphony	Retrograde Inversion	Pitch Class
Prime	Reihe	Matrix
Retrograde	Row	Set (Series) Segments
	Series	

THE TWELVE-TONE SERIES (DODECAPHONIC SERIAL COMPOSITION)

Schoenberg provided the following guides for his twelve-tone serial technique:

Order

All twelve tones of the octave scale in a particular order form the basis for the method. A particular tone may be repeated only when no other tones of the series intervene.

Register

The tones of the series may be in any octave.

Forms

The tone series may appear in any of the following four forms:

P	= *Prime*	—the series as it is originally constructed.
I	= *Inversion*	—starting with the first tone of the prime series the direction (up or down) of each successive tone is reversed (contrary motion).
R	= *Retrograde*	—the prime series sounded in reverse order.
RI	= *Retrograde Inversion*	—the inversion of the series is sounded in reverse order.

Transposition

Any of the four forms of the series can be transposed. The prime form untransposed is P^0, one-half step up is P^1, another one-half step up P^2, etc. As a further illustration:

P^8 = Prime form of the series transposed up eight half steps (m6th).

RI^2 = Retrograde inversion transposed up two half steps (M2nd).

I^{11} = Inverted series transposed up eleven half steps (M7th).

Row, Series, and Set

The term "row" derives from the German word *Reihe* and is a somewhat literal translation. Other terms such as "series" and "set" are used by later authors who believe that "row" denotes certain properties not in keeping with the true nature of the original German term. Despite controversies over subtleties in translation "row," "series," and "set" are used synonymously.

Numbering

Earlier writers also numbered the series from 1–12, but later authorities adopted the 0–11 numbering to facilitate mathematical calculation.

Pitch Class

"Pitch class" is another term frequently found in contemporary writing. This term is used in preference to "tone" or "pitch" since it is broader in meaning and includes a single pitch together with its octave duplication.

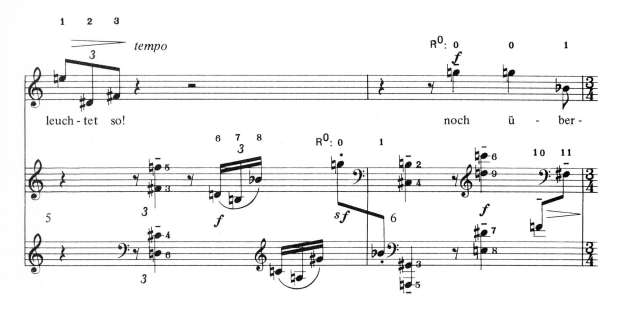

Wie Bin Ich Froh, No. 1 of Drei Lieder, Op. 25

About the Composer

Anton Webern (1883–1945) became a student of Arnold Schoenberg in 1904 and remained with him until 1910. Webern wrote in such a concentrated style that most of his works are quite brief, and his complete works could be played in less than six hours (any two of Wagner's operas would consume more). The three songs that comprise Opus 25 are the last of his vocal works and were composed in 1934–1935.

This work is an excellent example of the use of a twelve-tone series plus various forms and transpositions of the series.

The Matrix

The following illustration (known as a "matrix") will help to show the possible series forms and their transpositions (48 possibilities in all). This particular matrix represents the series that is the basis of the Webern composition analyzed here.

For Prime Series (P): Read from Left to Right
For Inverted Series (I): Read Down
For Retrograde Series (R): Read From Right to Left
For Retrograde Inversion Series (RI): Read Up

	I^0	I^{11}	I^8	I^{10}	I^9	I^6	I^3	I^7	I^2	I^5	I^4	I^1	
P^0	F#	F	D	E	Eb	C	A	C#	G#	B	Bb	G	R^0
P^1	G	F#	Eb	F	E	C#	Bb	D	A	C	B	G#	R^1
P^4	Bb	A	Gb	Ab	G	E	Db	F	C	Eb	D	B	R^4
P^2	Ab	G	E	Gb	F	D	B	Eb	Bb	Db	C	A	R^2
P^3	A	G#	F	G	F#	Eb	C	E	B	D	C#	Bb	R^3
P^6	C	B	Ab	Bb	A	Gb	Eb	G	D	F	E	Db	R^6
P^9	Eb	D	B	Db	C	A	Gb	Bb	F	Ab	G	E	R^9
P^5	B	Bb	G	A	Ab	F	D	Gb	C#	E	Eb	C	R^5
P^{10}	E	Eb	C	D	Db	Bb	G	B	F#	A	Ab	F	R^{10}
P^7	C#	C	A	B	Bb	G	E	G#	D#	F#	F	D	R^7
P^8	D	Db	Bb	C	B	Ab	F	A	E	G	F#	Eb	R^8
P^{11}	F	E	Db	Eb	D	B	Ab	C	G	Bb	A	F#	R^{11}
	RI^0	RI^{11}	RI^8	RI^{10}	RI^9	RI^6	RI^3	RI^7	RI^2	RI^5	RI^4	RI^1	

Selected Forms and Transpositions

Webern selected the following series forms and transpositions (from the matrix above) for *Wie bin ich froh!*

Prime Series untransposed (P⁰)

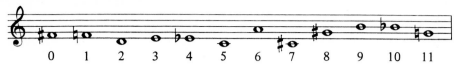

Retrograde Series untransposed (R⁰)

Inverted Series untransposed (I⁰)

Inverted Series transposed up one whole step (I²)

Inverted Series in Retrograde Transposed Up One Whole Step (RI²)

Set (Series) Segments

The series itself is very carefully planned to include a three-tone figure (*trichords*) with two transpositions.

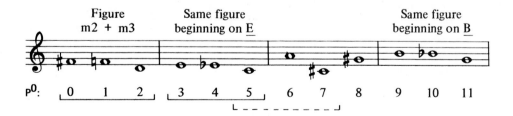

The Text

The composition is based on a poem of two strophes by Hildegarde Jone.

Wie bin ich froh!	How happy I am!
noch einmal wird mir alles grün	Once more all around me grows green
und leuchtet so!	and shimmers so!
noch über blühn die Blumen mir die Welt!	Blossoms still cover the world for me!
noch einmal bin ich ganz ins Werden hingestellt	Once again I am at the center of Becoming
und bin auf Erden.	and am on earth.

Voice Line

1ST STROPHE
a   The retrograde inversion (RI) of the series.
b   Followed by the first 4 notes of the same.

2ND STROPHE
a   The retrograde of the original series.
b   Followed by the complete retrograde inversion.

Form

This produces a three-part form:

A (retrograde inversion) RI^2
B (retrograde) R^0
A (retrograde inversion) RI^2

Accompaniment

The order of use in the accompaniment is as follows:

1ST STROPHE (MEASURES 1–5)   *2ND STROPHE* (MEASURES 6–12)
    P^0 RI^2 P^0 RI^2 R^0 I^2 I^2 P^0 R^0

Rhythmic and Harmonic Figures

The accompaniment consists for the most part of three figures, two of which are rhythmic and the other harmonic:

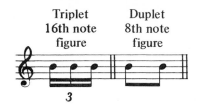

Triplet 16th note figure   Duplet 8th note figure

Four tone chord

There is a direct relationship between the figures and the pitches contained in them:

THE SIXTEENTH NOTE TRIPLET FIGURE
All sixteenth triplet figures (all are based on a minor 2nd + minor 3rd)

Measure:	1	2	3	4	4	5	5
Series Type:	P^0	RI^2	RI^2	P^0	P^0	RI^2	RI^2

Series Number: 0 1 2 . 0 1 2   9 10 11   5 6 7   9 10 11   6 7 8   9 10 11

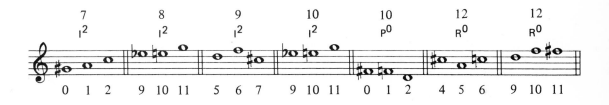

	7	8	9	10	10	12	12
	I^2	I^2	I^2	I^2	P^0	R^0	R^0

0 1 2   9 10 11   5 6 7   9 10 11   0 1 2   4 5 6   9 10 11

THE EIGHTH NOTE FIGURE
All two-tone eighth note figures are made up of one-half step intervals (with the exception of 2 examples*).

Measure:	Up + 1	1	2	5-6	6	7	10	12
Series Type:	P^0	P^0	*RI^2	*R^0	R^0	I^2	P^0	R^0

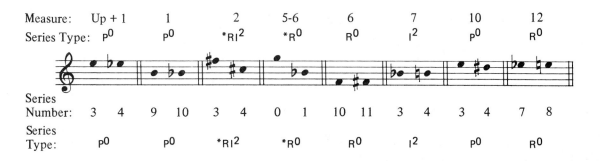

Series Number:	3	4	9	10	3	4	0	1	10	11	3	4	3	4	7	8

Series Type:	P^0		P^0		*RI^2		*R^0		R^0		I^2		P^0		R^0	

THE FOUR-TONE CHORD FIGURE

All four-tone chord figures:

A   Lower two tones form a major 7th (exception, measure 2)
B   Upper two tones form a major 7th (3 exceptions)

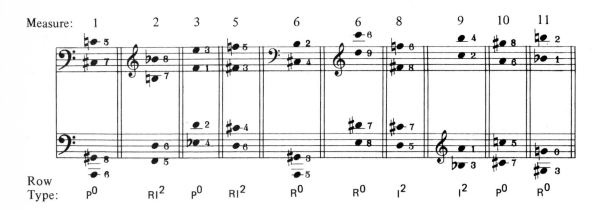

Dynamics and Tempo Indications

A   The third line of each strophe is marked with a soft dynamic.
B   The first line of each strophe begins loud and ends soft.
C   Accompaniment at the beginning, between strophes, and at the end,
     begins loud and ends soft.
D   Each line of strophe contains a ritard near the end.

ASSIGNMENT 1   On a separate sheet of paper make a complete analysis of the following composition using the same approach as is used above for *Wie bin ich froh*.

Before preparing the analysis have a vocalist and an accompanist from the class perform the composition two or three times or listen to a recording until the work is thoroughly familiar.

Webern: No. 2 of Drei Lieder, Op. 25. Copyright 1956 by Universal Editions, Ltd. A. G. Wien. Used by permission.

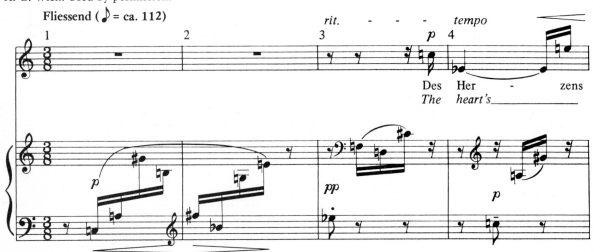

Assignment 1 (continued)

Assignment 1 (continued)

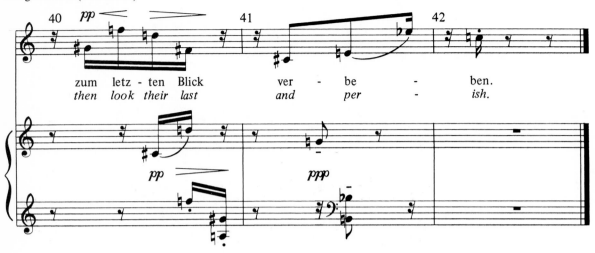

zum letz - ten Blick   ver - be - ben.
then look their last   and per - ish.

ASSIGNMENT 2   1   Write a short song employing the following twelve-tone series:

P^0:

0   1   2   3   4   5   6   7   8   9   10   11

2   Examine the series for motivic cells that might lend themselves to the technique found in the Webern song.
3   Then, prepare a matrix for this series (see page 468).
4   Select four compatible series forms.
5   Prepare (without score paper) a plan for the form of the composition. Use techniques discovered in the Webern song analyzed in this chapter.
6   Select two rhythmic figures for the accompaniment.
7   Sketch in the voice part and add the accompaniment.
8   Add dynamics and other marks of interpretation as well as phrasing.
9   Perform the composition in class.
10   After each performance the composer will lead a discussion concerning the techniques he employed in the composition.
11   Write for solo voice and piano.

27
Modern Twelve-Tone Set Techniques

Pitch Class Numbers *Derived Set* *Pentad*
Order Numbers *Dyad* *Hexachord*
Interval Class *Trichord* *Subset*
Combinatoriality *Tetrachord* *Equivalence*

AFTER 1945

After 1945 major changes took place in both technique and attitude toward the technique of twelve-tone composition. For this reason the pre-1945 period was called the Classical 12T and the post-1945 period the Modern 12T.

In both Classical and Modern 12T an emphasis on absolute intervallic identity replaces the functionalism of pitch in the tonal system.

In discussing pitch-interval relations within this approach, it is advantageous to use number notation rather than standard musical notation. This is not due to any sort of mathematical attitude toward music, but rather that number notation is simply more clear and a less ambiguous way of expressing these relationships.

PITCH CLASS NUMBERS

Those numbers that represent the intervallic relationship between the first tone and any given tone of the twelve-tone series.

The following twelve-tone series will serve as an illustration:

12 tone series:

Select the first one of the twelve-tone series, and write a chromatic scale:

Pitch class numbers: 0   1   2   3   4   5   6   7   8   9   10   11

Transfer the pitch class numbers from the chromatic scale to the twelve-tone series in its given order. The relationship between each member tone and the beginning tone is made available in this manner.

ORDER NUMBERS

Those numbers that represent the position of any given tone in the series.

Write the order numbers above the tones since they provide important information also.

Order numbers: 0   1   2   3   4   5   6   7   8   9   10   11

Pitch class numbers: 0   11   9   2   10   7   1   4   8   3   5   6

NUMBERS

The advantages of number notation are: (1) intervals are more explicit since they can be expressed in only one way. For example: F to A♭ and F to G♯ are two distinct intervals where tonal function is concerned, but with the intervallic approach (devoid of tonal function) they are identical. Indeed, musical notation allows four different ways of expressing the above interval, but number notation has only one:

Music notation   Number notation

    m3   A2   m3   DD4   *03

*Pitch classes "0" to pitch class "3," the interval of three half-steps.

      These intervallic identities are irrespective of registral placement, which is a separate compositional consideration. As is obvious, the only difference between a minor 3rd and a major 6th is the registral placement of the two pitches. This purely intervallic approach precludes this distinction, and labels both interval class 03. Extending this concept, only six intervals are recognized: the equivalent of a m2, M2, m3, M3, P4, tritone. The remainder are simply inversions of these. Standard musical notation necessitates a registral commitment, but number notation allows the expression of absolute intervals.

Music notation   Interval class

It should be stressed that in using number notation, whether in full 12T sets or smaller subsets, that the integer 0 is assigned to the first pitch encountered and all others are measured from there. This does not in any way imply that the initial tone of a series is more important than any other or that a fixed "do" system is in operation.

Modern 12T composers extended and developed the following two basic tenets of the Classical 12T composers largely through the work of the American composer-theorist Milton Babbitt.

SCHOENBERG'S PRINCIPLE OF HEXACHORDAL COMBINATORIALITY

The first hexachord (first six tones) of two different set forms combine to produce the aggregate (all 12 tones).

Schoenberg: Variations for Orchestra, Op. 31

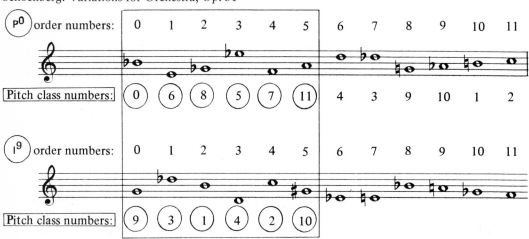

All 12 tones (aggregate) are found in the first six tones (hexachord) of these 2 set forms.

WEBERN'S PRINCIPLE OF THE DERIVED SET

An entire 12T set is generated from the intervallic content of a subset, most often a trichord (3 pitches).

Since the term "chord" has definite tonal implications, other terms must be used to identify groups of pitches.

> 1 pitch   = *pitch class*
> 2 pitches = *dyad*
> 3 pitches = *trichord*
> 4 pitches = *tetrachord*
> 5 pitches = *pentad*
> 6 pitches = *hexachord*

TRICHORD

For purposes of set derivation, there are twelve intervallically distinct trichords, distinguishable by means of the three intervals each contains.

SET NO.	NORMAL ORDER	EQUIVALENCES	NO. OF POSSIBLE PITCH SETS
1	0 1 2	None	12
2	0 1 3	(0 2 3)	24
3	0 1 4	(0 3 4)	24
4	0 1 5	(0 4 5)	24
5	0 1 6	(0 5 6)	24
6	0 2 4	None	12
7	0 2 5	(0 3 5)	24
8	0 2 6	(0 4 6)	24
9	0 2 7	None	12
10	0 3 6	None	12
11	0 3 7	(0 4 7)	24
12	0 4 8	None	4

Shown here are the above listed trichords as they relate to notation:

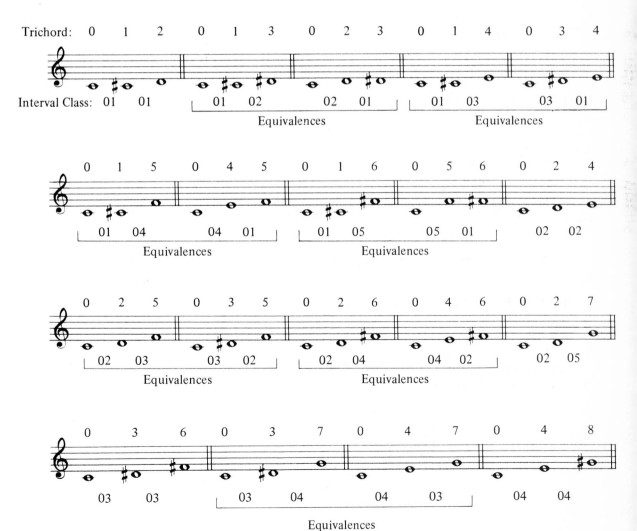

Tetrachords also serve as set generators, but the principle can be most clearly understood by means of trichords. The first trichordally derived set was used in Webern's *Concerto for Nine Instruments*, Op. 24. This set is derived from the 014 trichord.

Webern: Concerto for Nine Instruments, Op. 24

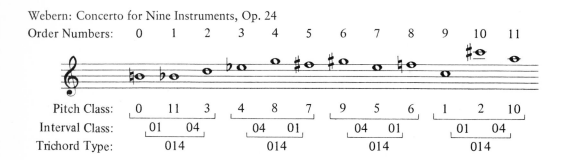

Order Numbers:	0	1	2	3	4	5	6	7	8	9	10	11
Pitch Class:	0	11	3	4	8	7	9	5	6	1	2	10
Interval Class:		01	04		04	01		04	01		01	04
Trichord Type:		014			014			014			014	

It is important always to bear in mind that both the hexachordal combinatorial principle and the derived set principle operate with respect to content alone, irrespective of both registral placement and temporal ordering.

In addition to the utilization of these properties handed down from the Classical 12T composers, the Modern 12T composers inaugurated other flexibilities largely through the use of set reordering and permutation, resulting in new sets being introduced within a work.

28

The Widow's Lament in Springtime by Milton Babbitt

ABOUT THE COMPOSER

Born in 1916, Milton Babbitt was educated at both New York University and Princeton and presently is professor of Music at the latter institution. He was active in the early days of electronic music and helped found the Electronic Music Center at Columbia University. His interest in both music and mathematics led him to develop new and original ways to utilize more of the potential inherent in the twelve-tone technique of musical composition.

ABOUT THE COMPOSITION

There are many interesting and intricate aspects of this composition, but it would be impossible to deal with all such occurrences in the confines of this chapter. Thus, only a few of the more basic facets will be discussed.

PROPERTIES

The Widow's Lament in Springtime is a particularly good example of Modern 12T technique because it contains the following properties:

A   Hexachordal combinatoriality
B   Derived sets
C   Permutation and reordering
D   Polyphonic treatment of sets
E   Trichordal context throughout
F   Set simultaneities and successions that are contextual and reflective of the A B A large form.

THE BASIC SET

The basic set that is heard first is combinatorial in two ways: P^0-P^6 and P^0-I^3. This set also contains a redundancy property that eliminates all retrogrades. In other words all retrogrades are duplicates of a particular P or I.

This quality of redundancy first appeared in the late works of Webern.

Webern: Cantata No. 1, Op. 29

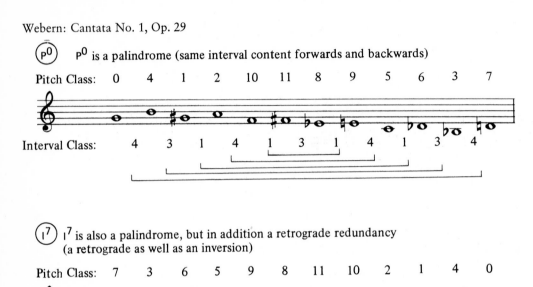

P^0 P^0 is a palindrome (same interval content forwards and backwards)

Pitch Class: 0   4   1   2   10   11   8   9   5   6   3   7

Interval Class: 4   3   1   4   1   3   1   4   1   3   4

I^7 I^7 is also a palindrome, but in addition a retrograde redundancy (a retrograde as well as an inversion)

Pitch Class: 7   3   6   5   9   8   11   10   2   1   4   0

Interval Class: 4   3   1   4   1   3   1   4   1   3   4

The basic set for *Widow's Lament in Springtime* is:

Order Numbers: 0   1   2   3   4   5   6   7   8   9   10   11

Pitch Class: 0   11   9   2   10   7   1   4   8   3   5   6

DERIVED SETS

From this basic set are generated four trichordally derived sets, utilizing the four trichords available in the first hexachord of the basic set.

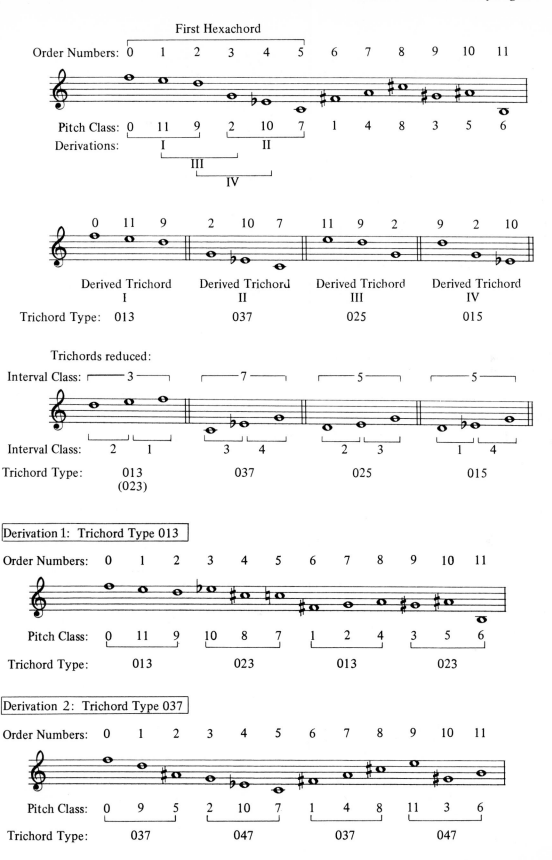

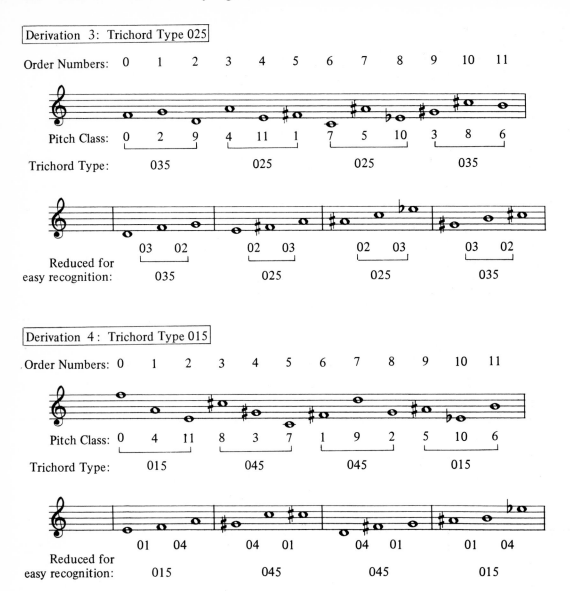

MATRICES

The four derived sets from the trichords above contain the same properties of combinatoriality and retrograde redundancy as the basic set.

The following illustrates all basic set forms plus all four derived set forms:

BASIC SET MATRIX:

	I^0	I^{11}	I^9	I^2	I^{10}	I^7	I^1	I^4	I^8	I^3	I^5	I^6	
P^0	0	11	9	2	10	7	1	4	8	3	5	6	R^0
P^1	1	0	10	3	11	8	2	5	9	4	6	7	R^1
P^3	3	2	0	5	1	10	4	7	11	6	8	9	R^3
P^{10}	10	9	7	0	8	5	11	2	6	1	3	4	R^{10}
P^2	2	1	11	4	0	9	3	6	10	5	7	8	R^2
P^5	5	4	2	7	3	0	6	9	1	8	10	11	R^5
P^{11}	11	10	8	1	9	6	0	3	7	2	4	5	R^{11}
P^8	8	7	5	10	6	3	9	0	4	11	1	2	R^8
P^4	4	3	1	6	2	11	5	8	0	7	9	10	R^4
P^9	9	8	6	11	7	4	10	1	5	0	2	3	R^9
P^7	7	6	4	9	5	2	8	11	3	10	0	1	R^7
P^6	6	5	3	8	4	1	7	10	2	9	11	0	R^6
	RI^0	RI^{11}	RI^9	RI^2	RI^{10}	RI^7	RI^1	RI^4	RI^8	RI^3	RI^5	RI^6	

DERIVATION 1 SET MATRIX

	I^0	I^{11}	I^9	I^{10}	I^8	I^7	I^1	I^2	I^4	I^3	I^5	I^6	
P^0	0	11	9	10	8	7	1	2	4	3	5	6	R^0
P^1	1	0	10	11	9	8	2	3	5	4	6	7	R^1
P^3	3	2	0	1	11	10	4	5	7	6	8	9	R^3
P^2	2	1	11	0	10	9	3	4	6	5	7	8	R^2
P^4	4	3	1	2	0	11	5	6	8	7	9	10	R^4
P^5	5	4	2	3	1	0	6	7	9	8	10	11	R^5
P^{11}	11	10	8	9	7	6	0	1	3	2	4	5	R^{11}
P^{10}	10	9	7	8	6	5	11	0	2	1	3	4	R^{10}
P^8	8	7	5	6	4	3	9	10	0	11	1	2	R^8
P^9	9	8	6	7	5	4	10	11	1	0	2	3	R^9
P^7	7	6	4	5	3	2	8	9	11	10	0	1	R^7
P^6	6	5	3	4	2	1	7	8	10	9	11	0	R^6
	RI^0	RI^{11}	RI^9	RI^{10}	RI^8	RI^7	RI^1	RI^2	RI^4	RI^3	RI^5	RI^6	

DERIVATION 2 SET MATRIX

	I^0	I^9	I^5	I^2	I^{10}	I^7	I^1	I^4	I^8	I^{11}	I^3	I^6	
P^0	0	9	5	2	10	7	1	4	8	11	3	6	R^0
P^3	3	0	8	5	1	10	4	7	11	2	6	9	R^3
P^7	7	4	0	9	5	2	8	11	3	6	10	1	R^7
P^{10}	10	7	3	0	8	5	11	2	6	9	1	4	R^{10}
P^2	2	11	7	4	0	9	3	6	10	1	5	8	R^2
P^5	5	2	10	7	3	0	6	9	1	4	8	11	R^5
P^{11}	11	8	4	1	9	6	0	3	7	10	2	5	R^{11}
P^8	8	5	1	10	6	3	9	0	4	7	11	2	R^8
P^4	4	1	9	6	2	11	5	8	0	3	7	10	R^4
P^1	1	10	6	3	11	8	2	5	9	0	4	7	R^1
P^9	9	6	2	11	7	4	10	1	5	8	0	3	R^9
P^6	6	3	11	8	4	1	7	10	2	5	9	0	R^6
	RI^0	RI^9	RI^5	RI^2	RI^{10}	RI^7	RI^1	RI^4	RI^8	RI^{11}	RI^3	RI^6	

DERIVATION 3 SET MATRIX

	I^0	I^2	I^9	I^4	I^{11}	I^1	I^7	I^5	I^{10}	I^3	I^8	I^6	
P^0	0	2	9	4	11	1	7	5	10	3	8	6	R^0
P^{10}	10	0	7	2	9	11	5	3	8	1	6	4	R^{10}
P^3	3	5	0	7	2	4	10	8	1	6	11	9	R^3
P^8	8	10	5	0	7	9	3	1	6	11	4	2	R^8
P^1	1	3	10	5	0	2	8	6	11	4	9	7	R^1
P^{11}	11	1	8	3	10	0	6	4	9	2	7	5	R^{11}
P^5	5	7	2	9	4	6	0	10	3	8	1	11	R^5
P^7	7	9	4	11	6	8	2	0	5	10	3	1	R^7
P^2	2	4	11	6	1	3	9	7	0	5	10	8	R^2
P^9	9	11	6	1	8	10	4	2	7	0	5	3	R^9
P^4	4	6	1	8	3	5	11	9	2	7	0	10	R^4
P^6	6	8	3	10	5	7	1	11	4	9	2	0	R^6
	RI^0	RI^2	RI^9	RI^4	RI^{11}	RI^1	RI^7	RI^5	RI^{10}	RI^3	RI^8	RI^6	

DERIVATION 4 SET MATRIX

	I^0	I^4	I^{11}	I^8	I^3	I^7	I^1	I^9	I^2	I^5	I^{10}	I^6	
P^0	0	4	11	8	3	7	1	9	2	5	10	6	R^0
P^8	8	0	7	4	11	3	9	5	10	1	6	2	R^8
P^1	1	5	0	9	4	8	2	10	3	6	11	7	R^1
P^4	4	8	3	0	7	11	5	1	6	9	2	10	R^4
P^9	9	1	8	5	0	4	10	6	11	2	7	3	R^9
P^5	5	9	4	1	8	0	6	2	7	10	3	11	R^5
P^{11}	11	3	10	7	2	6	0	8	1	4	9	5	R^{11}
P^3	3	7	2	11	6	10	4	0	5	8	1	9	R^3
P^{10}	10	2	9	6	1	5	11	7	0	3	8	4	R^{10}
P^7	7	11	6	3	10	2	8	4	9	0	5	1	R^7
P^2	2	6	1	10	5	9	3	11	4	7	0	8	R^2
P^6	6	10	5	2	9	1	7	3	8	11	4	0	R^6
	RI^0	RI^4	RI^{11}	RI^8	RI^3	RI^7	RI^1	RI^9	RI^2	RI^5	RI^{10}	RI^6	

CHART OF SET SIMULTANEITIES

The chart on the next page identifies set simultaneities and successions revealing the trichordal units and their constantly changing relationship to the set in its various forms. This, plus the intricacies of the four-voiced texture maintained throughout, produce a large array of formal affiliations within the composition going much beyond the simple idea first conceived by Schoenberg that one note follows another and is not used again until all others have been utilized.

The Widow's Lament in Springtime
SET SIMULTANEITIES

Columns 1–2 and 11–12: **Basic sets**; columns 3–10: **Derived sets**.

	P^0	I^9	D.1:P^0	D.1:I^7	D.2:P^6	D.2:I^1	D.3:P^9	D.3:I^{10}	D.4:P^8	D.4:I^3	I^3	P^6
VOICE:	P^0	I^9	D.1:P^0	D.1:I^7	D.2:P^6	D.2:I^1	D.3:P^9	D.3:I^{10}	D.4:P^8	D.4:I^3	I^3 CDAB	P^6 CDAB
UPPER PIANO LINE:	P^6 *DCBA	I^3 DCBA	D.1:I^1	D.1:P^6	D.2:I^7	D.2:P^0	D.3:I^4	D.3:P^3	D.4:I^9	D.4:P^2	I^3 BADC	P^6 BADC
MIDDLE PIANO LINE:	I^7 A C_r B D_r	P^8	D.3:I^7 *A_r C B D_r	D.3:P^0 A_r C B D_r	D.4:I^4 A_r C B D_r	D.4:P^3 A_r C B D_r	D.2:P^3 A C B_r D	D.2:I^4 A C_r B_r D	D.1:P^2	D.1:I^9	P^2 CDAB	I^7 C A_r D_r B
LOWER PIANO LINE:	I^1 D_r B C_r A	P^2 DCBA	D.3:P^6 A_r C B D_r	D.3:I^1 A_r C B D_r	D.4:P^9 A_r C B D_r	D.4:I^3 A_r C B D_r	D.2:I^{10} A C B_r D	D.2:P^9 A C_r B_r D	D.1:I^3	D.1:P^8	P^2 BADC	I^7 B D_r A_r C

* A, B, C, D refers to the four discrete trichords of the set form.

+ A_r means trichord A appears in retrograde form.

++ D = Derivation

The student is now encouraged to explore the composition exhaustively locating not only the set simultaneities and successions pointed out in the above chart, but other subtle complexities existing in the contents.

Milton Babbitt: The Widow's Lament in Springtime. Used by permission of the publishers, Boelke-Bomart, Inc., Hillsdale, N.Y.

grief___ in my heart   is strong - er than they;   for

though they were my joy   for-mer - ly,   to - day   I no - tice them   and

turn   a-way   for - get - ting.   To - day___ my son

496   *The Widow's Lament in Springtime*

like   to go   there   and fall   in - to those flow - ers   and

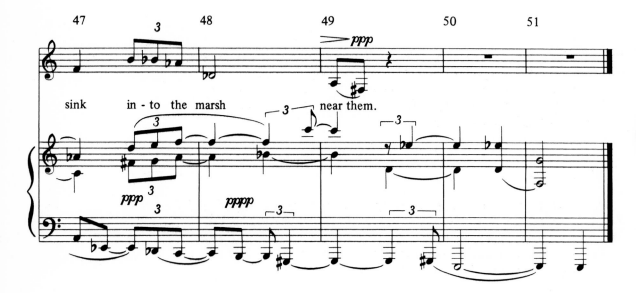

sink   in - to the marsh   near them.

Appendix

The analysis of chords, especially contemporary chords, is made easier through the use of the classification chart shown below. This system of analysis was developed by Paul Hindemith in his book, *The Craft of Musical Composition,* and is helpful in calculating chord tension, chord roots, chord strength, and tonality.

INTRODUCTION

1   Chords are to be considered simply as a combination of intervals.
2   The stability of a chord is determined by the intervals that make it up.
3   The intervals are listed in a decreasing order of stability (increasing order of tension). The perfect fifth is the most stable. The octave is considered only as a doubling of the lower note.

Interval stability

Interval roots

1   2   3   4   5   6   7   8   9   10   11

4   Intervals are considered to have roots (see above).
5   In the illustration above, the black notes indicate the root of each interval. The tritone has no root.
6   In any chord the root of the lowest best (most stable) interval is the root of the chord.
    a.   Doubled tones count only once. Use the lowest.
    b.   In case the best (most stable) interval appears twice in the chord, use the lowest.

497

Following is a chart that places chords into categories of increasing tension (excluding Group V and VI). The I_1 chord has the lowest tension, I_2 chord slightly more tension, and the II_{a1} even more. Chords of highest tension are those in Group IV_2 since Group V and VI are reserved for "indeterminate" chords—chords without roots.

TABLE OF CHORD GROUPS

A. CHORDS WITHOUT TRITONES	B. CHORDS CONTAINING TRITONES
I. Without seconds or sevenths	II. Without Minor Seconds or Major Seconds

1. Root and bass are identical.
    2. Root lies above the bass tone.
	A. With Minor Seventh only
	    1. Root and bass are identical.
	    2. Root lies above the bass tone.
	
	  B. With Major Seconds—with or without Minor Sevenths
	    1. Root and bass are identical.
	    2. Root lies above the bass tone.
	    3. Containing more than one tritone.

III. Containing seconds or sevenths or both	IV. Containing Minor Seconds or Major Sevenths or both

1. Root and bass are identical.
    2. Root lies above the bass.
	1. Root and bass are identical.
	    2. Root lies above the bass.

V. Indeterminate	VI. Indeterminate, Tritone Predominating

Illustrated examples of chord groups

I_1

I_2

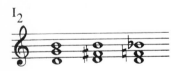

II_{A_1}

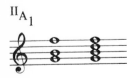

II_{A_2}

II_{B_1}

II_{B_2}

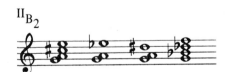

II_{B_3}

III₁

III₂

IV₁

IV₂

V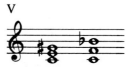

VI

SUMMARY

The following chart summarizes the various categories and the interval involvement.

GROUP I

MUST CONTAIN	MAY CONTAIN	MUST NOT CONTAIN
	3rds	2nds
	6ths	7ths
	4ths	Tritones
	5ths	

GROUP II

MUST CONTAIN	MAY CONTAIN	MUST NOT CONTAIN
Tritone	3rds	Minor 2nd
	6ths	Major 7th
Major 2nd or	4ths	
Minor 7th	5ths	

GROUP III

MUST CONTAIN	MAY CONTAIN	MUST NOT CONTAIN
2nds or	3rds	Tritones
7ths or	6ths	
both	4ths	
	5ths	

GROUP IV

MUST CONTAIN	MAY CONTAIN	MUST NOT CONTAIN
Tritone	3rds	no intervals prohibited
	6ths	
Minor 2nd or	4ths	
Major 7th or	5ths	
both		

For more detailed information, consult *Craft of Musical Composition* by Paul Hindemith.

Glossary

Aggregate	The total. Example: the first six tones of a twelve-tone series form an Aggregate with the second six tones.
Altered Chord	A chord that contains one or more factors that are not part of the prevailing diatonic system.
Altered Dominant	A dominant triad or 7th chord that contains a raised or lowered 5th and in one instance a lowered 3rd. Example: *G B D♯ F* = altered dominant (V7) in Am C major.
Answer (Fugue)	Imitation of the fugue subject usually at the interval of a P5th higher or P4th lower.
Answer (Real)	*See* Real Answer.
Answer (Tonal)	*See* Tonal Answer.
Asymmetric Meter	Meter in which the beats are not grouped into symmetric units. Examples: 7/8 and 5/4 meters.
Augmentation	A melody in increased (usually doubled) note values. Example: in augmentation a melody in quarter notes becomes a melody in half notes.
Augmented 6th Chords	A type of altered chord that contains the interval of an augmented 6th. The three most common types (up from the lowest sounding tone): (1) Italian —M3rd and A6th (2) German—M3rd, P5th, and A6th (3) French—M3rd, A4th, and A6th. The bass note is most frequently a M3rd below the tonic. Symbols: It⁶, Gr⁶, and Fr⁶.
Basso Continuo	Same as figured bass. Usually performed by a cello, viola da gamba, or bassoon playing the bass line while a harpsichordist or pianist plays the bass notes and adds the chords as requested by the figuration.
Basso Ostinato	Same as Ground. *See* Ground.
Bitonality	*See* Polytonality.
Borrowed Chord	A chord borrowed from the parallel major or minor key. Example: *A C E-flat* is a borrowed (from *G* minor) chord in *G* major.

Bridge (Fugue)	A short passage in the exposition of a fugue between entrances of the subject or answer. Acts as a modulatory passage for return to the tonic of the subject that ends in the dominant.
Bridge Passage	Another term for transition. Connects two themes. *See* Transition.
Cadence—Linear	*See* Linear Cadence.
Changing Meters	Meter changes within a composition to show rhythmic patterns more clearly than with a single constant meter.
Chord, Cluster	A chord with three or more factors of which each is no more than a whole step from its adjacent factor. Example: *C C♯ D E* when sounded together is a cluster chord.
Chords of Omission and Addition	Chords with added or deleted tones. Common example of an added tone chord: *C E G A*. The *A* is an added tone. Example of a chord of omission: *C G C*. The 3rd is omitted from the triad.
Chromatic Mediant Chords	The altered mediant and submediant triads (and 7th chords on occasion). Example: *E G♯ B* = III in C major. Not common in any style, but found most often in the late Romantic period.
Clausula Vera	The most common cadence in two-voice, sixteenth-century choral writing. The voices either expand to an octave (from a 6th) or contract to a unison (from a 3rd).
Cluster Chord	*See* Chord, Cluster.
Coda	Technically an expanded cadence. Occurs at the end of a composition and traditionally brings the composition to a convincing conclusion. May consist of a few measures or an entire subdivision in itself.
Combinatoriality	The first hexachord (first six tones) of two different set forms combine to produce all twelve tones. Example: when the first six tones of a particular P^0 and the first six tones of I^9 are combined the result is all twelve tones of the series with no duplications.
Contrary Motion	*See* Inversion—Melodic.
Countermotive	Counterpoint accompaniment to the motive in a two-part invention. In some inventions the countermotive is utilized in ensuing developmental material.
Countersubject (of a Fugue)	The continuation of counterpoint in the voice that has just completed the subject. In actuality it should be called counteranswer because it appears with the answer. In most fugues the countersubject is a fertile source of material for the remainder of the composition.
Derived Set	A twelve-tone set different in order from another but retaining some particular characteristics of the original. Example: deriving a twelve-tone set from a prime with a particular trichord type (016) as its first segment. The derived set might be manipulated to contain a series of four 016 trichords.
Development (in a Fugue)	After the exposition has been completed, the subject, answer, or possibly countersubject are stated in various keys connected by episodes (brief sections that contain neither the subject nor the answer).
Development (Sonata Form)	The middle section of a movement or composition in sonata allegro form. The function of this division is to develop the themes of the exposition through variation, alteration, fragmentation, modification, and mutation. The development section is characterized by restless modulation, agitation, and increased tension.
Diminution	A melody in decreased (usually halved) note values. Example: in diminution, a melody in quarter notes becomes a melody in eighth notes.

Dodecaphonic	Term used to describe twelve-tone serial writing.
Dual Modality	Simultaneous use of major and minor mode or combinations of Gregorian modes. Usually the two have the same tonic or final.
Duodecuple Scale	*See* Scale—Duodecuple.
Dodecuple Scale	*See* Scale—Duodecuple.
Dyad	Two pitches. Generally used when describing segments of the twelve-tone series. Has both melodic and harmonic connotations.
Eleventh Chord	A superposition of five 3rds—one 3rd above the 9th of a 9th chord. Example: $G\ B\ D\ F\ A\ C = V^{11}$ in C major.
Episode	A short interlude in the development section of a fugue that does not contain the subject or answer but connects entrances of either in various keys. Most development sections contain a number of episodes.
Equivalences	A trichord or tetrachord in two or more arrangements or registrations but having the same intervallic content.
Exposition (of a Fugue)	The first section of a fugue. Consists of an entrance in all voices of either the fugue subject or answer. When all voices have entered, the exposition gives way to the development.
Exposition (of a Sonata Form)	The first large section of sonata allegro form containing at least contrasting key relationships and more often two or three contrasting themes set apart by transitions.
Expressionism	A reaction to Impressionism. Actually the term has no intrinsic meaning, but its proponents hoped to create music that would be an expression of their inner world in contrast to the Impressionists who sought to represent their impressions of the external world.
Free Atonality	A kind of atonal writing that allows free use of the twelve tones of the octave, but does not order or prescribe the arrangement as in serial technique.
Free Tonality	Term used to designate music that contains a definite tonal center but is not key oriented. As opposed to Chromaticism, which also utilizes a wide variety of tones but is placed in a setting of functional harmony where each scale or nonscale degree has a traditional role in the operation of key-centered tonality.
French Augmented Sixth Chord	*See* Augmented 6th Chords.
Fugue	A contrapuntal composition in two or more voices, based on a subject (theme) that is introduced at the beginning in imitation and recurs frequently in the course of the composition. A monothematic composition except for double or triple fugues that contain two or three subjects.
German Augmented 6th Chord	*See* Augmented 6th Chords.
Hocket	Thirteenth century—Adjacent notes and rests alternating among different voices or parts in such a way that one voice is silent while the other sings. Sixteenth century—The overlapping of phrases at the cadence point where one voice rests and then immediately begins the new phrase.
Hexachord	Six pitches. Generally used when describing segments of the twelve-tone series. Has both melodic and harmonic connotations.
Inversion (of a Twelve-Tone Set)	Starting with the first tone of the prime series, the direction (up or down) of each successive tone is reversed (contrary motion). Symbol: I^0. Transposed up a half step the inversion becomes I^1, another half step up I^2, and so on.

Inversion (of the Vertical Order of Voices)   A device in counterpoint in which the vertical order of two simultaneous voices is reversed. When the counterpoint is purposely contrived to sound as well in the 'upside down" order, it is known as INVERTIBLE COUNTERPOINT. Inversion of vertical order is not to be confused with melodic inversion in which the direction (up or down) of a single melody is reversed.

Inversion—Melodic   Reversal of melodic direction. Upward direction in the original becomes downward direction in the inversion, an ascending 6th becomes a descending 6th, a descending 3rd becomes an ascending 3rd. In tonal music the inversion is usually diatonic rather than exact. Melodic inversion is synonymous with contrary motion.

Invertible Counterpoint   Two-voice counterpoint which is purposely contrived to sound as well in reversed (upside down) order. Inversion may be at any interval, but the octave is most common.

Italian Augmented Sixth Chord   *See* Augmented 6th Chords.

Linear Cadence   Melodic lines that converge or diverge at the cadence point. Oblique motion is also possible.

Melismatic   A style of vocal writing in which several or many pitches are set to a single syllable of the text.

Melodic Doubling   The doubling of melodic lines to create parallel movement. Also called *melodic parallel*.

Melodic Inversion   *See* Inversion—Melodic.

Monophony   A single line of melody with no accompaniment. Example: Gregorian Chant or folk music when performed without accompaniment.

Movement   A unit of a larger work that stands by itself as a complete but related composition. Such divisions are usually self-contained. Most often movements are arranged fast-slow-fast or in some other order that provides contrast.

Musica Ficta   Accidentals added to modal compositions of the sixteenth century and earlier. Such accidentals were not included by the composers but were used by singers to correct for tritones and provide leading tones for the modes that lacked them. Now musica ficta accidentals are usually written above the staff.

Neapolitan Sixth Chord   A major triad based on the lowered 2nd degree of the major or minor scale. Example: *D-flat F A-flat* = N in C major. Since the chord is most often found in first inversion it is called the Neapolitan Sixth.

Neoclassicism   A reaction to the freedom and lack of order in the form and content of compositions of the Romantic period. A return to discipline, form, and symmetry of the Classical period. Followed immediately after the Post-Romantic and Impressionistic period. Representative composer: Paul Hindemith.

Ninth Chord   A superposition of four 3rds—one 3rd above the 7th of the 7th chord. Example: *G B D F A* = V^9 in C major.

Nonaccentual Rhythms   Absence of dynamic accents.

Normal Order   In twelve-tone serial writing, the term indicates the ascending order of intervals (from small to large) of a trichord, tetrachord, pentad, or hexachord. Example: a trichord in normal order = 016 as against 0 6 1.

Nota Cambiata   A common dissonant melodic device of sixteenth century vocal music. The decoration of a descending 3rd. The figure consists of four tones: (1) dotted half note descending one step to a (2) quarter note, which is the *nota cambiata*, that then descends a 3rd to a (3) half note and up a step to another (4) half note.

Octatonic Scale	An eight-tone scale.
Order Number	The number that represents the position of any given tone in the twelve-tone series. Example: the 3rd tone in a given series is *order number* 2 (remember the first tone is always 0).
Palindrome	Reads the same backwards as forward. Example: Madam, I'm Adam. In the context of twelve-tone serial music it connotes the same interval content forward and backwards.
Pandiatonicism	The use of the tones of a diatonic scale in such a way that each tone is stripped of its usual function in the key.
Parallel Chords	Chords in which all factors or voices move in parallel motion. Parallel chords are sometimes diatonic (Example: *C E G* to *D F A*) and sometimes chromatic (Example: *C E G* to *D F♯ A*).
Pentatonic Scale	A five-tone scale. Example: *C D E G A* (*C*).
Permutation	Used in connection with the twelve-tone series and involves a changing of the order of a set.
Pentad	Five pitches. Generally used when describing segments of the twelve-tone series. Has both melodic and harmonic connotations.
Pitch Class	A more recent term for pitch. Considered more broad because pitch class includes octave duplications while pitch designates only a single sound.
Pitch Class Numbers	Those numbers that represent the intervallic relationship between the first tone and any given tone of the twelve-tone series. Example: PITCH CLASS 3 means a tone in the series that is three half steps above the prime (first) tone.
Planing	*See* Parallel Chords.
Polychord	Simultaneous use of two chords. Spacing is important in the use of polychords since the chords must be spaced sufficiently apart to be heard as two distinct entities.
Polyphony	Simultaneous interacting melodies. A texture of independent melodies sounding at the same time. Examples: a Bach fugue, a Bach two-part invention, a Palestrina mass. Music of both the Renaissance and the Baroque period was predominantly polyphonic. The terms "polyphony" and "counterpoint" are used interchangeably.
Polytonality	Simultaneous use of two or more tonalities.
Portamento	A common dissonance found in sixteenth century vocal writing resembling the anticipation of harmonic counterpoint in the eighteenth century. Most often of quarter note value in 4/2 meter. Approached by step and left by repetition.
Prime Series (in 12-Tone Technique)	The twelve-tone series as it is originally constructed. Symbol: P^0. The same series transposed up a half step is P^1, another half step is P^2, and so on.
Primitivism	A reaction to the refined and fragile music of such composers as Debussy. Its proponents sought to eliminate the subtlety and gentility of previous music and emphasize the mechanistic, the violent, the animal nature, and the more earthy aspects of music.
Quartal Chords	Chords constructed through a superposition of 4ths rather than the conventional 3rds as in tertian harmony. Example: *B E A* or *B E A D*.
Real Answer	An exact transposition (usually interval by interval, but in any case by diatonic interval) of the subject usually at the P5th above or P4th below. In a fugue or other contrapuntal composition.

Recapitulation	The third section of a movement or composition in sonata allegro form. Contains the return of the themes stated in the exposition. Conventionally all themes in the recapitulation are returned to the tonic key.
Recapitulation (of a Fugue)	The third and final part of the fugue containing the return of the subject and/or answer in the tonic key of the composition. Not all fugues have recapitulations, and in some the recapitulation is quite abbreviated.
Retransition	A transition at the end of the development section in sonata allegro form that leads back to the first theme of the recapitulation.
Retrograde	A melody, subject, motive, etc., in reverse order (backwards). Example: a melody *C D G E F* in retrograde is *F E G D C*. *Cancrizans* is another term meaning retrograde.
Retrograde (of a 12-Tone Series)	The prime series sounded in reverse order from last to first. Symbol for the retrograde set: R^0. Transposed up half step is R^1, transposed up another half step is R^2 and so on. It is important to remember that R^0 begins on the last pitch of P^0.
Retrograde Inversion (of a 12-Tone Set)	The inversion of the prime series in reverse order from last pitch to first. Symbol for the Retrograde Inversion is: RI^0. The retrograde inversion transposed up a half step is RI^1, another half step up to RI^2 and so on. It is important to remember that the RI form begins on the last tone of I^0.
Romanticism	The period of musical writing from roughly 1825 to 1900. Characterized by a tendency to accentuate the impulsive, the unusual, the adventuresome, the impetuous, and the passionate attitudes toward musical composition.
Scale—Duodecuple	The twelve tones of the octave each with equal status. Although the older term *chromatic scale* also denotes twelve tones, its relation to key and tonal systems makes it inappropriate for the purpose intended. The term *duodecuple* is used in connection with serial music.
Shifted Tonality	Sudden tonality change without preparation or modulation in the traditional sense.
Sonata	A composition usually in three or four movements for (1) piano or harpsichord solo, or (2) for solo instrument and accompaniment. These multi-movement compositions developed in the mid-eighteenth century.
Sonata Allegro (Form)	A compositional structure used most often in the first movement of a sonata, symphony, string quartet, or trio consisting of three main sections: (1) an exposition (2) a development, and (3) a recapitulation.
Stretto	Overlapping of subjects (or answers) in different voices. A subject in one voice is not completed when the same subject is introduced in another voice.
Subject (of a Fugue)	A short melody that is used as the basis for a fugue.
Syllabic	A style of vocal writing in which one pitch is used for each syllable of the text. Contradistinction of *melismatic*.
Tetrachord	Modern interpretation: A four-tone scale segment. Example: *C D E F* is the lower tetrachord of the *C* major scale. The term was adapted from Greek music where it referred to a four-tone scale segment in descending order.
Third Relationship	Relationship of a 3rd between roots of adjacent chords. When prominent progressions employ 3rd relationship in concentration or in succession, particularly ascending, tonal emphasis is decreased.
Third Relationship Cadence	A cadence in which the roots of the two chords lie in 3rd relationship. Example: *E G♯ B* progresses to *C E G* in a cadence.

Thirteenth Chord	A superposition of six 3rds—one above the 11th of an 11th chord. Example: $G\ B\ D\ F\ A\ C\ E = V^{13}$ in C major.
Tonal Answer	The subject (of a fugue) transposed usually to the P5th above or P4th below. However, slight modifications are made in a tonal answer so that the intervallic distance is not always the same as in the subject. The modifications generally entail replacing tonic implications with dominant and vice versa. Thus, if a fugue subject begins on the dominant tone the answer begins on the tonic.
Total Serialism	All (or at least most) of the parameters or dimensions of a twelve-tone serial composition are serialized. Example: serialization of pitch, intensity, duration, and timbre.
Transition	Provides a musical link between one theme and the next. The term is used most often to designate passages in the exposition and recapitulation of sonata allegro form that furnish a smooth connection between themes.
Trichord	Three pitches. Generally describes segments of twelve-tone sets. Has both melodic and harmonic connotations. *Trichord* is used in place of *triad* by contemporary composers and theorists since *triad* has key and tonal implications.
Twelve-Tone Set	Same as twelve-tone series. Series, set, and row are used synonymously. Authors and composers of the 1960s and 1970s prefer the term *set*.
Variation—Continuous	A type of composition employing variation techniques in which the variations are fused together in the continuous flow of the music. The most common type employs a *ground (basso ostinato)*. The ground consists of a short melodic figure of four to eight measures maintained in the lowest voice and repeated throughout the composition.
Variation—Principle	The transformation of a melody, harmony, or rhythm with changes or elaborations. A modification of a melody, harmony, or rhythm especially using one of the techniques developing the potential of the theme or subject material.
Variation—Theme And	A theme usually in sectional form is stated simply and ends with a cadence. Variations of this theme, maintaining sufficient character of the original to identify them as variations, then follow.
Whole-Tone Scale	The harmonic or melodic use of a six-tone scale in which each degree is a whole step from the next. Example: $C\ D\ E\ F\sharp\ G\sharp\ A\sharp\ (C.)$

Index